Learning to Connect

Learning to Connect

*Relationships, Race, and
Teacher Education*

Victoria Theisen-Homer

ROWMAN & LITTLEFIELD
Lanham • Boulder • New York • London

Published by Rowman & Littlefield
An imprint of The Rowman & Littlefield Publishing Group, Inc.
4501 Forbes Boulevard, Suite 200, Lanham, Maryland 20706
www.rowman.com

6 Tinworth Street, London SE11 5AL, United Kingdom

British Library Cataloguing in Publication Information Available

Library of Congress Cataloging-in-Publication Data

Names: Theisen-Homer, Victoria, 1983– author. | Rowman and Littlefield, Inc.
Title: Learning to Connect : Relationships, Race, and Teacher Education / Victoria Theisen-Homer.
Other titles: Relationships, Race, and Teacher Education
Description: Lanham : Rowman & Littlefield Publishing Group, 2020. | Includes bibliographical references and index. | Summary: "Learning to Connect explores how two different teacher education programs—No Excuses Teacher Residency and Progressive Teacher Residency— attempt to prepare preservice teachers for meaningful relationships with students, especially across racial and cultural differences."—Provided by publisher.
Identifiers: LCCN 2019059374 (print) | LCCN 2019059375 (ebook) | ISBN 9781475855425 (Cloth : acid-free paper) | ISBN 9781475855449 (Paperback : acid-free paper) | ISBN 9781475855456 (ePub)
Subjects: LCSH: Teachers—In-service training—United States. | Teacher-student relationships— Social aspects—United States. | United States—Race relations.
Classification: LCC LB1731 .T474 2020 (print) | LCC LB1731 (ebook) | DDC 370.71/1—dc23
LC record available at https://lccn.loc.gov/2019059374
LC ebook record available at https://lccn.loc.gov/2019059375

To my dearly-missed mom, who taught me to see the person
behind the façade.
To my two daughters, whom I hope to teach the same.

Contents

Preface

Through the Thou, man becomes I.—Martin Buber, *I and Thou*, 1965[1]

Over the course of conducting and analyzing the research that informs this book, I became a mother—twice over. And while cliché, this experience changed me. For in addition to looking at life through the lens of an educator, I began to see it through the eyes of a parent. Like most parents, I love my two girls more than I could have ever fathomed. And more than anything, I want to raise them in a way that nurtures their unique spirits and enables them to thrive and grow into the human beings they were born to be. But I also realize that my husband and I will not be the only two adults raising these girls or shaping their experiences of the world. In fact, for a significant chunk of their lives, they will spend more waking hours in schools than they will with us. In these settings, teachers will be the adults who raise them, influencing their development at pivotal moments.

I can only hope their teachers will have been well trained, not just in matters of curriculum and pedagogy, but in connecting with students. Because I know that relationships with teachers can impact students' engagement in school, academic achievement, and resilience.[2] Even more than that, though, relationships with influential adults—which teachers absolutely are—can shape a child's sense of self and the world. As the philosopher Martin Buber puts it, "Through the thou, man becomes I." It is through relationships with others that we learn to define who we are.

I also know that my girls are extremely fortunate. Because not only do they have parents with the time and wherewithal to navigate the education system before them, but as white girls, my daughters also look like the vast majority of the teaching force.[3] This gives them a distinct advantage, for it is much easier for people to form relationships with those who visibly resemble

ix

themselves. But most school children are not so privileged. They represent
diverse racial, ethnic, linguistic, religious, socioeconomic, sexual orientation,
and gender identities that differ from those of their teachers. And these differences—specifically in race, which Christine Sleeter refers to as a "cultural
mismatch"[4]—can negatively influence the teacher's efforts to establish relationships with them, further disadvantaging students who come from historically marginalized groups. Teacher education programs should certainly recruit and prepare a more diverse cohort of teachers. However, all programs
should also be thoughtfully preparing their current teacher candidates with
the tools they need to form meaningful relationships with all students, especially those who don't look or think or behave like them.

While preparing teachers to form relationships across racial and cultural
differences seems like a daunting task, I know that it is possible because I
was the recipient of such an education. While attending UCLA's graduate
school Teacher Education Program, I learned to "see" students and examine
myself. I learned about the need to understand local histories, as well as the
historical legacies that continue to impact the students I would serve. I
learned to design curricula and instruction that responded to students, with
authors that reflected their cultures, subject matters that piqued their interest,
and active and varied lessons that elicited their own expertise. I learned to
treat students as human beings first, students second.

Had I walked into the large Title-1 high school in central Los Angeles
where I taught without this preparation, I am convinced that I would have
become a statistic—yet another white, idealistic teacher who left the profession after a year or two when daily classroom challenges seemed insurmount-
able. Instead, I was named one of Los Angeles Unified School District's
Teachers of the Year after my first two years of teaching. I do not presume to
have become an expert teacher in this short time; instead, I have come to
realize that the tools I acquired at UCLA enabled me to form authentic
relationships with students of color from low-income backgrounds that advanced their engagement and achievement, as well as my own.

I took all of this for granted, but when I left the classroom to pursue
doctoral studies, I was surprised to learn that the broad field of teacher
education rarely addresses the critical relational aspects of practice.[5] This
book is my attempt to bring more attention to teacher–student relationships
and the ways programs from different pedagogical standpoints are already
approaching this work, with lasting consequences. I argue that the field of
education more broadly needs to better conceptualize, support, and practice
the formation of meaningful relationships with *all* students.

My daughters, and the children of most people in this country, will be
influenced by the connections they have with various teachers in their lives.
And the ability to foster meaningful connections with students will likely
impact the teachers, too, in their professional efficacy and job retention, but

also in their own sense of self. I certainly know it did for me. I still keep in touch with many of my former students, across hundreds of miles and several years. They inspire this work. For truly, it is through connecting with these students that I became who I am today.

NOTES

1. Buber, Martin. (1958). *I and thou*. New York: Scribner & Sons, p. 28.

2. See Cooper, Kristy. (2013). Eliciting engagement in the high school classroom: A mixed-methods examination of teaching practices. *American Educational Research Journal, 51*(2), 363–402; Fredricks, Jennifer A., Blumenfeld, Phyllis C., & Paris, Alison H. (2004). School engagement: Potential of the concept, state of the evidence. *Review of Educational Research, 74*(1), 59–109; Martin, Andrew J., & Dowson, Martin. (2009). Interpersonal relationships, motivation, engagement, and achievement: Yields for theory, current issues, and educational practice. *Review of Educational Research, 79*(1), 327–365; Sosa, Teresa, & Gomez, Kimberley. (2012). Connecting teacher efficacy beliefs in promoting resilience to support of Latino students. *Urban Education, 47*(5), 876–909.

3. Throughout this book, I intentionally capitalize Black but not white. This is because Black is a proper noun, referring to a formal culture or group of people from the African diaspora. White, on the other hand, is not generally thought to be a culture in and of itself, and white people often think of themselves in terms of their specific cultural origins (e.g., Irish American). To understand more about this, see https://radicalcopyeditor.com/2016/09/21/black-with-a-capital-b/.

4. Sleeter, Christine. (2008). Preparing white teachers for diverse students. *Handbook of Research on Teacher Education: Enduring Questions in Changing Contexts, 3*, 559–582.

5. Grossman, Pam, & McDonald, Morva. (2008). Back to the future: Directions for research in teaching and teacher education. *American Educational Research Journal, 45*(1), 184–205; McDonald, Morva A., Bowman, Michael, & Brayko, Kate. (2013, April). Learning to see students: opportunities to develop relational practices of teaching through community based placements in teacher education. *Teachers College Record, 115*, 1–35.

Acknowledgments

The journey to write this book has been an arduous and incredible one, rife with many twists and turns, trials and tribulations. And I would not have reached my destination without the support and assistance of so many people who inspired me, bolstered me, guided me, listened to me, let me cry on their shoulders, read my profuse prose, watched my children, and nourished me—body, mind, and soul. There are so many people who deserve appreciation.

First, this book would not exist today had it not been for the three incredible scholars who served on my dissertation committee, supporting and guiding me throughout the course of the study that informs these pages. These distinguished professors include Jal Mehta, Sara Lawrence-Lightfoot, and Meira Levinson. As my advisor, Jal encouraged an ambitious research agenda, one that led to this book. Throughout the last 8 years, he has been my "guide on the side," always asking questions first, sharing insight in the form of personal anecdotes, exposing me to life-changing scholarship, and cheering on my efforts. Through his generous attention, I was able to hone my analytic abilities, improve my writing, and generate meaningful scholarship. Meira, too, generously guided me, with her critical insights and sympathetic concern for me as a person. Her incredibly high standards helped me conduct and report research that was both innovative and rigorous. I am further indebted to both Jal and Meira for continuing to support my work after I graduated from the doctoral program, reading drafts of my book proposal and chapters and helping me think through the process of publishing this work. Moreover, Professor Lawrence-Lightfoot served as both an inspiration and guide throughout this research; she exemplified what is possible in methodology and artistry, while offering genuine warmth and subtle advice to help me find my way to portraiture and through this study. Her incisive questions and keen aesthetic sensibility helped me craft a more thoughtful and beautiful narrative. Overall, I feel honored to have had the opportunity to learn from these amazing people.

The study documented here would not have been possible without the research sites that star in this book. A special thank-you to the faculty and residents from "Progressive Teacher Residency" (PTR) and "No Excuses Teacher Residency" (NETR), who allowed me to observe and examine their thoughts and experiences. In particular, I want to thank "Taylor" from PTR and "Sara" from NETR for taking a great deal of time to sit with me and answer questions. And of course, I must thank my four focus residents—"Julie" and "Casey" from NETR and "Elisabeth" and "Leah" from PTR—for allowing me to interview and observe them multiple times in their programs and then in the field, their first year in the incredibly demanding teaching profession; these four teachers generously gave me hours of their lives, access to numerous documents, and a seat in the back of their classrooms. I am also grateful to the Harvard Graduate School of Education for awarding me various small grants to aid in the collection and analysis of the data represented here.

I have also been extremely fortunate to be surrounded by brilliant friends and colleagues who have shed their time, attention, and insight upon this work by reading drafts and offering comments. In alphabetical order, I want to thank Mildred Boveda, Chris Buttimer, Amy Cheung, Maleka Donaldson, Sarah Fine, Jenna Gravel, James Noonan, Stuti Shukla, Lynneth Solis, and Beth Swadener. They have all offered me encouragement, seen things in the data that I overlooked, helped interrogate my assumptions, pushed my thinking, and cared about me a person outside the work. I am also grateful to my childhood best friend Adriane Ackerman, the only person outside of the academy who willingly read hundreds of pages of my writing while providing feedback and support. Additionally, I would like to thank Shirley Fedorak, who helped edit a rough draft of this manuscript. This book would not be what it is today without all of their insights and encouragement.

I want to acknowledge Elsie Moore for believing in this work and leading me to the postdoctoral research position at Arizona State University's School of Social Transformation that made space for me to complete this book. Her support and guidance has been invaluable. Within this position, I have also been fortunate to be advised by Bryan Brayboy, who has generously shared his experience and expertise to help me navigate the waters of academia. And before I ever entered academia, I was fortunate to have many wonderful teachers through elementary and secondary school, college and beyond who modeled meaningful teacher-student relationships. Some of these educators–including April Chambers, John Palmer, Rae Jeane Williams, and Samuel Joo–fostered connections with me that changed my life.

I am fortunate to have good friends who provided moral support, camaraderie, advice, and even child care. Cynthia Pepper has been there every step of the way, helped with my children, and listened attentively to my challenges. Rachel Blaine, who plowed this path before me, helped guide me through this academic and parenting journey. Ashli Jones let me crash on her couch for weeks during my initial data collection experiences in Los Angeles and was always there to listen and empathize. My fellow working moms—including Leslie Armstrong, Sheena Chiang, Pearl Esau, Whitney Leinin, Jennifer Stein, and Sabrina Villagran—provided me needed moral support on this journey of writing while parenting. And to those who went through the doctoral journey alongside me, including my fellow *Harvard Educational Review* editors and cohort mates: thank you for being there, for listening and understanding, for showing me that I was never alone. My friends have been like family.

And then, of course, there is my wonderful family, who has supported me throughout this process. I am so grateful for my mom, Marissa Theisen. Although she battled pancreatic cancer for two years, she continued to ask about my research, listened to my forming theories, turned me on to Martin Buber, and made it across the country with cancer in her very bones to watch me walk across the stage to collect the doctoral degree for the research that informs this book. She passed away in September 2018, and though it has been hard to move forward without her, she never let anything inhibit her passion for knowledge and I know she would be proud that I have persisted with this work. I also want to thank my dad, Chuck Theisen, who has always believed in me, encouraged my academic trajectory, and cared for my personal well-being. Without his support over the years, I would not have been able to pursue learning the way that I have. My stepmom, Anita Theisen, has also helped support my growth as a person and offered a great deal of moral support as I navigated the worlds of motherhood and professional employment. I appreciate my brothers, Nick Theisen and Alexander Theisen, for their enthusiasm and love. I am also lucky to have my parents-in-law, Eva and Chuck, who have provided moral support, generous childcare when they visit, and understanding. I also want to thank my East Coast family—Pat Bicchieri, Erica and John Boudreau, Kelly Brooks, Judy and Jack Davidson, Jim Davidson, Lisa Davidson, Jill Mirman, Sheila Ouellette, Brian and Courtney Ouellette, and Diane Roche—for being there for me while I conducted this study, for nurturing my heart with food and song, for helping me stay connected to my mom, and for reminding me that I am never alone. And to my extended family in Phoenix—Lisa and Karl Knickmeyer, and Cathy Theisen and Denise DiLallo—for helping sustain me with good company and food.

Thank you to my longtime love, Nils Homer. Over the course of nearly 17 years of partnership, Nils has encouraged, supported, and endured this journey alongside me. In college, when I was a teacher, and throughout this academic journey, he has always seen me for the best version of myself, pushing me to do and be more. He has also been a loving father to our two girls, enabling me time and space to get this done while parenting very young kids. Above all, I could not have done this without him. My daughters are my most profound inspiration. I want them to be proud of their mama. And they also inspire me to imagine a better world with better relationships in and out of the classroom. And before my girls came along, my students in Los Angeles set the stage for this work by showing me the power of teacher–student relationships; they continue to inspire me.

During the 5-year journey of researching and writing this book, all the people named above have encountered their own challenges and transitions, as is part of the human condition. My knowledge of this makes their support all the more meaningful, as they made time to ensure I did not feel alone in my own challenges. No one can do something like this alone; it truly takes a village. I feel so lucky for "the village" that has led me to this point and now buoys me forward. As I have researched and experienced, human connection truly is a powerful force for good.

Introduction

I've learned that people will forget what you said, people will forget what you did, but people will never forget how you made them feel. —Maya Angelou

When people talk about their favorite teacher, it is often the teacher who took a special interest in their work, identified their potential in a particular area, helped counsel them through a personal issue, made a piece of literature relevant to their lives, or even attended their quinceañera, bar mitzvah, choral performance, sports game, or other activity. These are the teachers who formed relationships with students, and sometimes influenced the trajectory of their lives. Research also supports the power of meaningful teacher–student relationships to advance students' social and emotional learning and academic outcomes.[1]

But it cannot be assumed that forming meaningful connections with students is innate, especially when most teachers come from very different embodied perspectives (in terms of race, ethnicity, class, socioeconomic status, religion, language, sexual orientation, gender identity, etc.) than their students. In fact, connecting across lines of race might be particularly precarious for teachers.[2] Although race is a social construct, and a single racial category can incorporate several different cultures and ethnicities, skin color is one of the most apparent signifiers of difference and "racial considerations shade almost everything in America."[3] For example, research suggests that white teachers often carry "deficit" perspectives of students of color into their practice, impeding the development of meaningful relationships with them.[4] Because the vast majority of teachers—and those in teacher education pipelines—in the United States are white women, but most students today are not, it is imperative that teacher education programs equip beginning teachers with the relational tools to overcome this "mismatch."[5] Unfortunately, there is not enough empirical work on teacher–student relationships, particularly in the field of teacher education.[6]

There are a few prominent conceptual works of scholarship that focus on teacher–student relationships as a crucial aspect of good teaching across racial and cultural differences.[7] Moreover, some qualitative scholars have explored what meaningful social justice teaching or culturally relevant pedagogy looks like and found that forming fluid, caring, and humanizing relationships with students of color is an integral part of this.[8] There are also a number of empirical studies, particularly in the field of educational psychology, that attempt to measure and address the impact of teacher–student relationships on student outcomes; nearly all of these studies find a significant link between meaningful relationships and positive student outcomes.[9] But we know little about how teacher education programs seek to prepare novices for such relational work.[10] We know even less about how this preparation translates to beginning practice once teachers are in the field.

Instead, most of the empirical research on teacher education focuses on the "cognitive" aspects of the profession—topics like content knowledge, pedagogical content knowledge, and appropriate scaffolding for students.[11] What we see as "soft skills" often take a backseat to what are perceived to be harder skills. But this imbalance is unjustified for a few reasons. First, as Carol Lee points out, forming relationships with students involves a great deal of cognition; it requires concerted attention to students' sense of identity, emotional states, personal goals, learning history, and culture.[12] Additionally, the basis for these so-called cognitive competencies is often established by teachers' relational abilities, as they are better able to design curricula and instruction that is appropriate for students when they really know them. And when students leave schools, they are more likely to remember the teacher who "saw" and connected with them on an individual level, than the teacher who was adept at something like lesson plan sequencing and transitions. Truly, most teachers, too, thrive on these connections, which contribute to what Dan Lortie would call "intrinsic rewards."[13]

But how do we conceptualize meaningful teacher–student relationships?

MEANINGFUL TEACHER–STUDENT RELATIONSHIPS IN THEORY

Martin Buber offers theoretical guidance on human relationships. In his most seminal book *I and Thou* (1958), he makes the distinction between two different kinds of relationships in which humans engage.[14] First, there are "I–It" relationships, which are transactional and superficial. In an I–It relationship, one party uses another for a particular end or interacts with them in a limited capacity. *New York Times* columnist David Brooks provides this example: "A doctor has an I-It relationship with a patient when he treats him as a machine in need of repair."[15]

Buber contrasts this with the idea of "I–Thou" relationships, which are trusting, reciprocal, dialogical, and caring. In I–Thou relationships, a person meets and accepts another person, is fully present to that meeting, listens and responds to that person's "whole being," and views the other's thoughts and feelings as equally valuable as their own. Drawing on Buber, scholars like Guilherme and Morgan have sought to further explain the difference between these two relationships: "It could be said that the I–It relation is an objective or instrumental relation that allows human beings to provide for and fullfil their basic needs and desires because we are material entities, but it could also be said that the I–Thou relation is a subjective or spiritual relation that allows human beings to fulfil themselves creatively, emotively and spiritually because we are also subjective entities."[16] According to Buber, I–Thou relationships require more energy, but are inherently more meaningful for both parties.

In schools, the power differential between teachers and students necessitates a unique kind of I–Thou relationship, one that Buber suggests requires a fine balance of "giving and withholding oneself, intimacy and distance."[17] Instead of perfect mutuality, the educator is responsible for taking the lead in working to recognize and receive all children as human beings (not just as students) before even attempting to teach them, modeling for students the foundation of meaningful relationships with others. But this can and should still be an I–Thou relationship, one built on dialogue, trust, responsiveness, and some degree of reciprocity, where teachers draw students into learning through personal connections and students engage and contribute in ways that inform the teacher.

In contrast, Buber criticizes educational relationships of "compulsion," where teachers require students to regurgitate the knowledge they have dispensed without engaging with students. Buber believes that establishing I–Thou relationships with students will help them go on to contribute to building a better "community," whereas relationships of compulsion will contribute to "disunion . . . humiliation and rebelliousness."[18]

Both Nel Noddings and Paulo Freire explicitly draw upon Buber's idea of an I–Thou relationship in schools in their own conception of teacher–student relationships. For example, Freire evokes Buber in his description of dialogical relationships between teacher and students. He describes this as a horizontal "I-Thou Relationship" that is "nourished by love, humility, hope, faith, and trust."[19] Like Buber, Freire warns of the perils of more rigid, perfunctory, and hierarchical forms of teacher–student relationships: "Each time the 'thou' is changed into an object, an 'it,' dialogue is subverted and education is changed to deformation."[20] Freire further insists that humanizing teacher–student relationships are especially important for students from "oppressed" groups, who must learn that their voice matters, too.[21] Noddings also cites Buber in her early work, as her conception of care ethics depends on the way that teachers see and receive their students. She, too, distinguishes between two types of caring in schools: (1) the active and engaged form of "caring as relation," which follows the form of the "I–Thou" relationship, and (2) the passive virtue of "aesthetical caring" in which a person generally "care[s] about" another as they would an "object."[22] And in recent work, Noddings acknowledges that her conceptualization of care ethics is very much in line with Buber and Freire in that she thinks teacher–student relationships should be trusting, affirming, and responsive.[23]

Buber, Freire, and Noddings all view teacher–student relationships as an active and dynamic exchange that is central to the enterprise of teaching. To them, relationships with students should not be passive or shallow, and they all warn against objectifying students. Instead, they establish the idea of humanizing relationships that are active and dynamic, caring and responsive.

These scholars do not advocate for an equal relationship per se, but a reciprocal one in which the teacher seeks to really "see" and respond to each student as a human being. But these responsive relationships with individual students are not intended to advance student individualism or narcissism. Instead, these theorists suggest that meaningful human relationships with teachers can prepare students to care for others, cultivate community among people, and fight for what Freire calls our "full humanity." To them, meaningful teacher–student relationships are necessary to create a better world.[24]

Scholars of culturally responsive teaching, culturally relevant pedagogy, and critical pedagogy have also taken up the call for more humanizing teacher–student relationships.[25] Since schools have failed to serve students of color for generations, these traditions of educational scholarship call on teachers to reenvision the way they teach and interact with students from historically marginalized groups. Prominent educational scholars—like Geneva Gay, Gloria Ladson Billings, Jeff Duncan-Andrade, and Angela Valenzuela—assert that students of color need teachers who are not simply "nice" but can form critical relationships with them. These scholars conceptualize such relationships as stemming from deep knowledge about individual students, coupled with social awareness and self-reflection on behalf of the teacher; such relationships manifest in active care for students as human beings and curricula and instructional practices that help empower students' understandings of self and the world. While meaningful and humanizing teacher–student relationships are important for all students, these may be particularly important for historically marginalized students.[26]

STUDYING TEACHER EDUCATION FOR RELATIONSHIPS

Theorists and researchers alike emphasize the weight of teacher–student relationships, but the field of teacher education lacks clear answers to a multitude of relevant questions about how teachers learn to form relationships. How are different teacher education programs approaching this work? How do programs take into account issues of race and racism when preparing preservice teachers to form relationships with all students? What practices seem particularly powerful for these teachers? How do new teachers carry relational learning into the field? And what factors might influence the degree to which teachers use what they have learned to form these relationships? In this book, I address these questions and shed further light on this critical aspect of teaching practice as it is implemented in teacher education programs.

To do so, this book focuses on two well-respected teacher residency programs located in the same city that intentionally tackle relationships and race but in very different ways. Teacher residency programs, which are expanding nationwide, offer a "third way" to educate teachers that attempts to improve upon the shortcomings of both traditional and alternative preparation programs.[27] For example, residencies pair novices with excellent mentor teachers in extended field placements that last up to a full year, often interweave theory and practice in coursework, and employ a cohort model that supports collaboration and discourages traditional teacher silos.[28] In these ways, teacher residencies are designed to resemble medical residencies, in a step toward further professionalizing teaching. Moreover, these features— particularly the extended proximity to students in supportive field placements—seem to make teacher residencies uniquely promising sites for student–teacher relationship development. Early research on residencies indicates they effectively recruit more racially diverse teachers, promote teacher retention, and ultimately improve students' academic outcomes.[29] However, limited scholarship documents the interworking of these programs, and none of it specifically attends to relationship development.

To explore relationship development in residency programs, I draw upon data from a 2-year ethnographic study of two such programs: one based in a well-established progressive independent school (Progressive Teacher Residency, or PTR), the other in a relatively recent no excuses charter school (No Excuses Teacher Residency, or NETR).[30] I selected these two programs because both espouse distinct missions and have an intentional and explicit focus on the development of teacher–student relationships, something that is not common among teacher education programs. They each also have excellent reputations within their respective circles (no excuses or progressive).[31] In many ways, these two programs reflect the potential of "mission-driven" residency programs to help novice teachers learn to form meaningful relationships with students.[32] However, they approach this work very differently, offering an illuminating contrast that exposes the complexity of relational work and the way it is deeply intertwined with context. [33]

In the first year of this study, I embedded myself in these two programs. I observed coursework and activities, interviewed faculty and residents, and collected documents along the way. The stark juxtaposition between No Excuses Teacher Residency (NETR) and Progressive Teacher Residency (PTR)—which one of my colleagues referred to as "whiplash"—enabled me to see aspects of each approach to teacher education that I might not have otherwise identified. Then in the second year, I followed two white residents from each program (four in total) into their first full-time school sites.

Although I intentionally interviewed residents of color to shed light on their responses to residency coursework, I chose to follow white teachers into their first classrooms because not only do they represent the vast majority of the teaching force, but research also suggests they have more work to do to form meaningful relationships with students of color. [34] In the process, I got to know the four focal teachers, which allowed me to better understand how they brought their biography, personality, and goals into their work. Focusing on these teachers also allowed me to discern how they carried their program learning into the field and whether school factors influenced their ability to connect with students in line with their training.

There is much to learn from the portraits of the two different residency programs in this book, especially when presented in relief. Over the years, numerous similar teacher education programs have molded themselves off the example set by both these programs. Thus, while both NETR and PTR demonstrate idiosyncrasies, they are both largely reflective of the no excuses or progressive approach to relationships, teacher preparation, and education overall. And because both standpoints represent influential educational ideologies, vestiges of which continue to permeate a range of schools across the United States and abroad, it is worth exploring how these programs structure relationships at the fundamental level of teacher education. For readers unfamiliar with these educational approaches, I describe them briefly here, but will render each approach in much more depth throughout the chapters.

Progressive Education

In the early 20th century, John Dewey and a series of other prominent educators led a new movement in education toward the individualization of curricula and instruction to better suit the needs and interests of students, which became progressive education. Progressive education eschews traditional didactic modes of instruction in which the teacher dispenses predetermined lessons upon all children. Instead, progressive education is "student centered" in that it focuses on each child's individual needs and attempts to respond to these through varied experiences in the classroom. [35]

As Rugg and Shumaker—champions of progressive education in the 1900s—espoused in their 1928 text *The Child-Centered School*, progressive education "has coursing through it a unitary integrating theme: individuality, personality, experience."[36] While it rose to prominence over 120 years ago, progressive education is still practiced in many schools and classrooms across the world, particularly independent, charter, and magnet schools. Some prominent examples include Theodore Sizer's "Essential schools," Expeditionary Learning schools, High Tech High and its network, and many Montessori, Waldorf, and Reggio Emilia schools.

In action, progressive education favors a constructivist approach to learning that involves cooperative assignments, inquiry-based projects, "hands-on" activity, and real-life application.[37] Different students may be concurrently working on different activities and moving forward at different paces, depending on what each child needs. Students not only have a great deal of agency over what they are learning, but also how they want to approach it.

No Excuses Education

In contrast, the no excuses approach to education is a fairly recent phenomenon, geared around "closing the achievement gap."[38] It expanded prolifically after the enactment of the federal No Child Left Behind Law of 2002, which attached rewards and penalties to school performance on state standardized exams. No excuses schools represent approximately 25% of urban charter schools (which are publicly funded and do not charge tuition but often hold a lottery for entrance) and a scattering of public turnaround schools; these schools often implement longer school days and extended test preparation and have subsequently had more success than many other models in advancing the standardized exam scores of students from historically marginalized backgrounds.

As a result, many no excuses models have expanded into wide networks including KIPP, Relay, Uncommon Schools, Yes Prep, Success Academy, Achievement First, and others. In these schools, teachers and administrators "sweat the small stuff," closely monitoring students' attire, posture, behavior, and academic work, and enforcing strict discipline policies (through demerits, "sendouts," in-class suspensions, etc.) when any of these fall below expectations.[39] Every detail matters, everything must be controlled, so that students can direct all their attention to academic achievement.

In the process, no excuses schools maintain that forces like poverty, racism, and hunger are no excuse for falling below these expectations, hence the moniker "no excuses." Rituals, mantras, and timers often characterize daily activities, as students work in unison. Classrooms feature efficient instruction in a preestablished canonical curriculum that closely aligns with state standardized tests. Students learn what the teacher, school, and state designate is important.[40]

OVERVIEW OF THE BOOK

This book explores the complex, textured, and human side of relationship formation in teacher education programs and schools. It is primarily organized in three parts, each featuring three chapters. Parts I and II offer multifaceted portraits of NETR and PTR, respectively. Considering these programs holistically illuminates the intricate fabric that informs relational learning and the way each program makes consequential trade-offs in pursuit of its coherent mission. Because racial competence is critical for forming relationships with students across racial differences, I devote a chapter in each of these two parts to exploring how each program addresses issues of race and racism. The profound contrasts between these two programs are made more explicit in Part III, which considers how residents carry learning into the field from each program and the implications of each approach.

Part I of the book (Chapters 1–3) explores relationship development in a no excuses setting. Chapter 1 provides background on NETR and explores its strikingly instrumental vision of relationships and the discrete coursework that supports this; in the process, it considers the tensions that emerge between maintaining personal authenticity while establishing authority and the call for efficiency in messy human interactions.

Chapter 2 describes NETR's coursework on race and inequality, addressing its heavy emphasis on "the culture of power," and the ways that teaching students to "navigate" this system in schools could possibly perpetuate it. And Chapter 3 focuses on the residents: the explicit expectations they must follow, their aligned student teaching experiences, and their less structured tutorial experiences with a small group of students; while this latter experience feels more salient to residents, its application for no excuses teaching is uncertain.

Part II (Chapters 4–6) depicts relationship-building in a very different educational environment, PTR and the unique school it inhabits, which I call Xanadu. Chapter 4 depicts the immersive experience of learning to teach at Xanadu, where teaching and relationships are student centered and reciprocal, focused on critical thinking and self-advocacy; however, learning in this unique space may not sufficiently prepare residents for the range of schools the program intends to serve. Chapter 5 explores the challenges of confronting issues of race and racism in this sheltered and privileged space. The PTR director seeks to challenge oppression through curriculum and pedagogy, but the white homogeneity of the resident cohort, the privileged group of students residents serve in fieldwork, and the lack of an explicit mission or framework around this work limits how far the director can push residents to challenge racism.

Chapter 6 centers around PTR residents' fieldwork experiences and how they absorb profound lessons about teaching and classroom management from their teaching placements at Xanadu, but struggle in their spring public school placements because education in these sites is not coherent with PTR's philosophy; this has the ironic effect of dissuading most residents from teaching in public schools.

Finally, Part III (Chapters 7–9) explores how residents carry their distinct lessons on teaching and relationship development from their preparation program into the field. Chapter 7 serves to transition from the portraits of programs to the cases of teachers in the field: it compares the different educational and relational approaches in each program outlines ten relational competencies for teachers, reviews research on the impact of teacher education in beginning practice, and introduces *interactional culture* as a framework for studying relationships in school contexts.

Chapter 8 features cases of the four focal residents (two from each program) and how they attempt to connect with students in contexts that are both similar to and different from their programs; across contexts, residents display program learning in all aspects of their teaching, but the teachers in schools with less coherent cultures end up feeling less able or willing to implement all of their relational tools. In the final chapter, Chapter 9, I consider the implications of each program's approach to relationships and how this played out in the classroom, and conceptualize how teacher education programs, schools, and teachers themselves might better support more humanizing teacher–student relationships in schools.

Through rich portraits and cases, careful analysis, and aspirational discussion, this book illustrates how teacher education programs currently train teachers to connect with students, especially across cultural differences. It challenges readers to reflect on their own relational practice, or that enacted by programs or schools with which they are affiliated, with the idea that we all can, and should, do better.

NOTES

1. Cooper, Kristy. (2013). Eliciting engagement in the high school classroom: A mixed-methods examination of teaching practices. *American Educational Research Journal, 51*(2), 363–402; Fredricks, Jennifer A., Blumenfeld, Phyllis C., & Paris, Alison H. (2004). School engagement: Potential of the concept, state of the evidence. *Review of Educational Research, 74*(1), 59–109; Martin, Andrew J., & Dowson, Martin. (2009). Interpersonal relationships, motivation, engagement, and achievement: Yields for theory, current issues, and educational practice. *Review of Educational Research, 79*(1), 327–365; Schonert-Reichl, Kimberly. (2017). Social and emotional learning and teachers. *The Future of Children 27*(1). Retrieved from https://files.eric.ed.gov/fulltext/EJ1145076.pdf; Sosa, Teresa, & Gomez, Kimberley. (2012).

Connecting teacher efficacy beliefs in promoting resilience to support of Latino students. *Urban Education, 47*(5), 876–909.

2. I use the term "race" throughout this text to indicate a social construct, not a biological reality, that has a weighty meaning in the United States in particular. Race in this context is often seen as a binary, either white or nonwhite, with the latter associated with historical legacies of oppression and the former with privilege and supremacy. These ideas are so deeply embedded into the culture that skin color alone can trigger a slew of assumptions about a person, especially by white people, who happen to represent the majority of the teaching force. And because skin color is so apparent, this perceived signifier of difference will be the one I focus on most throughout this book.

3. Bonilla-Silva, Eduardo. (2014). *Racism without racists: Color-blind racism and the persistence of racial inequality in America.* Lanham, MD: Rowman & Littlefield.

4. Sleeter, Christine. (2008). Preparing white teachers for diverse students. *Handbook of Research on Teacher Education: Enduring Questions in Changing Contexts, 3,* 559–582; Picower, B. (2009). The unexamined whiteness of teaching: How white teachers maintain and enact dominant racial ideologies. *Race Ethnicity and Education, 12*(2), 197–215; Matias, C., & Zembylas, M. (2014). "When saying you care is not really caring": Emotions of disgust, whiteness ideology, and teacher education. *Critical Studies in Education, 55*(3), 319–337; Hyland, N. (2005). Being a good teacher of black students? White teachers and unintentional racism. *Curriculum Inquiry, 35*(4), 429–459.

5. Ingersoll, Richard, & Merrill, Lisa. (2014). *Seven trends: The transformation of the teaching force.* Philadelphia, PA: Consortium for Policy Research in Education.

6. Grossman, Pam, & McDonald, Morva. (2008). Back to the future: Directions for research in teaching and teacher education. *American Educational Research Journal, 45*(1), 184–205.

7. See, for example, Gay, Geneva. (2000). *Culturally responsive teaching: Theory, research, & practice.* New York, NY: Teachers College Press; Schultz, Katherine. (2003). *Listening: A framework for teaching across differences.* New York, NY: Teachers College Press.

8. Ladson-Billings, Gloria. (1994). *Dreamkeepers: Successful teachers of African American children.* San Francisco, CA: Jossey-Bass; Valenzuela, Angela. (1999). *Subtractive schooling: U.S.–Mexican youth and the politics of caring.* New York, NY: SUNY Press.

9. For example, Brinkworth, Maureen, McIntyre, Joseph, Juraschek, Anna D., & Gehlbach, Hunter. (2017). Teacher–student relationships: The positives and negatives of assessing both perspectives. *Journal of Applied Developmental Psychology, 55,* 24–38; Cooper, Eliciting engagement; Fredricks, Blumenfeld, & Paris, School engagement; Gehlbach, Hunter, Brinkworth, Maureen E., & Harris, Anna D. (2012). Changes in teacher–student relationships. *British Journal of Educational Psychology, 82*(4), 690–704; Martin & Dowson, Interpersonal relationships.

10. Grossman & McDonald, Back to the future; McDonald, Morva A., Bowman, Michael, & Brayko, Kate. (2013, April). Learning to see students: Opportunities to develop relational practices of teaching through community based placements in teacher education. *Teachers College Record, 115,* 1–35.

11. See, for example, Ball, Deborah Loewenberg. (2000). Bridging practices: Intertwining content and pedagogy in teaching and learning to teach. *Journal of Teacher Education, 51*(3), 241–247; Clark, Christopher, & Lampert, Magdalene. (1986). The study of teacher thinking: Implications for teacher education. *Journal of Teacher Education, 37*(5), 27–31; Lampert, Magdalene. (2001). *Teaching problems and the problems of teaching.* New Haven, CT: Yale University Press; Saphier, Jon, & Gower, Robert R. (1997). *The skillful teacher: Building your teaching skills.* Acton, MA: Research for Better Teaching.

12. Lee, Carol. (2017). *Opportunity and equity inside classrooms: Teacher–child relationships and educational success.* Invited speaker session presented at the American Educational Research Association, San Antonio, TX.

13. Lortie, Dan C. (1975). *Schoolteacher: A sociological study.* Chicago, IL: University of Chicago Press.

14. Buber, Martin. (1958). *I and thou.* New York, NY: Scribner & Sons.

15. Brooks, David. (2016, November 1). Read Buber, not the polls. *New York Times*. Retrieved from https://www.nytimes.com/2016/11/01/opinion/read-buber-not-the-polls.html

16. Guilherme, Alex, & Morgan, W. John. (2009). Martin Buber's philosophy of education and its implications for adult non-formal education. *International Journal of Lifelong Education, 28*(5), 565–581.

17. Buber, Martin. (1965). *Between man and man*. London, England: Routledge, p. 95.

18. Buber, *Between man and man*, p. 91

19. Freire, Paulo. (1973). *Education for critical consciousness*. New York, NY: Continuum, p. 45.

20. Freire, *Education for critical consciousness*, p. 52.

21. See Freire, Paulo. (1970). *Pedagogy of the oppressed*. New York, NY: Continuum.

22. Noddings, Nel. (1984). *Caring: A feminine approach to ethics & moral education*. Berkeley: University of California Press, p. 21.

23. Noddings, Nel. (2013). Freire, Buber, and care ethics on dialogue in teaching. In R. Lake & T. Kress (Eds.), *Paulo Freire's intellectual roots: Toward historicity in praxis*. New York, NY: Bloomsbury.

24. See Freire, *Pedagogy of the oppressed*; Freire, *Education for critical consciousness*; Freire, Paulo. (1998). *Pedagogy of freedom: Ethics, democracy, and civic courage*. Lanham, MD: Rowman & Littlefield; Noddings (1992), *Caring*; Noddings (2013), Freire, Buber, and care ethics on dialogue in teaching.

25. Duncan-Andrade, Jeff. (2007). Gangstas, wankstas, and ridas: Defining, developing, andsupporting effective teachers in urban schools. *International Journal of Qualitative Studies in Education, 20*(6), 617–638; Duncan-Andrade, J. M. R., & Morrell, E. (2008). *The art of critical pedagogy: Possibilities for moving from theory to practice in urban schools*. New York, NY: Peter Lang; Gay, *Culturally responsive teaching*; Ladson-Billings, *Dreamkeepers*; Valenzuela, *Subtractive schooling*; Villegas, Ana María, & Lucas, Tamara. (2002). Preparing culturally responsive teachers: Rethinking the curriculum. *Journal of Teacher Education, 53*(1), 20–32.

26. Also see Victoria Theisen-Homer (2020), Preparing teachers for relationships with students: Two visions, two approaches, *Journal of Teacher Education* for a more succinct presentation of this theoretical framing.

27. Papay, John P., West, Martin R., Fullerton, Jon B., & Kane, Thomas J. (2012). Does an urban teacher residency increase student achievement? Early evidence from Boston. *Educational Evaluation and Policy Analysis, 34*(4), 413–434.

28. Berry, Barnett, Montgomery, Diana, & Snyder, Jon. (2008). *Urban teacher residency models and institutes of higher education: Implications for teacher preparation*. Chapel Hill, NC: Center for Teaching Quality; Solomon, Jesse. (2009). The Boston teacher residency: District-based teacher education. *Journal of Teacher Education, 60*(5), 478–488.

29. For example, Guha, R., Hyler, M. & Darling-Hammond, L. (2016). *The teacher residency: An innovative model for preparing teachers*. Palo Alto, CA: Learning Policy Institute; Papay, West, Fullerton, & Kane, Does an urban teacher residency increase student achievement?; Solomon, The Boston teacher residency.

30. I use pseudonyms to anonymize the names of the programs and participants throughout this book.

31. I have decided not to capitalize "no excuses" throughout this book for a few reasons. First, progressive education is rarely capitalized, and the term "no excuses education" has become almost as ubiquitous. Second, I wanted to distinguish No Excuses Teacher Residency with capitalization. Third, capitalizing the phrase makes it seem more like a universal brand than it is; today, there are a number of different no excuses schools and while they share a number of common characteristics, there is notable variation between them.

32. Feiman-Nemser, Sharon, Tamir, Eran, & Hammerness, Karen. (2015). *Inspiring teaching: Preparing teachers to succeed in mission-driven schools*. Cambridge, MA: Harvard Education Press.

33. By context in this study, I mean the character and culture of each program and the people implementing the work in this space.

34. Sleeter, Preparing white teachers.

35. Dewey, John. (1900). *The School and society*. Chicago, IL: University of Chicago Press.

36. Graham, Patricia A. (2005). *Schooling America*. New York, NY: Oxford University Press, p. 53.

37. Mehta, Jal, & Fine, Sarah. (2019). *In search of deeper learning: Inside the effort to remake the American high school*. Cambridge, MA: Harvard University Press.

38. Despite calls to reframe this as an "opportunity gap" or "education debt," no excuses schools continue to focus on student achievement as the main problem; thus their solution is not on addressing a society that deprives them of opportunities, but of attempting to improve their individual achievement. For more on "opportunity gap" and "education debt," see Ladson-Billings, Gloria. (2006). From the achievement gap to the education debt: Understanding achievement in U.S. schools. *Educational Researcher, 35*(7), 3–12.

39. Whitman, David. (2008). *Sweating the small stuff: Inner-city schools and the new paternalism*. Washington, DC: Thomas B. Fordham Institute.

40. See Whitman, *Sweating the small stuff*; Mehta & Fine, *In search of deeper learning*.

Part I

No Excuses Teacher Residency

Chapter One

An Instrumental Approach

All your relationship-building has to be leveraged for the ultimate goal: the student's success in school and in life.—NETR handbook for the Relationships and Student Investment course

A FORMULA FOR PRODUCING EDUCATIONAL RESULTS

Occupying an unassuming industrial building with a façade of gray stucco and red brick, the charter school that houses No Excuses Teacher Residency (NETR) blends into the densely settled city block. When the bell chimes, announcing the end of first period, students (most of whom are Black and Latinx) and teachers and administrators (most of whom are white) stream into the lobby, progressing up and down the wide, angled staircase at the building's center. Both teachers and students wear some variation of the uniform for Excellence Preparatory High School (EPHS): a blue or gray shirt or sweatshirt with khaki pants or shorts.

Opposite the grand staircase sits the Big Hall, an expansive white room separated from the hallway by a wall of glass. Neat rows of large tables and blue plastic chairs span the width of the room that doubles as a meeting room for both NETR courses and EPHS students. I settle into an inconspicuous plastic chair in the very back of the room and glance around; tall off-white Grecian pillars, ornate designs on the white ceiling, bare walls, and cold tile floors characterize the formality of the space. Instead of sunlight, recessed fixtures in the raised ceiling illuminate the room with yellow light, giving the space the feel of a warehouse, perhaps reminiscent of the auto parts distributer that formerly inhabited this building.

As newly minted teacher residents stream in through the glass doors, they briefly chat with one another and quickly populate the rows of tables throughout the room. There are 74 residents, most of whom are dressed in some type of monochromatic professional attire: cleanly pressed dark blazers and matching slacks or skirts. Most appear quite young, likely right out of college. And I am surprised by the number of men and people of color in attendance, as they are generally underrepresented in the nation's teaching force; according to NETR data, 33% of these residents are people of color (compared to only 18% of teachers nationwide), and 31% are male (versus 24% nationally).[1]

All seven of the principal program faculty stand in the room for this opening day; all of them are white. When the clock strikes 9:00 a.m., Todd, the program's founding director, confidently strolls to the front of the hall and immediately captures the attention of the large group. He is dressed in a gray business suit, a navy-blue tie, and a crisp, blue, checkered shirt, neatly tucked into his slacks. His shortly cropped salt-and-pepper hair and goatee reflect his age in a way his unlined face does not. Before joining NETR, Todd spent years leading an Ivy League teacher training program and before that, he was a teacher himself. When I first met with him to gain access to researching NETR, he welcomed me with genuine warmth and spoke about his work with unabashed pride. I found him very charismatic.

As the residents gaze up at Todd, he begins lightheartedly, "This is year 19 for me, and I still get teacher nerves and have teacher dreams before the first day." The residents laugh. Todd continues his introduction with passion and enthusiasm, his hazel eyes flashing as a smile brightens his face. "The last degree that you earned was about how smart you were; this next one is about getting other people to learn," he adds.

Then Todd moves on to introduce a formula to help guide residents' thinking about their beginning teaching practice (see Figure 1.1 at bottom of page).

Some of the residents nod, having seen this formula during their interview for the program. I, however, find myself staring incredulously at the screen up front. I have never seen learning represented in such starkly quantitative terms before, and I immediately attempt to deconstruct the reasoning behind this formula.

According to one of the NETR handbooks, lesson quality and individual student effort are both rated on a scale of 1–10 units, with 1 representing very low quality or effort, and 10 representing very high. Meanwhile, the "misbehavior tax" refers to the percentage of class time "lost" due to student misbe-

Classroom Learning = Lesson Quality×$\sum$**Individual Student Effort** ×(**1 − Misbehavior Tax**)

Figure 1.1.

havior. The average goal for graduates of the program is a "tax rate" of around 5%, losing approximately 3 minutes of a 56-minute class. The handbook further explains, "High Lesson Quality and Student Effort will never compensate for a high Misbehavior Tax. You have to lower the tax in order to generate significant gains in your students' Classroom Learning. You have to. You must. There is no other way." From these assertive lines, I get the sense that themes of classroom management, constructed as a quantifiable experience, will permeate *all* coursework here at NETR.

Todd next asks the residents to silently respond to a "Do Now" that challenges teachers to apply this formula to their own neophyte instructional experiences in Tutorial. Tutorial is an integral part of NETR in which residents tutor the same group of 5 to 10 students Monday through Thursday throughout the year, using a scripted curriculum provided by the no excuses school where they are placed. Although today is the first day of coursework, residents have already been tutoring for a couple weeks.

After the residents have typed silently for 5 minutes, Todd asks for a show of hands: "Did anyone generate 90 units of learning? Eighty?" No one raises a hand. "At least we are being honest. Seventy?" Still, no hands climb into the air. "All right, I guess the honeymoon period is over," he says with a chuckle and tells the residents to engage in a brief "turn-and-talk" with peers at their tables about their respective learning outcomes. Chatter erupts from the tables—a stark contrast to the previous pin-drop silence—as novices excitedly discuss their Tutorial experiences with a partner. I overhear the following disclosures from residents in the room:

"I have no idea how to teach the struggling students."
"I feel like it's so stigmatizing to always be saying, 'No. No. No.'"
"Every 5 minutes there is an outburst."
"Write your name, write your name. . . ."

Then Todd's clear voice echoes across the room: "Take about five more seconds." When the last of the chatter dies away, he begins his group questioning: "How many would attribute the issues [in Tutorial] to lesson quality?" A couple of wayward hands lift into the air.

"Student effort?" A few more hands ascend in a slightly less tentative fashion.

"Misbehavior tax?" The vast majority of the hands shoot up. Todd smiles knowingly.

Like Todd, I am not surprised by this. I recognize how common it is for new teachers to struggle with classroom management, as I myself initially struggled. In fact, inadequate training in classroom management is the most common complaint of new teachers.[2] But I am beginning to get the sense that this will not be the primary complaint of NETR graduates. Instead, they will learn to approach it like a science, or a formula for that matter, and in ways that will likely shape their relationships with students.

As Todd continues the lesson, he introduces three levers residents can use to increase classroom learning by increasing effort and reducing misbehavior: "lesson tightness," which has to do with how efficiently time is used in the class; "lesson legitness," which relates to the rigor of the lesson and its outcome, and how well students are supported to achieve this; and "professional relationship capital."

Todd explains this last idea: "The better you have relationships with students, the more they are going to be willing to work hard when they don't want to. [For example,] if I don't want to let Ms. X down, I will work harder for her." While faculty link "relationship capital" with increased student effort and reduced misbehavior, they do not link this to lesson quality. Relationships are thus established as unidirectional, altering the behavior and effort of the student, but not that of the teacher. The word "capital" also frames relationships in financial terms, accumulated to achieve desired ends. Still, relationships play an important role in NETR's formula for education.

When I interviewed Todd before the school year began, I asked him about the program's vision for the development of relationships between the teachers they are preparing in NETR and their future students. He explained:

> On an individual level I think the foundation of the relationship is that my job [meaning, the teacher's job] is to try to generate maximum effort in thinking from you. That's my job. It's not to be your friend. It's not to learn everything that's going on in your life, although at times I do need to know those things in order to get to the other [stuff]. If I'm learning that or investigating that, it's only to get to the end goal of how I get you to work and think as hard as you can in the time that I have you.

In this way, NETR conceives of forming relationships with students as instrumental: as process that must be thoughtfully undertaken to inspire maximum effort and proper behavior from students. This vision is antagonistic to a relationship of "friend[s]," which Todd implies would be too close, too informal, too messy.

Contrary to what might be expected of a no excuses institution, NETR intentionally aims to prepare residents to develop relationships with students and has a course entirely devoted to this end. In this course on relationships, coupled with the course on classroom management, residents learn moves and strategies to help them connect with students, promote student investment, and improve behavior. But how will this distinctive conceptualization of relationships play out in coursework? How will residents respond to it?

SUPPLY AND DEMAND: A TECHNICAL RESPONSE TO A SOCIAL PROBLEM

No excuses schools like EPHS emerged in response to one particular social problem: the "achievement gap."[3] But they soon had to contend with another issue: a shortage of effective teachers who could readily implement no excuses pedagogy. As education reformers and parents demanded an increased number of these schools, which appeared to have unique success in advancing test scores, administrators had to find a way to increase their supply of teachers. It is within this context that NETR was born.

Although a relatively recent addition to the teacher education landscape, NETR has received many accolades (and perhaps an equal amount of criticism) for its practical, moves-based, and context-specific coursework. Like the conceptualization of teacher–student relationships, every aspect of the program directly maps backward to its mission of preparing effective first-year teachers for no excuses schools. Todd explains their goal as: "trying to essentially reduce the penalty, if you will, that students experience with a first-year teacher."

This mission is directly related to the program's broader vision for social justice. As Joe, the director of curriculum, tells residents on the first day, "We believe social justice is best enabled through good teaching technique." He adds that NETR's proxy for social justice is economic advancement in society. To address the social problem of reproduced poverty—which they feel is represented in the form of the "achievement gap"—NETR maintains that "high-needs" students must acquire the skills and knowledge to attend college and secure higher-paying jobs. Thus, their social justice vision is narrowly conceived: advance the achievement of students in no excuses schools to improve students' social mobility.

NETR's mission is also constructed as an urgent one. Faculty indicate that residents have a lot to learn before they can adequately serve students who have had fewer educational opportunities, and thus there is no time to waste; everything in the program must directly advance this mission.

To continuously improve, faculty constantly reevaluate the program, collecting and analyzing copious data from their residents. Several faculty members have also offered to help support my research in any way they can, providing me complete open access to all program documents online and over email, a reflection of the value they place on transparency, feedback, and objectivity. This unwavering dedication to program evaluation and constant improvement is uncommon in teacher education, which is sometimes criticized for lacking accountability and failing to evolve.[4]

Achieving NETR's mission begins with intentional recruitment. Program affordability, coupled with nearly guaranteed employment upon completion of the residency year, allows NETR to recruit a high-achieving and racially diverse cohort of residents. NETR only accepts 17% of those who apply, compared to what is perceived to be low admission standards in most teacher education programs.[5] Once admitted, residents pay no tuition during the residency year. Moreover, NETR staff members support all graduates to interview and secure jobs at nearby "high-poverty," mostly no excuses schools. Over the course of the second year—residents' first year of full-time teaching—they complete online coursework toward their master's degree through NETR's affiliated graduate school of education, and for a fraction of the cost of most graduate degrees.

Throughout the residency year, NETR residents follow a grueling schedule of coursework, fieldwork, and additional responsibilities. Residents spend 8–12 hours a day Monday through Thursday in schools, serving as tutors for the same small group of students. During these days, they also complete secondary responsibilities as teacher's assistants or other school support staff, for which they receive a small stipend. And their responsibilities do not end when they leave campus, as residents must call parents and attend supplemental NETR activities. Then on Fridays and Saturdays, residents complete NETR courses and engage in practice teaching simulations from 8:00 or 9:00 a.m. until 5:00 or 6:00 p.m. Each class comes with required reading from the lengthy NETR-authored course guides and practical homework assignments. Residents tell me that Sunday is their only uncommitted day, and even this day is often consumed by NETR homework. NETR faculty seem to have a dual rationale for this intensive schedule: there is extensive training to cover in limited time, and since teaching in no excuses schools is relentlessly demanding, residents should get used to it now.

If the program does not seem to work for residents, there are two ways that they can (or will be asked to) leave the program. The first is through the Gateway, a high-stakes performance exam that measures residents on a series of teaching standards (which I will discuss more in Chapter 3); in the past, up to 10% of the residents have failed out of NETR through this structure. Meanwhile, several other residents might leave voluntarily through a process termed "healthy exit." Healthy exit occurs when residents realize that they do not want to be a teacher or teach at a no excuses school, or want to focus on other priorities, or perhaps just cannot handle the workload; these individuals can exit the program within the first semester on dates designated as "off-ramps," without being responsible for any tuition. NETR leverages the Gateway and healthy exit as means of ensuring their graduates are competent and committed to teaching in a no excuses setting. But NETR is not committed to advancing every resident, because they do not believe everyone should be teaching in this particular context. As a result, the program feels a bit like trial by fire: only the extremely determined will remain.

Over 7 years, NETR coursework has continued to improve in line with its own mission, demonstrating a particularly strong capacity for "single-loop" learning.[6] But from the beginning, the program has operated with some version of its three anchoring courses: Classroom Management, Instructional Methods, and Building Relationships with Students and Families, more recently titled the Relationships and Student Investment course.

This course on relationships is part of the legacy of the late founding principal of EPHS, John Scott, more commonly known as "Johnny." Prior to leading EPHS, Johnny Scott taught in local public schools for 30 years, during which time he was named state Teacher of the Year. He brought his wealth of experience to the daily administration of EPHS, focusing on the relational side of his duties. One of his first acts as principal was to call every single parent or guardian for the students enrolled at the school, which won him quick regard among those he served. His perception of school was different from most: "School is not a building. It is a collection of relationships—kids, parents, teachers, staff." With this in mind, Johnny displayed seasoned expertise at developing "strong, lasting" relationships at EPHS. When he died a few years later, his impact on the culture of the school remained, making EPHS a special kind of no excuses charter school—different from those that prioritized discipline without developing relationships[7]—and this transferred over to the teacher residency that grew out of EPHS.

NETR has continued this focus on relationships because they think it also advances their mission. As stated above, faculty believe that if students feel more "invested" in the teacher and the class, they will behave better and put forth more effort in their academic work. Scholarship also seems to confirm the importance of teacher–student relationships in no excuses settings. In her book *Building a Better Teacher*, Elizabeth Green notes that the best no excuses schools she found had an explicit focus on teacher–student relationships. Joanne Golann corroborates this in her ethnographic study of one no excuses school, noting that the one teacher she observed who actively demonstrated care for her students seemed to be the most successful.[8] Thus, the NETR relationships coursework is designed to advance their bottom line: student achievement. But in the context of urgency, with teacher residents dropping out through the Gateway or healthy exit, and amid the focus on strict, technical- and moves-based coursework, how will NETR integrate a subject matter that is often considered "soft" or "touchy-feely"?

CUTTING TO THE POINT WITH PEDAGOGICAL AND RELATIONAL EFFICIENCY

As I observe coursework, I soon notice that most of the NETR sessions follow a similar format. First, there is a "Do Now," followed by a Power-Point presentation of relevant concepts. Next, residents watch videos of teachers in action and discuss with peers how well the teachers in these videos fulfill the concepts introduced previously, which is often followed by a controlled whole-group discussion. Usually, the session concludes with an opportunity for residents to practice skills related to the concepts introduced that day and a short debrief of this practice.

Every activity within this format is timed, and during transitions, faculty quickly secure residents' attention by modeling a ritual like a rhythmic clap. To select residents to share their responses with the whole group in the discussion and debrief, faculty often "cold-call" residents (without giving them prior warning) by drawing a white plastic knife with the name of a resident inscribed on it from a paper cup. Angela, the director of training, later jokes about this tool: "Never apologize for using your cup of knives." To me, these knives seem the embodiment of an unapologetically efficient manner of cutting right to the point without ceremony; and like the timer and the rhythmic clap, the knives serve as a symbol of relational efficiency.

Efficiency reverberates throughout the program. One of the three "foundational ideas" about teaching content in the NETR Instructional Methods course guide is: "My job is to increase student learning in the most efficient way possible." This focus on efficiency is reminiscent of the way Frederick Winslow Taylor's ideas of "scientific management" permeated the education system in the United States in the early 20th century. Among other things, Taylor recommended the use of a stopwatch, the standardization of practices across industries, the establishment of set tasks "each day for each worker," and the use of external motivators in the form of rewards and punishments "given immediately" to encourage workers to complete these tasks.[9] When implemented in factories, scientific management increased workers efficiency, but it also increased their stress.[10]

As Callahan observes in *Education and the Cult of Efficiency*, school leaders began to take cues from industry, viewing education in terms of its inputs (funding) and outputs (measurable "achievement"). In applying principles of scientific management to schools, leaders began to eliminate anything perceived as superfluous, in relentless pursuit of advancing outputs. I notice vestiges of this mentality woven throughout NETR's coursework, in the form of timers, prescribed teaching moves, and the use of external motivators for students and residents, all driven by a sense of urgency to advance their mission.

NETR's approach to instruction reflects the cult of efficiency in other fundamental ways, too. Instead of spending time learning how to design lessons "from scratch," residents simply learn to lesson plan by modifying existing scripted curricula to support efficient instruction. The Instructional Methods class recommends residents further "streamline" this lesson modification process according to "The Machine." Again, I can't help but recognize the industrial imagery at play in this term.

This "no-frills approach to literacy" is established as a quintessential structure in English language arts (ELA) classes, but all the residents learn it, as some version of this is also considered useful in other subjects. It looks like this (emphasis original):

The Machine is:
READ
THINK
DISCUSS
REVISE
WRITE
[REVISE]
[RE-WRITE]

NETR estimates that 80% of a beginning teacher's lessons will follow this format. And interestingly, it seems that if "write" were replaced with "practice," nearly the same percentage of NETR sessions could be seen as following an analogous format.

Later in the year, some of the residents comment upon the pedagogy espoused by and employed in NETR. Ellen, a white secondary English resident, acknowledges that the format often results in a fairly repetitive class for the students at no excuses schools: "The kids, every day, all they do is listen to you annotate, turn and talk, stop and jot. They're okay with that, if that's what they do every day." Furthermore, Ellen makes the connection between the structure of classwork for students and NETR's structure of coursework for residents: "We've gotten very used to [doing the same] and we've gotten very bored by it. . . . We feel ourselves doing what the kids do." Although Ellen claims to be "bored" by the pedagogical structure of coursework, she acknowledges the symmetry between how residents and students are taught; it is repetitive, but because of its repetition, people begin to accept it.

Modeling pedagogy is thought to be an effective way of reinforcing it; as Pamela Grossman asserts, "In the professional preparation of teachers, the medium *is* the message."[11] The pedagogy employed and promoted in NETR effectively communicates the importance of lesson efficiency to the residents. However, I also notice that this expedient and ordered format contrasts what many pedagogical theorists like Dewey espouse: namely, that meaningful learning requires a bit more "messing about."[12]

In anticipation of my thoughts around this, Joe tells me, "John Dewey's name has never been said in NETR . . . because we think the teachers need coherency." Instead of exploring deeper pedagogical knowledge, lessons efficiently teach practical and prescriptive knowledge and skills that directly align with no excuses pedagogy. After all, NETR seems to feel that "messing about" is a luxury that residents learning to teach, and the "high-needs" students they will serve, cannot afford in no excuses schools.

Themes of urgency and efficiency extend to NETR's concept of teacher–student relationships. The Relationships Course Guide (RCG) focuses heavily on employing relational moves to advance "student investment." But this was not the original focus of the Relationships course.

Sara, NETR's director of coaching, explains, "It started more on the individual relationship building level, and has evolved more into both that and how to invest [students] into your class. . . . How to build class culture, how to create goals for your class, how to incentivize students, how to make their class interesting and engaging. . . ." Once a class about forming "individual" relationships with students and parents like EPHS principal Johnny Scott did, the Relationships course now focuses on providing residents with specific strategies to engage students in their instruction so students will "work hard and be nice in your class." Like other aspects of the program, this too has evolved to more clearly advance NETR's mission.

In applying ideas of efficiency to relationships, NETR focuses on their desired ends. The four outcomes of the teacher–student relationship are described as getting students to feel "love" for: (1) "you" (the teacher), (2) "the team" (their classmates), (3) "the journey" (school), and (4) "the destination" (college or future employment). While faculty suggest that getting students to "love you" requires some "charisma" or "the cult of personality," they characterize the other loves as by-products of effective teaching.

In emphasizing these "loves," and in having a course on relationships to begin with, NETR seems to acknowledge that in order for teachers to engage students in a context that emphasizes strict behavioral norms, they must find ways to bring warmth, and even love, into the classroom. However, the love that NETR proposes is again unidirectional. Instruction toward this end encourages the student to love the teacher, group, and subject matter; it is not about the teacher doing the loving. This is very different from conceptions of "radical love" proposed by Paulo Freire, Jeff Duncan-Andrade, and Shawn Ginwright, who describe love between teachers and students as reciprocal, dialogical, and antiauthoritarian.[13] Just as NETR does not feel there is space to "mess about" pedagogically, they do not seem to feel there is time for messier forms of love or connection in schools.

Additionally, I begin to notice that this last love, "love the destination," is perhaps the most explicitly and implicitly emphasized throughout NETR. Residents learn to teach students to believe that if they work hard and behave, they can achieve their own version of the American dream. The deployment of such hope is a powerful tool to motivate students within the classroom. However, the advancement of "hokey hope"—in which students uncritically accept the possibility of achieving their desires by simply working hard—can lead to pain and disappointment because "the playing field" is indeed "uneven."[14] This mentality places blame on the individual if they do not achieve, not a system rife with barriers.

As human beings, we don't usually think of relationships in terms of their ends; instead, our focus is often on the experience of both parties within relationships. But because there is so much urgency at NETR, teacher–student relationship coursework cuts right to the point: student achievement. And it is explicitly designed to advance this end with moves that are as efficient as those prescribed in the instructional methods and classroom management courses.

THE BUSINESS OF RELATIONAL MOVES

Six weeks into the school year, I observe a session that lays out some of these very concrete strategies. Mark is leading this session, which surprises me. He is the chief operating officer of NETR, and I did not expect him to be facilitating course sessions. But at NETR, all faculty were once practitioners and actively engage in teaching the residents.

As someone who ascended the ranks in other well-known no excuses schools prior to helping start NETR, Mark strikes me as an imposing figure. Today, he wears a serious expression under his dark, closely trimmed beard and stands perfectly erect with an orange tie that appears to have been quite tightly tied. Mark begins the session promptly at 12:15 p.m., the exact time by which residents were told to be back from lunch. He means business.

In this course session, Mark provides residents with additional tools to leverage their "professional relationship capital" with students to increase their classroom learning. These include "relationship-building moves" and the "one-on-one conversation." I am intrigued by the idea of relationship-building moves as a deliberate approach to connect with students, and it reminds me of Dale Carnegie's classic self-help book *How to Win Friends and Influence People*. This book emphasizes strategies to "make people like you" such as smiling, expressing curiosity about others' interests, actively listening, and remembering names. And it suggests that anyone can form connections by following the strategies presented.

The unpredictable nature of the classroom—which is shaped by interactions with multiple students simultaneously—seems to complicate the implementation of universal strategies aimed at developing relationships with students. And these strategies are not easy when a teacher must manage relationships with over 70 students. Nevertheless, NETR seems to have borrowed a page from Carnegie's book in the creation of their own universal moves.

The four "proactive" relationship moves are: (1) the sneeze, (2) high five, (3) private check-in, and (4) chat for no reason. Mark describes "the sneeze" as remembering little things about students—like a distinctive sneeze—and seeking out more information about this or repeatedly mentioning it so students feel their teacher knows them. The RCG includes an example of a teacher who systemized a way to achieve "the sneeze" with a large roster of students by keeping a spreadsheet in which he "capture[d] little nuggets" about each student and reviewed these later so he could "work" them into their interactions. Like the strategies suggested by Carnegie, this "sneeze" example is a move that any teacher could adopt and implement to display some knowledge of students. And it occurs to me that with 74 residents, NETR staff might have established a "sneeze" spreadsheet of their own.

The other moves are also framed as simple strategies that all teachers should employ. The high five is described as voicing appreciation or offering a friendly gesture like a high five to a student when he or she does "something great or for no reason at all." The private check-in is reserved for when a student seems to be struggling with an assignment or something else. Both of these moves aim to display academic care for students through affirmation for good work or in-school support. Finally, the chat for no reason is exactly as it sounds, encouraging teachers to talk to the students for no reason and find out about them, outside of instructional time, of course. To me, this last move seems a sort of "catchall" move for everything else involved in forming relationships with students, and neither Mark nor the RCG dwells upon it in any depth.

Mark then tells the residents, "We are going to get out of the little moves to the big one." He introduces the "one-on-one" conversation, a move that is accompanied by a guide and a rubric. The guide suggests one-on-ones should follow this format: "1) Identify the problem and its impact, 2) Ask questions to better understand, 3) Discuss solutions, 4) Check for understanding." This format systematizes an approach that is clear, solicits student perspectives and opinions on the situation, and ends with a mutually understood and agreed-upon solution. This process is explicitly instrumental, geared around solving a "problem," presumably one that impedes academic achievement and desired behavior.

NETR does not spend time exploring the emotional side of these conversations. As Todd notes, NETR is "of the mind that you change actions first and that changes beliefs." And Rachel, a secondary science resident, affirms that NETR teaches a lot about the "what to do" in class, but does not often focus on the "why" or the "research to support the why" teachers should do what NETR is proposing. By changing teachers' behavior in these interactions with students, and not dwelling on any theory or research around why this approach might be efficacious for students, NETR seems to believe residents will soon begin to understand the complexities and importance of utilizing particular moves and engaging in "one-on-ones" by actually doing them.

When I speak with the residents later, they offer varying perspectives on this explicit relational coursework. Rachel summarizes her view of the class:

"It's almost like keeping students on your side without being like buddy-buddy with them." Given that one of the desired outcomes of the course is to get students to "love you" so they will work harder and behave better, this seems like an apt observation. Alina, an outspoken white elementary resident, suggests, "It makes you kind of cringe because you're like, 'Oh God, there shouldn't be a textbook about having relationships.' I would die if any parent ever saw this booklet and read it, it's so embarrassing. [But] I do think some of the bare-bones, you absolutely must do this or you won't have a good relationship, are right." This, too, is my initial reaction to the coursework; I find myself cringing at the methodical approach to connecting with students, but I also acknowledge that I may have employed some similar strategies in my interactions with students, without the benefit of explicit training around this process. [15]

Other residents suggest that learning these discrete relational strategies is essential for them. For example, Jose, a Latino secondary English resident, admits that he appreciates this straightforward coursework because he is "older" and "more introverted" than the other residents, and feels relational moves "don't come innately for me." This indicates that for some, this explicit, to-the-point coursework in relationship building might be powerful, just as Carnegie's work has been for many.

Residents in NETR learn how to make an effort to connect with their students by acquiring and "leverage[ing]" some knowledge of individuals with the "sneeze" and displaying care through the other moves. But while these moves may seem uncomplicated, they must be executed in the context of a strict disciplinary imperative that could threaten to strain nascent relationships between teachers and students.

MAINTAINING A "TRICKY BALANCE" IN A WORLD OF "BROKEN WINDOWS"

No excuses schools are notorious for their emphasis on student compliance. Much of this stems from the "broken windows" theory, originally applied to policing, which suggests that if even one window is left unrepaired in a neighborhood, many more will follow and the neighborhood will fall into decline. [16] Opponents of "broken windows" policing suggest that it has severe consequences for people of color from low-income neighborhoods, including mass incarceration, the destruction of families, and police brutality. [17]

In applying the "broken windows" theory to the classroom, advocates of no excuses education emphasize the importance of "eliminating the tiniest signs of disorder" by enforcing all rules, including those that require students to tuck in their uniform shirts, sit up straight in their chairs, and track whoever is speaking with their eyes. [18] Violations result in everything from "demerits" to suspensions and expulsions. It's not just about establishing a safe classroom environment, but a highly controlled one. Critics of this approach point to its disproportionate application to students from historically marginalized groups and suggest that it essentially criminalizes these students. [19] But supporters make the distinction between "broken windows" behavior management and "zero tolerance" policies and claim that "broken windows" is more about maintaining "unrelenting expectations" for students and upholding a culture that supports this. [20]

NETR and other no excuses institutions refer to the urgency of their mission to justify this focus on order; they claim that because the students they serve are so "behind" their affluent peers, they cannot afford to waste a single second of class time on misbehavior. While NETR acknowledges that students must put forth maximum effort if they are to learn what they need to advance in line with their peers, and that teachers' lessons must also be high quality, behavior is often framed as the utmost priority. And when these residents become teachers of record the following year, the "street-level bureaucrats," if you will, they will be responsible for enforcing school rules. [21] Through the Classroom Management course, NETR equips residents with the tools they will need to exert their authority, and in ways that cannot be disentangled from their relationships with students.

The Classroom Management Course Guide lists six foundational beliefs about classroom management. These state that teachers: (1) are the "ultimate authority" in their classrooms, (2) should strive for "100%" student compliance, (3) must learn to see and respond to student misbehavior automatically, (4) have the "right" and "responsibility" to correct misbehavior, despite their inexperience, (5) must enforce rules from "the first day," and (6) should believe that all students "want to be good and do well." These six beliefs harken back to the "broken windows" theory, justifying teachers' role in maintaining meticulous order in their classrooms.

On a sunny fall day, I observe Angela, the director of training, leading an early course session on this topic. I find her simultaneously approachable and intimidating. Her stance is firm in her gray pencil-skirt suit, the expression on her lightly freckled face pleasant but serious. After making a relatable pop culture reference to the TV show *Battlestar Galactica*, Angela directs residents in a loud and clear voice to "turn and talk" to their surrounding peers about these six beliefs: "What are reasonable objections to these beliefs? How would a demanding no excuses teacher respond to those objections?"

After a few minutes of discussion, Angela begins to clap in a recognizable rhythm from the video game Super Mario Bros. Residents finish the rhythm with the last clap in unison. This is so well executed that the cohort must have practiced this clap, as they practice everything they learn at NETR. But I also notice that the claps, snaps, and other rituals are so catchy that even I find myself unintentionally mimicking these gestures at times. Maybe there is something in the water, or as a couple of the residents joked to me, "the Kool-Aid" at NETR. And it occurs to me that the rituals, mantras, and routines used by NETR are also highly potent forms of maintaining order, of preventing "broken windows."

The whole-group discussion begins with the belief "The teacher is the ultimate authority." One resident offers a "reasonable objection" to this belief, suggesting that if teachers teach students to think critically, they might question teachers' authority. This comment implies that strict discipline and critical thinking are poor bedfellows. However, the resident who said this seems to feel the need to qualify this comment, quickly adding the caveat that a "true demanding teacher" would likely be able to address any critical questions students might have about the reasons for such rules. This prompts one more resident to make the distinction between "authoritative and authoritarian," adding that being "authoritative can't limit student thought."

Next, residents focus upon the belief that "100%" of the class must be on task and compliant with rules at all times.

A female resident ventures, "One of the critiques [of this belief] is that you are teaching students to be followers. It seems a little bit controlling."

Because this comment provides no defense for the belief, Angela urges this resident and others to consider, "So what do you say to people like that when you are all being asked to 'row in the same direction'?"

A resident, whose name I later learn is Stephanie, enters the conversation. She offers with passion, "I am going to be really unpopular soon, but we have to critically evaluate the student population, evaluating your own privilege and why you are teaching students from low-income backgrounds and how you are *commanding* them."

Angela pauses, seemingly taken aback by this comment. Instead of defending the six beliefs, Stephanie has implied that the mostly white and relatively affluent teachers who enforce these beliefs in no excuses schools are essentially "commanding" their low-income students, almost all of whom are people of color, to reproduce power structures in society. When I later interview Stephanie, who is Asian American, I learn that she has spent a lot of time thinking about the ways NETR coursework might perpetuate racist ideologies (which I will discuss more in Chapter 2).

In an attempt to assuage Stephanie, Angela suggests that future NETR coursework on the culture of power[22] will address these concerns. Then she prompts the residents to further defend the belief about 100% compliance: "How do we as a group of teachers respond to these objections?"

One resident insists, "I do not think that anyone is born a leader, and those who became leaders, were good followers first; they were part of the whole and later [emerged]." This statement upholds what NETR preaches: to be successful, students (and residents) must first learn to be followers; or, to succeed by NETR's estimation, they must first learn to behave.

To close the discussion, Sara (the director of coaching) assures the residents, "We are not asking you to buy all of these beliefs right now, and nobody hates you, and we are going to try to answer and address a lot of the things you brought up over the next couple of months. . . . And part of the fall [work] is deciding whether the program has addressed your concerns enough that you decide to stick with it."

Because it is early in the year, residents still have leeway to voice opposition to NETR's beliefs. But if they ultimately choose not to "buy" into these beliefs (and Stephanie has indicated that she might not), Sara implies they should probably exit NETR. For those who remain must find a way to exert control over students while simultaneously connecting with them.

In no excuses schools, the way in which teachers establish relationships with students is inseparable from the way they manage behavior; but the strict enforcement of behavioral norms by teachers can lead to "strained relationships" with students.[23] NETR emphasizes several different moves and strategies to deal with this tension. For example, in the Classroom Management course, residents learn how to have "rebuilding conversations" with students when they have had to send them out of class for disciplinary infractions. The Relationships course guides residents to "authentically" invest students in the class and culture of the school, in part so they can prevent the need for a heavy hand.

The RCG and associated coursework outlines 12 "investment moves" toward this end. Some of these are explicitly designed around promoting school values by visibly "tracking" progress toward these, establishing class "décor" that corresponds with them, using "rituals or mantras" that emphasize them, or "embedding values" in class directions and content. Other investment moves are more general, like creating "hooks" to draw students into content (like the pop culture references that faculty often use in NETR coursework), using "games and competitions" to promote academics, and holding "little" and "big celebrations" for successes.

All these moves are in some way designed to encourage students to behave in line with the same set of values. Such values generally support the teacher's daily instruction by emphasizing student behavior and effort. And given how seductive the use of mantras, rituals, and routines seems to be within NETR, I get the sense that investment moves are just as powerful as classroom management moves in ensuring order in the classroom.

When teaching residents about implementing investment moves, Sara emphasizes that they are not expected to implement all 12 moves but should undertake particular investment strategies that are "genuine and authentic to you as a person." Sara underscores the idea of authenticity because she and the other faculty openly acknowledge that students can "see through" anything that feels inauthentic or contrived. Authenticity, too, is thus considered instrumental to ensuring student engagement.

However, Sara acknowledges that achieving pedagogical authenticity in a no excuses setting with a strict authoritative approach may feel precarious: "The ability to communicate who you are and what's important to you, in front of your class, to be authentic in front students, while also being an authority figure. . . . That's a really tricky balance for new teachers."

The "tricky balance" also presents itself in NETR's emphasis on becoming "warm/strict." In his book *Teach Like a Champion*—which is commonly used in no excuses schools—Doug Lemov characterizes "warm/strict" as a teaching strategy where teachers display warmth through their interactions with students, but remain unwavering in their behavioral and academic expectations for them. [24] Timothy, a secondary resident, explains, "I think what NETR has prepared us really well [for] is to have a good, genuine, warm presence in the classroom while also being firm and strict and holding 100% of students accountable." NETR seems to promote some sense of warmth through relationship-building moves and investment moves, which can all be "authentically" tailored to the individual teacher. But the "strict" enforcement of rules and punishments remains concrete and nonnegotiable.

To avoid "broken windows," residents must accept the necessity of strict authority and find a way to balance this with their own ideas of warmth and authenticity. Some of residents I interview justify their use of firm "authority" with the belief that they are enforcing rules in this manner because it will enable students to "actually learn"; and in believing in the necessity of this approach, residents' authority becomes more "authentic" for them. But other residents might find this process requires cognitive dissonance, or causes a division within themselves as they try to reconcile their required outward behavior with inward beliefs that might contradict this. [25]

Ultimately, though, there is no space in NETR to question this approach. Aside from a "Relationships and Student Investment Plan" that asks students to briefly list how they will integrate their own "ways of being" into their use of NETR moves, residents have little opportunity to reflect on who they are and how they want to show up in the classroom. They must then achieve this "tricky balance," not in thought, but in deed. And those who cannot find a way to achieve this balance—not even on the surface—might opt to utilize "healthy exit" routes, thereby maintaining their own sense of integrity and that of the program. For if they remain, they will become the voice of their institutions, the primary figures who will interface with students and their parents.

CONSULTING WITH STAKEHOLDERS: BRINGING PARENTS INTO THE CONVERSATION

On a brisk fall morning, Todd stands at the front of the Big Hall, a smile stretching to the crinkles around his eyes. He begins by outlining "seven nonnegotiable times to call [parents]." Then with a proud conspiratorial smile, he adds, "This is very NETR." As Todd acknowledges, the program is particularly proud of the way it teaches residents to call students' homes.

The "nonnegotiable" times fall into two different categories: "introductory calls" and "corrective calls." For example, in August, teachers must call all parents to introduce themselves, and in September, they should call/text/email parents to voice some kind of "praise" for students. Todd suggests these two introductory calls are like "putting money in the bank," in terms of garnering parent goodwill. The remaining five corrective calls are used to notify parents if their child: is "in danger of failing," was "sent out of class," "was involved in a major behavioral incident" (e.g., fighting, cheating), seemed "emotionally distressed" in class, or has begun to make "negative choices in behavior or academics."

Like they did for the student one-on-one conversation, NETR also provides a structure to help sequence parent phone calls. The format follows these six steps:

1. Greet: Start with a quick greeting where the teacher introduces themself.
2. Time check: Ask the parents, "Is this a good time?" and state how long you think the conversation might take.
3. State the reason for call: Provide the reason in a clear and direct way.
4. Talk: Include relevant details and explain more about why you are calling.
5. Next steps: Address what both of you will do next, if anything is agreed upon for this.
6. Bye: End the call on a positive tone and/or by thanking the parent for their time.

Given the nerve-wracking nature of calling parents—who likely have more life experience and wisdom than most new teachers—such an outline could prove quite valuable.

Teachers often feel that their preservice programs do a poor job of preparing them to work with parents and families.[26] But that is not the case at NETR. Lizzeth, an elementary resident, observes, "I feel like one of NETR's hugest priorities is building that relationship with families and making sure you're on the same team." Moreover, the emphasis on calling home appears influential. As Stephanie later reflects, "The thing that stuck with me most from [the Relationships course] was the idea of calling all of your [students'] parents on a very regular basis." Residents cannot escape the program without some sense of how to connect with parents, and this likely gives them a leg up on their peers from other teacher education programs.

After Todd has completed his explanation of mandatory phone calls, Mark introduces a panel of three parents who will speak to the residents today: Ms. Harper, a middle-aged Black woman with a soft smile; Mr. Antonio, a Latino man with a dark goatee; and Ms. Jones, an older Black woman with gray hair and a feisty spark in her eye.

Each parent begins by briefly describing their experiences with no excuses schools. Ms. Harper explains that her daughter is dyslexic and struggled in private schools, but that she is "very happy" with EPHS. Mr. Antonio explains that he also happily moved his two sons from private schools. He adds without a hint of irony that his younger son actually did not pass ninth grade here last year so he is now repeating it. "But it wasn't a failure of EPHS," he defends. "The amount of support that we received [here] was amazing. Sometimes it's really up to the children to take responsibility."

Then Ms. Jones tells an especially compelling story about her experience with her foster daughter. When the local public school put her in "low-level classes" because she was "troubled," Ms. Jones got her into a no excuses elementary school that not only taught her how to read and brought her math skills up to grade level, but also convinced her that she could go to college. Ms. Jones beams that the school "has done a wonderful job with my child." These brief personal anecdotes serve to reinforce residents' no excuses path into the teaching profession.

Later, Mark asks the panel to share their experiences with teacher and tutor communication. The parents relate heartwarming stories about interactions with teachers and tutors, voicing appreciation for how often no excuses employees communicate with them about their children. They also convey a few anecdotes about failed teacher–parent communication—most of which took place at other schools. For example, Mr. Antonio tells a story about a teacher from another school who called and "used big words" to essentially belittle him and his child. Across all the anecdotes, the parents emphasize the importance of establishing "trust" with them, maintaining a warm and respectful tone, and balancing positive and "negative" calls.

To my surprise, Mark also asks the parents to discuss their thoughts on the discipline and structure emphasized by their no excuses schools. Mr. Antonio suggests his son "needs that structure." And adds that it allows teachers to focus more on teaching content. Ms. Harper echoes this sentiment: "It really is about academics." And Ms. Jones praises the structure: "I live in structure. I am just happy that the school has structure so it won't look out of the ordinary when they come home."

These comments illuminate an important point: parents, particularly those from historically marginalized backgrounds, choose schools like EPHS intentionally. As Elizabeth Green observed of the no excuses schools she encountered, "It was discipline that captivated parents most: a promise to keep their children safe."[27] While numerous critics have likened no excuses schools to prisons and characterized their common practices—especially those around discipline—as inherently racist,[28] many low-income parents of color continue to seek out these schools for their children, in part *because of* their strict policies regarding behavior and their unrelenting academic standards.

However, new research indicates that once their students are at no excuses schools, Black and Latinx parents have a more complicated relationship with the discipline policies, often coming to believe these may promote academic achievement but inhibit student autonomy and self-advocacy.[29] Mark admits that the three parents who braved Friday traffic to speak to NETR today also represent some of their most "passionate" advocates and that there is also a "cross section of parents who might be more ambivalent" about the school.

Overall, NETR establishes relationships with parents as distinctly different from those with students. Todd tells me:

> A big part of what you're trying to do with the family is demonstrate that this is a place that is going to be responsive to you, that cares about your child's progress, that's welcoming to you, and that you can trust. . . . That requires a whole other set of strategies and effort on the part of the teacher to build that relationship.

Throughout this session, faculty insist that forming relationships with parents requires "trust," "care," "empathy," "responsive[ness]," "respect," and "partnership." Students are not considered partners in their own learning, but parents are. When presenting this to the residents, Mark emphasizes respect as the most important facet of these calls: "Respecting the relationship is paramount. Parenting is emotionally loaded business." In relationships with parents, faculty imply that teachers should employ competencies that are more emotional than the discrete moves they promote in forming relationships with students.

But why do parents deserve more emotional warmth than students? Perhaps it is partially because NETR faculty better understand parents. As a parent himself, Mark speaks with a sort of reverence for parents. He suggests, "You are at best a peer with them, but to the parents you haven't known [the kids] nearly as long as they have, so to say peer is even a stretch." And relationships with parents must be formed outside the controlled classroom context. Faculty might also treat this relationship differently because parents are the stakeholders with the most investment in their children's learning; they are the ones making the decisions about where to send their children, and no excuses schools need parents to choose them or they will go out of business. As adults with life experience, parents might also require more than moves like "the sneeze" to feel valued. Therefore, faculty encourage residents to treat parents like multifaceted human beings.

Still, NETR views relationships with parents, too, as instrumental in advancing the bottom line: student achievement. A small-scale study of NETR's phone call strategy in Tutorial indicates that it results in increased student engagement and homework completion. Todd further explains that if teachers reach out to parents in a constructive way, "the parent then is going to support the teacher in the teacher's efforts to make the student effortful . . . because it's coming from multiple adults in the child's life." Since they see parents as powerful advocates for student effort and achievement, and likely because they want parents to continue choosing their schools, NETR systematically prepares residents to reach out to parents multiple times over the course of the year with ideas of respect and partnership in mind.

INSTRUMENTALISM AS AN APPROACH TO RELATIONSHIPS

At times, I feel lulled into NETR's approach to coursework and relationships, clapping along with the residents in a way that suggests I, too, buy into the program. In some ways, it is seductive. As Alina told me in our interview, "It's easy to convince yourself that the population of students that we serve do in fact need schools with this type of structure. Then you have to ask yourself, what are they missing?"

In NETR, teacher–student relationship development is viewed as instrumental: a process that teachers must undertake to elicit "maximum effort" and better behavior from students. Relationships are also constructed as teacher centered and unidirectional; teachers foster "professional relationship capital" with students—an input into the formula to increase student behavior and effort—but there is no acknowledgment that such relationships might also influence teachers, their behavior, their lesson quality, and/or their effort. There is no emphasis on reciprocity. Additionally, relationships with students here are undeniably hierarchical, formed in a context in which the teacher has "ultimate authority." Thus, these relationships cannot be disentangled from the disciplinary imperative placed on teachers, who are given explicit "right" and "responsibility" to ensure "100%" compliance from their students.

Relationships with parents are not constrained by the need to enforce strict rules, for teachers do not have the "authority" in this interaction; if anything, parents do. So instead, teachers are tasked with forming a respectful partnership with parents, one built on "trust." Even so, this relationship is also instrumental to advancing NETR's mission. Parents can help support student achievement, and it is imperative to the survival of no excuses schools that parents continue to choose these institutions for their children. So teachers—in many ways, the voice of no excuses schools—must form relationships that make these critical stakeholders feel valued.

Most of the coursework on relationship development is almost indistinguishable from coursework on other topics: it is efficient, methodical, formulaic, and prescriptive. Throughout the program, NETR prepares residents like "technicians."[30] They learn moves and strategies to modify preestablished curricula, employ efficient instructional techniques, enforce school policies, and leverage "relational capital" to keep students engaged. Faculty teach all of this in a one-size-fits-all manner, so residents can learn to "row in the same direction" when they begin teaching. There is little room for individuality. And because modeling is a powerful form of teaching, residents learn how to be efficient in everything from instruction to relationship development.

Many teacher education programs promote self-reflection and self-knowledge, with the idea that teachers cannot really understand students, or interact with them authentically, until they understand themselves. But NETR does not operate on this assumption and is in fact admittedly wary of programs that spend too much time "thinking and feeling," perhaps because this is hard to prescribe. Instead, NETR coursework focuses on actions. Residents acquire frameworks and rubrics for calling parents and moves that display care (like "the high five" and the "private check-in"). They are taught to systematically use rituals, mantras, and "the sneeze" to efficiently connect with students and subtly condition them to uphold the values of the school. Personal "authenticity" is only addressed as a counter to "authority," with little opportunity to explore who residents feel they are in the first place. And before residents have time to question the practices prescribed by NETR, they are already implementing these. As NETR suggests, actions do change beliefs.

But actions alone can be superficial; deeds simply performative without thought or feeling. And maybe, truly meaningful relationships require more emotional energy, more reciprocity, more mess. As Nel Noddings insists, "Caring cannot be achieved by a formula. It requires address and response; it requires different behaviors from situation to situation and person to person."[31] Noddings would argue that meaningful relationships, those based on care, cannot truly be prescribed, nor can they be conditional or unidirectional. In NETR, though, the urgent ends—student achievement—justify a shallow and controlled means of relationship development, one that more closely resembles Buber's concept of an I–It relationship, or even a relationship of "compulsion," than an I–Thou relation. While efficient and methodical, NETR's limited vision of teacher–student relationships might have unintended consequences. I consider this further as I explore the program's approach to coursework on race and racism in Chapter 2, and their approach to fieldwork with "actual" students in Chapter 3.

NOTES

1. Ingersoll, Richard, & Merrill, Lisa. (2014). *Seven trends: The transformation of the teaching force.* Philadelphia, PA: Consortium for Policy Research in Education.

2. Levine, Arthur. (2006). *Educating school teachers.* Washington, DC: Education Schools Project. Retrieved from http://www.edschools.org/pdf/Educating_Teachers_Report.pdf; Mason, Kevin O. (2014). *Preparing for the classroom: What teachers really think about teacher education.* Lanham, MD: Rowman & Littlefield.

3. Educators have criticized the use of the term "achievement gap," as it seems to imply that the blame for this "gap" rests on the students who do not move up. Instead, Gloria Ladson-Billings suggests that it is more of an "education debt" or an "opportunity gap," in that schools and society are the ones responsible for any discrepancy between children from high and lower socioeconomic backgrounds, between white students and students of color. Ladson-Billings, Gloria. (2006). From the achievement gap to the education debt: Understanding achievement in U.S. schools. *Educational Researcher, 35*(7), 3–12.

4. Levine, *Educating school teachers.*

5. For example, college graduates who had lower grades and test scores. See Levine, *Educating school teachers.*

6. Argyris, Chris. (1977, September). Double loop learning in organizations. *Harvard Business Review.*

7. Golann, Joanne W. (2014). The paradox of success at a no-excuses school. *Sociology of Education, 88*(2), 102–119.

8. Golann, Paradox of success.

9. Callahan, R. E. (1964). *Education and the cult of efficiency:* Chicago, IL: University of Chicago Press, p. 31.

10. Graham, Patricia A. (2005). *Schooling America.* New York, NY: Oxford University Press.

11. Grossman, P. (2005). Research on pedagogical approaches in teacher education. In M. Cochran-Smith & K. M. Zeichner (Eds.), *Studying teacher education: The report of the AERA panel on research and teacher education* (pp. 425–476). Mahwah, NJ: Erlbaum.

12. Hawkins, David. (1974). *The informed vision: Essays on learning and human nature.* New York, NY: Algora.

13. Duncan-Andrade, Jeff. (2007). Gangstas, wankstas, and ridas: Defining, developing, and supporting effective teachers in urban schools. *International Journal of Qualitative Studies in Education, 20*(6), 617–638; Ginwright, Shawn A. (2015). Radically healing black lives: A love note to justice. *New Directions for Student Leadership, 148,* 33–44; Freire, Paulo. (1970). *Pedagogy of the oppressed.* New York, NY: Continuum; Freire, Paulo. (1998). *Pedagogy of freedom: Ethics, democracy, and civic courage.* Lanham, MD: Rowman & Littlefield.

14. Duncan-Andrade, J. M. R. (2009). Note to educators: Hope required when growing roses in concrete. *Harvard Educational Review, 79*(2), 182.

15. Also see Theisen-Homer, 2020.

16. Wilson, James Q., & Kelling, George L. (1982). Broken windows. *The Atlantic Online.* Joanne Golann also discusses this in "The Paradox of Success."

17. Harcourt, Bernard. (2005). *The illusion of order: The false promise of broken windows policing.* Cambridge, MA: Harvard University Press.

18. Green, Elizabeth. (2014). *Building a better teacher: How teaching works (and how to teach it to everyone).* New York, NY: Norton, p. 159.

19. Ofer, Udi. (2011). Criminalizing the classroom: The rise of aggressive policing and zero tolerance discipline in New York City public schools. *New York Law School Law Review, 56,* 1373–1411.

20. Livermore, Craig. (2008). Unrelenting expectations: A more nuanced understanding of the broken windows theory of cultural management in urban education. *Penn GSE Perspectives on Urban Education, 5*(2).

21. Lipsky, M. (1980). *Street-level bureaucracy: The critical role of street-level bureaucrats.* New York, NY: Russell Sage Foundation.

22. The culture of power comes from Lisa Delpit's work and refers to the dominant culture in society that has its own rules and values, which must be learned in order to advance in this society.

23. Golann, Paradox of success.

24. Lemov, Doug. (2010). *Teach like a champion: 49 techniques that put students on the path to college.* San Francisco, CA: Jossey-Bass.

25. Palmer, Parker. (1998). *The courage to teach: Exploring the inner landscape of a teacher's life.* San Francisco, CA: Jossey-Bass.

26. Levine, *Educating school teachers*; Mason, *Preparing for the classroom.*

27. Green, *Building a better teacher*, p. 161.

28. For example, Horn, Jim. (2016). *Work hard, be hard: Journeys through "no excuses" teaching.* London, England: Rowman & Littlefield.

29. Golann, Joanne W., Debs, Mira, and Weiss, Anna Lisa. (2019). "To be strict on your own": Black and Latinx parents evaluate discipline in urban choice schools. *American Educational Research Journal, 56*(5), 1896–1929.

30. Kumashiro, K. K. (2010). Seeing the bigger picture: Troubling movements to end teacher education. *Journal of Teacher Education, 61*(1–2), 56–65.

31. Noddings, Nel. (1992). *The challenge to care in schools.* New York, NY: Teachers College Press, p. xi.

Chapter Two

License for Navigation

If we think it's important for adults to know about white privilege or systemic oppression, I think it's also important for kids to know about that as well. They need to know what they're up against.—Stephanie, elementary resident from NETR

I begin my observations in No Excuses Teacher Residency (NETR) in the fall of 2014. A month before the program's opening day, Michael Brown, an unarmed 18-year-old Black adolescent, was shot and killed in Ferguson, Missouri, by a white police officer who was never indicted for Brown's death. A few weeks before that, bystanders in New York City filmed Eric Garner, an unarmed Black man, being put in a chokehold by a white police-man while Garner cried out 11 times, "I can't breathe!"; Garner died and the police officer was not indicted. Over the course of the year ahead, several more Black men, women, and children across the country—including 12-year-old Tamir Rice in Ohio, Walter Scott in South Carolina, Freddie Gray in Maryland, and Sandra Bland in Texas—die at the hands of police who are not indicted. The widespread media coverage that reports each of these inci-dents and the subsequent protests that they inspire serve as a wake-up call for numerous (mostly white) residents of this country: racism still exists and it is systemic and recalcitrant.

It is within this context that I conduct observations in teacher education programs with an eye toward how they attempt to prepare their mostly white teachers to connect with and serve students who regularly face the trials of racism in the United States. Although no excuses schools primarily serve students of color, many have shied away from explicitly addressing issues of race and racism. When NETR began several years earlier, it, too, omitted coursework on this critical subject. Joe (the director of curriculum) admits there was "a complete absence of teaching anything regarding race." For the first 2 years, the program focused on "the lowest-hanging fruit," meaning the basic skills faculty believed teachers would need to advance student achievement on day one. Faculty did not include race because though admittedly important, NETR did not view it as "the *most* important thing" for first-year teachers' "survival."

In the third and fourth year of NETR, faculty integrated one 4-hour course session that addressed race in no excuses schools. Joe describes these early sessions on race as "making the case to our teachers for the ways in which the schools they would go on to work in, including EPHS, implicitly thought about issues of race and power . . . [but] didn't have a very deep [or] really any existent curriculum on it at all." In this one session, residents did not have a chance to explore issues of race but instead heard what Joe calls "an affirmative case" for why no excuses schools rarely talked about race: there was simply no time to address this complicated issue amidst the urgency they felt to promote academic skills. In presenting this in debate terminology (affirmative case), Joe seems to anticipate an opposing argument from residents or from me—perhaps one he has heard before regarding the urgency of discussing race in a country where racism permeates every institution, including schools. But I simply listen as he continues to explain.

NETR's coursework on race expanded in year 5 for a few reasons. First, residents began to ask for more discussions of race in class. Second, faculty began to realize that residents were not having as many individual conversations about race as NETR hoped. Third, it seemed that residents sometimes struggled to connect with students and parents because of what Sara (the director of coaching) referred to as "race and class issues . . . that the teacher doesn't understand." Fourth, the faculty generally felt they could and should be doing more to address racism; Joe reflects, "I think we had this internal sense that there was more that we could do about it. We're all deeply progressive people at heart." Given the increasing attention to racism in white "progressive" circles, it is also possible that faculty were feeling social pressure to do more.

Finally, faculty began to think that first-year teachers did in fact need to develop awareness about issues of race and privilege to be effective in an urban school. Joe explains NETR's theory behind this:

> If our teachers are more comfortable talking about issues of race in their schools, they'll make better relationships with their kids. . . . Race is always present. Naming it and having our teachers be more comfortable talking about it with their kids we think will improve their relationships with kids, which in turn will improve their ability to teach kids and get them into college and successful postacademic careers. It all backwards maps from there.

While the program has not addressed other social injustices that may affect students (like discrimination based on gender identity or sexual orientation), faculty added more coursework on race when they began to view residents' racial competence as instrumental to advancing their mission. Acknowledging the difficulty of "prescribe[ing] specific strategies" to address race in the classroom, NETR began holding one and then two "alumni panels" a year, where teachers could share how they work to serve students of color in their no excuses classrooms.

When I arrive in NETR's seventh year, faculty have planned to take yet another step into coursework on race through "Culturally Affirmative Teaching" (CAT). Angela (the director of training) explains that the white female principle of one of NETR's affiliated schools came up with this term because she did not like the terminology "culturally relevant" or "responsive," and was "adamant" that this coursework should be about "actively valuing" students' cultures. Angela admits that she does not necessarily agree with the shift, as it "raises a whole other level of issues for me in terms of the act of the white teacher assigning value to something; I think [it] is problematic." But it stuck.

The term Culturally Affirmative Teaching also reflects a digression from scholarship around culturally responsive or relevant teaching. Before I begin observing, Todd (the program's founding director) explains that the CAT coursework might look different from what I expect:

> We don't go hard on "You have to make sure you wake up every day thinking about how students can see their own culture as reflected in the curriculum that you bring to bear." What we do go really hard on is making transparent to students the idea of this culture of power. That what you are trying to do is help them gain the tools that they need to succeed in this academic culture called school.

This indicates that coursework on race, like the rest of NETR coursework, is deliberately geared around preparing students to navigate the school's academic culture, and later, society's dominant culture. This aligns with NETR's broader vision for "social justice": equipping residents with better teaching techniques to advance students' academic achievement and presumably their social and economic outcomes.

I begin my observations with an awareness that the program's coursework around race is also still in flux, ever evolving like the rest of the program. I also wonder how will NETR manage to reconcile its highly efficient and directive approach to instruction with a topic that often compels dialogue?

MOVING FORWARD WITHOUT LICENSE

On a sunny Friday afternoon in October, I observe NETR's first CAT session of the year. Joe, who is white like the other six principal NETR faculty, opens the session after lunch with a warm, enthusiastic smile expanding across his face. To begin, he acknowledges the absence of explicit talk about race in most no excuses charter schools; as he did in our interview, he justifies this by explaining that these schools are focused on a "social–political problem," that of "poverty" (which is also a coded word for racial inequity here), but that their answer is a "technical one," using prescriptive teaching solutions. He adds that NETR is wary of programs that spend most of their time just "talking and feeling" in response to issues like race, but that ultimately don't show results. Thus, no excuses charters have shied away from sociopolitical discussions because they did not know how to talk about this in a way that translated into action. But now, Joe suggests, "NETR has begun to figure it out."

After introducing the session, Joe turns the floor over to John (the chief operating officer of NETR) and a facilitator who has just entered named Matt. Matt, a tall Black man in a matte black tailored suit and vest with a confident gait, is the first person of color that I have seen lead any of NETR's coursework this year. He is not an NETR faculty member, but rather the dean of students and the athletic director at Excellence Preparatory High School (EPHS), the school from which NETR emerged. Given this position, and NETR's instrumental approach to increasing student and resident effort in class, it seems faculty may have asked Matt to introduce this session because they felt a person of color would help bring legitimacy to their CAT lessons.

As Matt begins, he jokes with one of the residents, "Ernest, as the other brother in the room, you feel me, right?" This receives some laughter and seems to lighten the mood on a heavy subject; but as I look out across the room, where a third of the residents are people of color but few are Black, it also occurs to me that education might often feel lonely for Black teachers in particular, who are underrepresented in the teaching force.

Matt leads residents through a brief discussion about the idea of "culture." Reading from the PowerPoint slides, he introduces the stated goal of CAT work: "empowering culturally proud, socially and economically mobile students to succeed in life and transform the culture of power." This is a derivation of NETR's broader program vision, which aspires to advance individual social and economic mobility, but lacks reference to the ideas of "culturally proud" and "transform[ation]."

Matt glances at the screen he has just read and admits, "That is a tall order. A number of us in this room, no matter what our backgrounds, will attempt to do this in different ways." He then goes on to qualify this with his own story of growing up and working in an area of Newark, New Jersey, where "things were bad." He adds, "Somehow, some way, whether it was taught to us, whether our family taught us, we learned that, how to navigate the culture of power, fill out a college application, advocate for ourselves, navigate power." His tone is passionate, and the residents gaze at Matt in rapt attention as he uses a personal story to segue into the main point for today's session: navigating the culture of power.

Seizing on the silence, John moves toward the front of the room, stating, "We are going to go slightly academic . . . discuss some of the readings in table groups . . . to get a shared vocabulary." For this session, residents read Lisa Delpit's "The Silenced Dialogue"[1] and an excerpt from Prudence Carter's book *Keepin' It Real*.[2] NETR very rarely assigns residents reading from educational scholarship, favoring their own highly distilled, intentionally curated, and conversationally written course guides. But there is no NETR course guide on race, and so the program has borrowed from Carter and Delpit, two Black scholars. But based on my earlier conversations with faculty, I already know NETR will lean more heavily on Delpit's ideas.

In her article, Delpit advises teachers not to assume students from nondominant groups understand the culture of power. Instead, she advises teachers to explicitly address with students how power is constructed by white middle- and upper-class people who in turn construct the codes or rules of power; this makes these codes arbitrary but also powerful as they govern schools and society. Therefore, Delpit suggests teachers should "initiate true dialogue" with students about the rules of the dominant culture so they can understand and enact them when needed.

Matt asks residents to "debrief" these articles for 15 minutes with surrounding peers. I observe as three white residents process ideas from the articles. Drawing from Delpit, they consider how students adopting dominant norms from the white middle class is like "play[ing] this game" to achieve their desired goals; two of the residents emphasize the importance of being "transparent" about this in their instruction, "all while affirming their [students'] culture." Then, just before the timer sounds, one of the residents named Hailey observes a contradiction between the readings and what she observes in her fieldwork: "At EPHS, we are hiding that we are training them to become a certain kind of student." This astute observation implies that adopting the codes of power is synonymous with behaving in line with no excuses norms and school rules, and that the school is not actually transparent about who benefits when students adopt these norms. Hailey's words hang in the air as John moves to the front and silence descends on the room again.

John briskly leads the residents through PowerPoint slides that summarize the main points of each article. This ensures that despite the likely variability across small-group conversations, residents come away with a shared understanding of these texts, one that aligns with what NETR wishes to address today. The slide on Delpit summarizes the idea that the "culture of power is a set of codes or rules required to participate in a powerful subgroup of society" and that "being told the rules makes acquiring power easier." The slide on Carter is briefer and suggests that both "dominant cultural capital" and "nondominant cultural capital" have value. While both these scholars offer an implicit critique about the "arbitrary" nature of the rules of power and whose cultural capital receives more social value, facilitators quickly simplify the message: students need to acquire dominant cultural capital, the codes of power.

John distinguishes CAT from other NETR coursework: "This is an unusual NETR session because there is not like one takeaway; it's not that clean." While NETR maintains that other aspects of teaching can be distilled to a single "clean" "takeaway," race seems to be a complex and messy (or even dirty) subject that challenges NETR's attempt at prescription—hence the lack of a corresponding course guide. But that does not mean they will not try to make it what they feel will be "clean[er]."

John next introduces one of the "deliverables" for this session: the "personal cultural inventory." It asks residents to reflect upon their own culture in comparison to the culture of their students, addressing the following points:

- "Culture" of your students, as you understand it now.
- Possible points of common experience, community partnership, or potential interests with your students. There will always be some. Think.
- Areas in which you perceive your students' culture is most different than your own.
- Authentically interested questions you have about your students' culture.

However, Joe suggests that residents should just "get it done" and upload the assignment today, that it is not something they should continue to refine. And John agrees with this point. This independent assignment is the only part of the lesson that attempts to push residents to consider students' home cultures, reflect upon their own identities, or develop understanding of their differences. But as faculty have acknowledged, NETR is wary about spending too much time thinking and feeling about issues like race; what they really want is "action."

When Matt prepares to leave, the residents offer him enthusiastic farewells, as John gives residents a few minutes to work on this cultural inventory in the Big Hall. Initially, there is a lot of chatter as residents work on this; perhaps they feel the need to process aloud. John insists, somewhat lightheartedly, "We are silently working." And then he points what he refers to as "the disco finger" out at the audience, saying "this finger is tracking silent workers." The residents quiet down. There is simply not much space for informal or messy discussions about race here.

After a brief break, Sara (the NETR director of coaching) introduces a "video panel" that sparks a provocative discussion, the likes of which I have not observed in NETR. Unlike the live alumni panels of the past, faculty can curate what information is dispensed to residents through these videos. The teachers and staff featured on the video discuss their experiences with race in a school setting, some implying that it is possible to find common ground with all students. In one of the clips, a white female assistant principal recounts having a discussion with a student of color who sagged his pants about the need to "code-switch" into (meaning to strategically adopt behavior from) the "culture of power" while at school so he could succeed in society. When the video concludes, faculty lead residents through a debrief.

A few white residents offer laudatory comments about the video, appreciating how the stories helped them think about finding shared experiences to discuss with their students of color. Then Stephanie, an Asian American elementary resident, raises a hand and states in an impassioned voice, "Maybe we do or don't have shared experiences. [But] I don't think it's appropriate for a white lady to be teaching a child of color about code-switching. How can teachers in the culture of power teach students in nondominant groups about code-switching?"

I look up from my keyboard at this remark. When I was studying to be a teacher at UCLA, Delpit's "culture of power" was often referenced in coursework. It never would have occurred to me to question the use of this text in teacher education. But like many of Stephanie's previous comments, her question is rich and provocative, challenging whether it is morally justifiable for white teachers, who come from the culture of power, to explicitly teach students to mimic their dominant cultural norms in the way that NETR is advising. Is NETR's particular deployment of Delpit's work akin to teaching assimilation?

Wendy, a white secondary English resident, challenges Stephanie's assertion: "I respectfully disagree. As a white woman working in a school with students who are so many different colors, [the AP]'s job is [to teach] code-switching."

Sara moves into the discussion: "I think Stephanie raises a good point, [but] I also disagree. While [the AP] might not intuitively understand, there is a level of intellectual understanding you can gain about your students' experiences. In the mess we are in, it is important that we teach students that different contexts require different experiences, even if we don't fully understand that experientially. And if I don't teach him, college will expect completely different behavior that will disadvantage him. I can tell him this is the reality, it is unfair . . . the ultimate goal is to make it more inclusive of other cultures, but it's just not the reality right now." I note the emphasis on the current reality, while the "ultimate goal" falls into the subtext.

Another white female resident adds with a self-assured tone, "I think you should be careful of assuming something is a race thing. I don't think the pants thing is a racial thing. I think it is about neighborhood." Some residents snap their fingers in response to this comment, indicating their support for her thoughts.

Jessica, a Black resident, responds with exasperation in her voice, "I think there is no context in which she can understand what it means to sag your pants in a low socioeconomic neighborhood." A couple other residents snap their fingers at this comment, supporting a different viewpoint than the one previously stated.

I sense that this conversation could go on for hours, especially with so many different people and perspectives in the room. And perhaps it should. Nonetheless, Sara moves on without missing a beat, indicating that it is time to end the discussion. I later learn that Sara does this because the conversation has caught her off guard and she is unsure about how to respond to the unfamiliar dissonance. She also does not feel she has the freedom to sacrifice the "practice component" of the day's session, the "action" step, to continue the discussion; they must stick to their itinerary.

In moving forward with CAT this year, NETR has designed a practice component that asks residents to role-play having conversations with students about "code-switching." Faculty provide a rubric to help guide one-on-one conversations with students, two possible scenarios that might warrant a "code-switching" conversation, and 10 minutes to generate some "talking points" to practice. Then they will role-play their conversation with a partner.

I approach Kara, a young white woman, and Ernest, a young Black man, and ask if I can observe their discussion. They nod. They choose to discuss a scenario in which a teacher asks an African American student to "speak more quietly," but the student responds, "I'm from Africa and this is how we talk there."

Ernest begins as the teacher first. He seems to offer a personal take on the NETR message: "In my experience, if I talked the same way at home as I do at school, it wouldn't be professional." The student that Kara role-plays complains that the school is "just try[ing] to make us robots." To which Ernest responds: "You don't have to change yourself, but at school, you just have to tone it down a little bit."

When it is Ernest's time to role-play the student, he insists, "This is how we talk at home and I feel like students should be able to talk like this here." As the teacher, Kara initially tries to personalize the code-switching message, too: "But when I come to EPHS, I use different versions of myself: I dress differently, act differently, talk differently." Ernest responds to this. "I only have one version of myself!" Kara tries again, adopting an approach that sounds more like the AP from the video: "When you are at home, you can talk as you want to, but when you are at EPHS, you can practice using language that will help you in the future. Now what can you implement in school?"

As the acting commences, Ernest praises Kara overall but suggests maybe bringing it back to something else that matters to the student, not just a presumable future of college and employment. He suggests, "Who's your favorite artist? [pause] When Jay-Z walks into a meeting, do you think he acts like that? . . . Ask how he behaves with his friends, and then pull out a good example of a student who code-switches effectively."

In this interaction, both Ernest and Kara reify ideas of learning to navigate the culture of power. Neither resident voices any overt resistance to the ideas presented earlier. Although they do integrate hypothetical student perspectives that question why a school would try to make them "robots," their teacher responses indicate that the full "version" of the student that seems most authentic or most like home is unwelcome in the school setting, and perhaps in broader society, too; to be "professional," the program suggests students must adopt white middle-class norms. The residents also do not refer to the contentious conversation that Stephanie prompted. Like good NETR residents, they soldier through this practice component without digressions. However, Ernest seems to feel more comfortable leading such a conversation and naturally encourages Kara to employ a more responsive approach with students, by bringing the conversation back to something that personally matters to them now. In this way, he pushes Kara to step slightly beyond the NETR narrative about learning to navigate the culture of power to achieve something in the future. But as I look around the room and notice several all-white pairings, I question how many residents have the opportunity to extend their thinking about race and culture beyond what is presented to them.

When 10 minutes have passed, Sara asks the residents to focus up front. Time has run out, and instead of trying to debrief these role-play conversations, she briefly addresses the previous discussion: "These kinds of conversations bring up difficult things for everyone. And the worst thing that could happen is that we stop talking about it. The worst things happen in silence. These are anxiety producing things to talk about, but even with our kids, we need to talk about them. We will make mistakes, but it's worse if we don't bring them up. We connect by talking about difficult things." Her tone is sincere, her expression pensive, but while her words support the idea of "connect[ing]" with others through difficult conversations, Sara has suppressed a potentially rich conversation by moving on to the practice component. And many of the residents voice complaints about this session overall.

After Joe has had time to reflect on this first CAT session, he tells me that NETR tried to have an "unlicensed conversation" about race, one in which the faculty "hadn't done the work that we needed" to explicitly endorse conversations between teachers and students about "code-switching." He feels they should have spent more time unpacking terms and getting on "the same page" before prescribing actions. Despite feeling that NETR had begun to "figure it out" before this session, Joe acknowledges afterward that they have more work to do.

ADJUSTING COURSE

In the first CAT course session, NETR established a few of their core beliefs about race and equity. They acknowledged inequity in the form of the "achievement gap," but they did not analyze *why* this exists. This suggests that like in previous years, faculty did not feel it was worth spending time "talking and feeling" about social problems like racism and cultural/social reproduction. Instead, faculty jumped right to their proposed solution to inequity, their own vision of social justice: supporting students with the skills required to achieve in school and society. These skills are not just academic, but also social, as NETR faculty maintained that students must learn to "code-switch" into the culture of power so that they can more readily mimic dominant ways of dressing and behaving to get ahead.

This vision is consistent with ideas of "navigation," a word mentioned countless times throughout NETR coursework. According to Aliyah El-Amin, navigation is an approach to educating students of color that occurs when educators seek to provide individual students with the "tools" of academics, economic knowledge, and social capital so students can achieve social and economic mobility despite the obstacles they face. She suggests that a navigational approach to schooling is likely indicative of the commonly held belief that racism is a consequence of individual, not structural, prejudice.[3] And perhaps this is the case here, as NETR did not explore the structural and institutional forces that contribute to an unjust social system in the first CAT session. Instead, they took the current reality as a given and focused on how to teach the students to work within this system. But residents' critical reactions to this approach surprised Sara and the other NETR faculty, and residents' online evaluations of the session were uncharacteristically negative.

I hear a variety of responses to this first CAT session in individual interviews. Julie, who is white, remembers Stephanie's comment as: "I don't think that [white] teacher has the right to be talking about code-switching." She adds, "And I completely get where she was coming from, 'cause that's like a real issue, but I think that the issue people took with it was [that] you can't tell someone they don't have a *right* to do something." While Julie acknowledges the racial dynamics at play in code-switching conversations as a "real issue," she suggests people were affronted because they felt like Stephanie was denying white people a license to do something that NETR deemed important. As some research suggests, white people, having been denied very little in the past, may respond negatively to indications that there are things they cannot do or understand.[4]

However, Alina—a friend of Stephanie's who is white and often voiced dissonant opinions in other coursework—recalls the incident differently. She remembers, "Thank God, Stephanie's hand shoots up into the air and she was like, wait a minute. Can we process for a second whether or not it's even morally permissible or helpful for any teacher, regardless of race or back-ground, to be having this conversation with their students in the first place?" She adds that many "problematic dynamics" and assumptions "could be perpetuating power in that interaction" and needed to be unearthed before they could determine whether it was "permissible" for white residents in particular to practice having conversations about code-switching. Alina fur-ther laments how Sara "completely shut down" Stephanie and the conversa-tion at large by trying to "salvage" the practice component. Many of the residents seemed to walk away from the session feeling disappointed. As Alina notes, "People lit up the Zooms"—NETR's feedback surveys about each session—to voice negative feedback. This proved a humbling moment for NETR, causing them to reassess the way they approached CAT.

Because NETR places value on practice, feedback, making mistakes, and learning from these, faculty bring Stephanie in to help them plan a session to more thoroughly address her concerns and those of her peers. Stephanie remembers, "I helped them write that [follow-up] session and I feel like they were receptive because I think they don't have a strong core knowledge in this area [of race]." This course adjustment feels like a monumental step for a program that religiously avoids detours from its urgent mission.

In the follow-up CAT session, Sara opens by acknowledging NETR's many missteps in their first attempt at addressing race with cohort 7. In NETR style, she enumerates each perceived mistake, the first of which is: "We didn't plan nearly enough time to discuss bigger picture ideas; we tried too quickly to get to practice." The second is that the session did not begin with a clear and accessible shared understanding of important terms. The third is that they know it is easier to talk about these issues in small groups, but they attempted it in a large group and she "botched the response" to Stephanie's earnest inquiry. And fourth, she "could have thrown off the plan and moved to small group discussion, but I didn't." She frames this as an important lesson for teachers, who should "respond to what students do in the moment." Sara concludes, "But reflecting on it has been kind of a blessing, because we have had some great conversations among our team and with some of you, and we got to process a lot of these issues, and I think our program will be better [for it]."

These acknowledgments are somewhat surprising because although NETR usually establishes clear definitions for terms, none of the sessions spend much time discussing big ideas, feature extensive (unstructured) small-group discussions, or "throw off the plan" to "respond" to residents in the moment. Aside from the repeated use of numbered points to convey a message, this doesn't sound like NETR's efficient pedagogy. Perhaps faculty have come to believe that discussions of race require a different approach.

This reinvented CAT session continues by defining terms like race and culture, which were only briefly mentioned in the previous session. And the slides now present a new concept: white privilege. Privilege is a term that implies that there *are* structural forces that systematically grant some advantage over others, and are purely based on the color of a person's skin. In defining these terms, NETR begins to acknowledge that racism is likely not just an individual problem.

Next, residents take a "privilege quiz" based on Peggy McIntosh's *Knapsack of White Privilege*, a seminal text used in many teacher education programs that explores the many benefits white people take for granted in everyday life. After residents complete the quiz online, NETR immediately tallies the results, distinguished by the race of the residents, and projects these on the screen:

> White people: AVG: 108, Range: 89–115
> People of color: AVG: 44, Range: 6–91

This approach to discussing privilege is distinctly NETR: quantifying something that is usually qualified. Nonetheless, the difference in "privilege" between residents in the same cohort, purely based on skin color, is stark and undeniable. And for residents who have been taught to think explicitly and quantitatively, this representation might seem especially convincing.

Then faculty ask residents to discuss their reactions to this as a whole group, which unfolds in waves for 20 minutes or so. The conversation never explicitly addresses Stephanie's previous question about whether it is morally permissible for white people to teach students of color to "code-switch," but residents bring up general issues of privilege and how this is related to race. Next, residents are invited to continue this discussion in small groups facilitated by NETR alumni—many of whom are people of color—whom NETR has invited here to help residents explore these issues from a practical standpoint. Sara asks me not to observe the small-group discussions, as these might feel especially vulnerable for the residents. But what I hear from others indicates that this small-group continuation allows residents space to explore these difficult topics without a prescribed outcome. There is no practice component whatsoever today, which is unlike NETR.

After the second CAT session, the "Zooms" appear overwhelmingly positive, thanks in part to Stephanie. In their comments, residents generally praise NETR for incorporating their feedback in this follow-up and many call it "so much better." However, not every resident feels good about the session. Ellen, a white secondary resident, later tells me in an interview, "We got bogged down on that discussion for quite a while. I know a lot of people feel it's better . . . [but] I didn't. I basically had the whole day telling me I was supposed to feel guilty because I was white. I actually felt extremely uncomfortable the whole day. It's okay, I get it. I have advantages. Now tell me what I can do about it or what I can do to help other people." In these comments, Ellen seems to voice a preference for NETR's original focus on solutions over exploring uncomfortable realities that might make her feel "guilty." But most of the residents favor the follow-up session. In fact, Casey, a white secondary resident, reflects that he wasn't "able to really accept fully what privilege means for me" until NETR confronted him with it in this format. And he thinks his ability to frankly acknowledge his privilege will be his "greatest tool" for connecting across cultural differences.

After learning from these first two CAT sessions, faculty decide to make the remaining sessions of the year live small-group and whole-group alumni panels like those they held in the past. These feature a racially diverse selection of no excuses teachers who respond to some NETR-generated guiding questions to explore how they personally deal with issues of race in their classrooms and schools.

Julie recalls one panel discussion that addressed her "uncertainty" about "Why am I teaching kids to comply with white rules?" Although they reinforced the importance of learning to "navigate" the "culture of power," a few of the panelists softened Julie's uneasiness about teaching navigation by suggesting teachers tell students that their culture is still "important" and they shouldn't change "who you are," but that they just need to learn to "turn off" their "identity" in certain contexts (like school). The notion of students' having to "turn off" their identities while learning contradicts scholarship on culturally responsive teaching, which embraces students' cultural identities within the classroom. Nonetheless, Julie takes comfort in these panelists' comments as evidence that a navigational approach to schooling can truly be affirming to students' home cultures (so long as any cultural expressions remain at home).

Other panelists stress the importance of acquiring some awareness of students' cultures. One story from a panel that particularly impacts Casey is about a Cape Verdean student who would never make eye contact with the teacher because in his culture, that was a sign of disrespect; but he kept getting demerits and detentions for not "tracking the speaker" with his eyes, which essentially punished him for showing respect. This serves as impetus for Casey to learn more about students' cultures when he realizes, "Oh my God, I am going to traumatize so many kids because I don't know [about their culture]." He does not communicate a sense of how he would respond if faced with such a discrepancy between home culture and school expectations, but the story does seem to increase his desire to learn more about his students.

The lessons that both Casey and Julie derive from these panels—that residents should seek to gain some understanding of students' cultures and how this influences their behavior—are important for white residents. These are not lessons NETR has planned for residents, but rather lessons that practitioners convey in small discussions. And residents generally voice appreciation for the lessons they learn in these panels, likely because the teachers speaking to them in small and large groups have more positional authority on this topic, as many are people of color and all are current teachers. But while the panelists seem to complicate the picture of teaching across culture differences, they continue to reinforce NETR's message about navigation.

NETR faculty maintain that the alumni panels not only allow for a practical discussion of how race comes into play in teaching, but also provide space for residents to learn from a range of experiences. However, it is also possible that faculty choose to rely on panel discussions to transfer the weight of confronting race from their own white shoulders to those of their racially diverse alumni. After having encountered so much pushback in their first foray into issues of race with this cohort, they might not feel as comfortable leading residents through further conversations, like the one they had originally planned on race in the curriculum. Analogous to the "guilt" that Ellen reports after the second CAT session, the all-white faculty might feel similar "fragility" around facilitating uncomfortable conversations about race.

Moreover, some of the residents no longer seem to feel the faculty have license to lead such discussions. Alina explains, "To be completely honest, I feel like the people who are my program directors and my professors at NETR are no further along in their racial identity development than any of the residents, so they can't act like mentors or people who are guiding us along in this process." While NETR holds one more session on race this year, the white faculty avoid facilitating this coursework because it is still not in NETR's wheelhouse and residents might have cause to challenge them. Instead, NETR continues to emphasize the importance of navigation through practicing no excuses teachers.

NAVIGATING OBSTACLES

While NETR readily acknowledges the need for students to learn to navigate the system of power, they rarely acknowledge the injustices inherent in that system. Their mission is exclusively focused on working within the current society, about preparing individuals who can succeed despite unacknowledged oppressive forces, not preparing teachers with tools to challenge these.

Most of the NETR residents accept it with without questioning it. Stephanie, however, initially voices her critiques. As she reflects upon the CAT coursework, she indicts NETR's approach to coursework for two primary shortcomings: (1) its lack of "internal work" and (2) its tacit perpetuation of an existing unjust system.

Stephanie explains, "A lot of people haven't done the internal work, so if you haven't done the internal work, you definitely can't do any sort of external work. Well, not . . . antiracist work." She follows this statement with an example of how she feels the program "brush[es] aside" important identity markers in favor of connecting over shallow similarities like "music" or "dancing." Instead, Stephanie feels that racial competence, a prerequisite to forming meaningful relationships with students across racial differences, starts with deep "internal work" that includes interrogating why teachers have decided to teach students of color.

Todd (NETR's founding director) acknowledges that NETR approaches this differently: "For us, being a reflective practitioner means you are really thinking about the nuances of your practice. You're disciplined about how you approach problem solving within your classroom. It's less about constant reflection of the big picture and who I am, and how I fit into my larger philosophy around social justice." The short cultural inventory that NETR assigns residents is merely used as a prelude to the discussions of navigation, an aspect of practice upon which residents could reflect. But as Stephanie observes, there is no deep internal work around this; for that is just not NETR.

Stephanie further criticizes NETR for "oversimplifying" social justice as "Oh, the way we fight racism is by getting kids really good test scores." She adds, "You won't be able to have transformative change if you are thinking that way, because you are kind of like supporting a preexisting system that is already inherently racist and oppressive, right?" Instead of teaching residents to educate students with a critical perspective and the tools for social change so they "know what they are up against" and can "break down systemic inequalities" when they "become decision-makers . . . in the world," Stephanie implies that NETR is failing its residents and their future students by tacitly endorsing the culture of power and all that accompanies it.

Relatedly, I realize that in all my hours of observation throughout the year, I have not once seen a faculty member address the recent succession of publicized police brutality. These real and incredibly disturbing incidents, which undeniably affect the children served by no excuses schools, do not make their way into NETR. During my observations of residents in Tutorial and student teaching, I do not witness any discussion of race at all; instead, the classwork is strictly and efficiently focused on academic content from the mostly white canon. When they need to address student behavior, NETR encourages residents to indirectly bring up race in structured conversations with students about how to code-switch into the culture of power. But within the classroom, there is a general lack of acknowledgment that the forces students are "up against" are pervasive, recalcitrant, and unlikely to be remedied with good test scores. Although NETR faculty now seem to view racial competence as somewhat instrumental in effective cross-cultural teaching, only the residents who have already done the "internal work" (like Stephanie) seem to be comfortable initiating critical discussions about this.

But Stephanie tells me, "I am too radical for NETR." And indeed, NETR faculty reprimand Stephanie, Alina, and one other resident named Edgar (who is a transgender man of color) for their own "unlicensed" comments in coursework. As I will discuss more in Chapter 3, all three of these residents are threatened with failing NETR's professionalism rubric—particularly the strand around "Affect and Appearance," which calls for "positive tone and presence" in coursework and fieldwork—for voicing challenges to coursework that are not "solution oriented." This disciplinary action reinforces an idea that NETR seems to perpetuate: the purpose of education is to learn predetermined knowledge, not to engage in open-ended critical dialogue that might challenge the established order. Although faculty acknowledged that Stephanie's question in the first CAT session challenged them all to have deeper conversations amongst themselves and better "process these issues" to improve the program as a whole—which in turn helped residents like Casey gain a better understanding of his own privilege—Stephanie almost fails the program for her vocal challenges and thus stops sharing her opinions.

Perhaps there really is no space for "transformative" thought like Stephanie's in no excuses schools, which rely upon uncritical compliance to a strict behavioral code. Jose, a Latino secondary English resident, observes, "In this kind of school . . . you are sort of like holding this very strict rule, that [is] just a reenactment of the culture of power, basically." However, Jose personally justifies this "reenactment" because he sees his students completing rigorous academic work under this system and feels that it is preparing them to succeed in the future. He adds, "If you don't teach your kids that it exists [and] how [to] navigate it, it's something that happens to them rather than something they navigate." And like Jose, most of the NETR residents hope that the no excuses approach to teaching will help their individual students navigate the culture of power so they can make it to college and attain individual economic and social mobility in life.

Still, not all of the residents are convinced by the no excuses approach to schooling. Most of the more critical residents likely leave the program through "healthy exit," as faculty acknowledge that this approach is not for everyone. This might be why the attrition rate for residents of color in the year I observe is approximately 50%, while the attrition rate for white residents is only 25%. But Stephanie, Alina, and Edgar all choose to remain.

And while they all express an aversion to the way students are "policed" in no excuses schools, they join EPHS-affiliated schools upon finishing the program, likely because they too have convinced themselves that the no excuses model has merit for historically marginalized students.

NETR faculty and residents generally believe that a strict and efficient approach to education will truly advance the academic and economic opportunities of the low-income students of color they serve. And parents of color seem to agree, as thousands choose no excuses schools for their children. But it is possible that these parents have more complex motivations for this choice. Ericka, a Black NETR coach who is also a scholar at a local university, explains with passion:

> This is something that's attractive to Black parents and Brown parents because they know how the world is. Because the world is really shitty to a Black person who doesn't know how to fucking follow rules. Like, "You will be killed if you're a Black boy and you don't follow rules. You will be killed." And so, there's something about a school like that that I believe is enticing to a number of Black families.

As Ericka acknowledges, parents of color might intentionally select no excuses schools for their children because they think these disciplined spaces might teach them to defer to white authority figures, which might help keep them alive in potential altercations with police, like those that ended the lives of so many over the course of year 7 of NETR alone. Some parents might want their children to understand obedience, for "unlicensed conversations" and transformative thought can be personally risky for people of color.

Throughout my observations and interviews, residents and staff in NETR found themselves confronting the potential limits of the no excuses model. Although seemingly effective for the acquisition of discrete skills and moves, the instrumental and practice-based pedagogy employed in NETR left little room for critical discussions about the realities of racism. Julie reflects:

> At the beginning of the year their rationale was, "We're not going to talk about big issues like the achievement gap, like culturally responsive teaching because our work is too urgent. We're going to tell you guys how to be a teacher in those environments, but if we spend all of our time talking about more philosophical aspects of teaching you're not going to be ready." That is true, but it's also just irresponsible, because most of us were white . . . with little to no culturally responsive knowledge.

As a white teacher, Julie acknowledges that she feels ill prepared to teach students of color in a responsive way, despite the once-suggested goals of CAT coursework including reference to "empower[ing] culturally proud" students who can "transform the culture of power."

(UN)CRITICALLY ADVANCING

NETR residents learned to have conversations with students about navigating the culture of power in school and beyond, but not to interrogate it, or to emphasize cultures other than the one in power. As a result, the program promotes a strictly navigational approach to schooling, which advances a "hokey hope" in meritocratic success without equipping students with critical awareness about the systemic forces that work against people of color.[5] But as Stephanie suggests, in order to develop racial competence all teachers should learn to have critical conversations about the system, and to challenge it by honoring nondominant sources of knowledge and ways of being, because racism is insidious.

In today's society, racist forces rarely manifest in explicitly derogatory speech directed toward communities of color. Instead, racism has largely become institutionalized and tacit: people of color—and Black people in particular—are subjugated by the lack of access to quality housing and subsequent residential segregation; racial gerrymandering of political boundaries and lack of representation in elected office; historical and continuing job and wage discrimination and subsequent lack of wealth or property to hand down between generations; and disproportionate rate of arrest, incarceration, and death by police or capital punishment.[6]

Despite this country's ideals about education serving as the great equalizer of race and class disparity, schools also perpetuate institutional racism through increasing segregation, lack of resources and quality teaching staff at schools serving predominantly students of color, deficit thinking by faculty and discriminatory course-tracking policies, and overassignment to special education programs.[7] We do not live in a meritocracy. As Stephanie so eloquently explains above, the students "need to know what they're up against." And teachers do, too, so they can be honest with their students. For if students enter society without an awareness of the institutional forces that seek to deny them license to navigate the system, they will face various obstacles along their way, obstacles that can cut their journeys short. Learning to navigate the system does not help if they are not really prepared.

However, there may never have been space to have critical discussions of racism and oppression at NETR. No excuses schools were predicated upon the belief that low-income students of color need strict and explicit instruction into how to assimilate into dominant culture. In this model, it is not the dominant culture that is interrogated or critiqued, but rather the students who do not readily fit this norm who are pathologized and deemed in need of urgent reform. Any challenge to dominant culture and the system of white privilege that sustains and reproduces this culture presents turbulence for both the culture of no excuses institutions and their raison d'être.

As such, the predominantly white faculty of NETR are unprepared for, and ultimately uncomfortable with, any challenge to this system. However, they justify their avoidance of these thorny conversations by reiterating the urgency of their mission, the need to teach residents (and by proxy their students) all the skills they will need to succeed by their standards. Hence the omission of any discussion of the systemic police brutality that dominated the media in the year I observed these programs, or any mention of LGBT issues for that matter. And when residents of color, and even some white residents, voice critical opinions that challenge NETR's hegemonic world-view, their voices are suppressed. The norms of the dominant culture, which are the same as the professional standards of NETR, triumph.

But perhaps there is some hope in the fact that NETR was trying to have a conversation about race and racism. They could have avoided it all together, as they did in the past, and starting a conversation is undeniably the first step. When their first CAT session went wrong, they also learned from their mistakes and retaught the lesson, and in ways that digressed from their standard approach and included residents' guidance. This is the greatest strength of no excuses institutions: they are constantly iterating and evolving, ever working to improve.[8] In the few years since I concluded this research, I have heard that the program has already redesigned their CAT coursework, probably multiple times.

However, one can only evolve so much through "single-loop learning," operating within the confines of their existing ideology. To truly evolve to the point where they may indeed be able to advance a more ambitious form of social justice—one that helps empower students to not only work within the current society, but lead the efforts to make it better—NETR may have to reexamine the no excuses approach to education as a whole.[9] For a system predicated on uncritically advancing dominant culture, of simply teaching students to navigate it, can never truly achieve any form of social justice.

NOTES

1. Delpit, Lisa. (1988). The silenced dialogue: Power and pedagogy in educating other people's children. *Harvard Educational Review, 53*(3).

2. Carter, Prudence. (2005). *Keepin' it real: Why school success has no color*. Oxford, England: Oxford University Press.

3. El-Amin, A. (2015). *"Until justice rolls down like water": Revisiting emancipatory schooling for African Americans—A theoretical exploration of concepts for liberation* (Unpublished doctoral dissertation). Harvard University, Cambridge, MA.

4. See DiAngelo, Robin. (2011). White fragility. *International Journal of Critical Pedagogy, 3*(3), 54–70; DiAngelo, Robin. (2018). How white people handle diversity training in the workplace. *Medium*. Retrieved from https://medium.com/s/story/how-white-people-handle-diversity-training-in-the-workplace-e8408d2519f

5. See El-Amin, *"Until justice rolls down like water,"* and Duncan-Andrade, J. M. R. (2009). Note to educators: Hope required when growing roses in concrete. *Harvard Educational Review, 79*(2), 181–194.

6. Alexander, Michelle. (2010). The new Jim Crow: Mass incarceration in the age of colorblindness. New York, NY: New Press; Bonilla-Silva, Eduardo. (2014). *Racism without racists: Color-blind racism and the persistence of racial inequality in America.* Lanham, MD: Rowman & Littlefield.

7. Bonilla-Silva, *Racism without racists*; Oakes, Jeannie. (1985). *Keeping track: How schools structure inequality.* New Haven, CT: Yale University Press.

8. Mehta, Jal, & Fine, Sarah. (2019). *In search of deeper learning: Inside the effort to remake the American high school.* Cambridge, MA: Harvard University Press.

9. Argyris, Chris. (1977, September). Double loop learning in organizations. *Harvard Business Review.*

Chapter Three

The NETR Brand

I imagine on their end, they're obsessed with only producing people who are gonna represent the NETR brand to the best of their ability.—Casey, NETR secondary resident

Fieldwork, in which preservice teachers get to practice what they have learned about teaching, is often thought to be more influential than most teacher education coursework.[1] This might be particularly true when considering the formation of student–teacher relationships, where knowledge about connecting with people can only go so far; at some point, teachers will have to interact with actual students.

NETR has taken this idea to heart, as Todd (the founding director) explains, "We try to maximize the amount of time that people spend practicing and getting feedback on that practice." In order to do so, NETR has established what Todd calls a "ladder" for residents to slowly ramp up their real-time teaching opportunities, but this is a very different ladder from the one used in traditional teacher education programs. Todd adds, "Typically . . . a student teaching situation is you're placed with a mentor and you gradually take on the mentor teacher's responsibilities. We do not do student teaching like that." Instead, the NETR ladder moves from Tutorial, to teaching simulations, to limited student teaching, and finally solo summer teaching. Throughout all these experiences, residents are responsible for upholding very particular standards for both instructional practice and professionalism—the NETR brand.

In Tutorial, residents begin practicing instructional strategies and classroom management before the program even officially begins. Tutorial is the backbone of NETR; it originated as a "gap year" program for college graduates who could provide additional support for no excuses students, and who would in turn get experience working in schools. NETR designed itself around this built-in daily fieldwork, in which residents tutor the same five to 10 students over the course of the year. Residents meet with these students individually or in groups of two to three throughout the day, Monday through Thursday, and draw their tutoring lessons from a scripted curriculum provided by the school where they are placed. Tutorial is identified as the "bottom rung" on NETR's ladder because it involves real work with students but does not realistically mimic the instructional and classroom management strategies teachers will be expected to perform with a large group. As NETR has evolved, it has added multiple practical experiences and standards for practice throughout the program.

After learning specific moves in coursework, residents have scheduled time each week with a group of five of their peers to role-play these strategies. In these teaching simulations, there are no students, but the residents take turns being the teacher while the others inhabit specific student roles. Then in the spring, residents student teach twice each week. On Fridays, they take over the classroom of one no excuses teacher to practice teaching; and then in a Saturday academy, they take on the lead role of providing one class of no excuses students with extra support. Finally—in what Todd calls their final "dress rehearsal"—residents teach classes on their own for a month in one of the local no excuses summer academies. In each of these experiences, they are observed and receive copious and coherent feedback from an NETR-trained coach or faculty member.

This system of feedback is distinctly different from most teacher education programs, which generally rely on one or two mentor teachers in the field to provide feedback to preservice teachers. In other programs, there is often great variability across mentor teachers,[2] which is something NETR hopes to avoid. Thus, NETR has devoted a great deal of its resources to coaching.

Todd explains the benefit of this approach: "You know at the end of every day of teaching you have someone who has been trained by us, who we oversee, who is coaching you with a specific protocol in mind, everyone using similar observation and evaluation tools, whose job is to set a goal for you, help you meet that goal, evaluate how you're doing on that goal." This creates a great deal more coherence and uniformity across preservice teachers than would be seen in other programs, and on everything from instructional approach to teacher–student interactions. The idea is that in the end, all the NETR teachers will learn to effectively "row in the same direction" as their colleagues in the field, collectively advancing student achievement.

CODE OF CONDUCT

At NETR, student learning is in many ways conceptualized as the result of a team, which means that teachers must work together, and alongside parents and administrators, to advance common ends. As two of the directors—Sara and Angela—acknowledged in Chapter 1, committing to teaching in the no excuses world requires that residents accept common beliefs, like those regarding the enforcement of school rules. Todd echoes this point in our interview, "A lot of what we do is getting people to buy into the idea that in the schools we're preparing them for—it goes back to this idea of being autonomous as a teacher—it's incredibly important that you are rowing in the same direction as your colleagues." NETR's conceptualization of teaching stands in contrast to the traditional "egg crate" model where teachers have full autonomy to educate in their own way, toward their own curricular ends, and in isolation from others.[3] Instead, NETR residents learn to accept a collective approach to schooling, in part through the program's explicit instructional and professional standards that are analogous to a code of conduct.

To guide and evaluate residents' instruction, NETR staff use a comprehensive teaching rubric named "the Kraken," a reference to the movie *The Clash of the Titans*. The Kraken evaluates residents in the following six categories: classroom presence, proactive management, reactive management, thinking tasks, student practice, and implementation of feedback. Halfway through the year, directors draw upon some of these evaluative categories for the Gateway: a high-stakes performance evaluation that determines which residents are invited to continue the program and which will be encouraged to leave NETR. In the past, up to 10% of residents have been asked to leave after the Gateway, regardless of whether they wanted to remain. If they are not cutting it by NETR's definition, they're out. Unsurprisingly, residents find the Gateway "stressful," and both Casey and Julie (the two white secondary residents I will follow into the field) even refer to it as the "most stressful" experience of their "entire life" thus far. Nonetheless, NETR believes requiring this performance exam prior to teaching is essential because "high-needs" students should not have to "pay the penalty" for an ineffective teacher.

Despite the existence of a whole course on relationships in NETR, the only space on the Kraken or in the Gateway to assess teacher–student relationship development is through the lens of classroom management. So while concepts like "Warm/Strict" from the Relationships and Student Investment course likely inform residents' behavior in fieldwork, they are not being evaluated on whether they use NETR's relational moves in practice. However, NETR has another structure in place to more explicitly guide residents in all the "other skills" they will need to become "highly employable" first year teachers: the Professionalism Guide.

As NETR admits, the Professionalism Guide has "a lot to do with all those different relationships that you'll need to navigate," specifically those "with parents, students, colleagues, coaches, and your principal." Like their instructional techniques, relationships in the program and field are not left up to individual style, but rather guided by a set of standards, with the aim of ensuring a collective approach to professional interactions. This guide states: "Your school will have a specific vibe or culture. You'll want to learn this quickly so that you're 'rowing in the same direction' as everyone else. . . . It might mean you need to change the way you do something, or develop a new habit. This is what teams do to be successful." To support residents' success in no excuses schools, NETR explicitly teaches them the codes of successful no excuses teaching.

Residents seem to quickly understand that their autonomy as a teacher is constrained by the no excuses context. Kelly (a white elementary resident) explains, "I also think you have to buy into like, this is a program to teach you how to be an effective teacher in a high performing, urban charter school." As teachers in no excuses schools attempt to get students to "buy into" school rules and values, faculty attempt to prepare residents to "buy into" the idea of following protocol in these schools through coursework and other structures like this Professionalism Handbook.

The Professionalism Handbook outlines a rubric on which residents will be scored throughout the year to ensure they learn these skills "as quickly (and completely) as possible." This rubric is called RAITT, an acronym that stands for Responsibility, Affect and Appearance, Irene (the program's short-hand for willingness to accept and implement feedback), Timeliness, and Teamwork. Along with "the Kraken"—which is focused on classroom management and the planning and implementation of effective lessons—RAITT is used to evaluate residents' overall suitability for teaching in no excuses schools. I summarize each component below:

- **Responsibility:** completing all assignments on time, minimizing absences from coursework and fieldwork, and remaining responsive to email and other program communication.
- **Affect and Appearance:** wearing "conservative and not overly casual" clothes for coursework and fieldwork; maintaining a "positive tone and presence" in body language, comments, and writing; and engaging pleasantly and constructively in all coursework and fieldwork.
- **Irene:** the ability to respond "productively and positively" to feedback on their teaching practice and (to bring it full circle) "professionalism feedback."
- **Timeliness:** in the words of the handbook, "You're developing your urgency-o-meter this year and it starts with being on time for, like, everything."

- **Teamwork:** supporting peers, remaining positive throughout challenges, "be[ing] solution oriented," and "contributing to the vibe and culture of NETR."

Upon reading this document well into the school year, I gain new insight into the attire of residents and faculty, the punctual course sessions, the graciousness with which residents give and receive feedback, and the attentiveness of the residents. These are not accidental by-products of an intense culture; they are the result of an explicit code of conduct. As Casey tells me in passing when I make a comment about how formally dressed everyone is, "We dress this way because we have to."

Alina (a white elementary resident) distinguishes NETR from a "college" environment because of RAITT standards, suggesting that residents cannot express uncensored opinions or challenge ideas with NETR faculty "because [they] are also the body that's going to be selling you to future employers." Instead, NETR functions as structured training for a very specific work environment. And they are able to maintain this unique approach because like the no excuses charter schools they serve, NETR is an institution "of choice": residents chose this program intentionally and can leave it via "healthy exit" if they do not like it.

The Professionalism Handbook presents behavioral norms that seem quite symmetric to rules and values guiding student behavior at no excuses schools. As the handbook states, "The same way we'll sweat the small stuff in your teaching. . . . You'll see us sweat the small stuff in all five RAITT categories." In an explicit reference to Whitman's book *Sweating the Small Stuff: Inner-City Schools and the New Paternalism*,[4] NETR communicates a belief that students and teachers alike can become "broken windows" if left unsupported, and small signs of chaos can multiply if left unaddressed. This approach impacts their relationships with various stakeholders, including students.

Throughout the year, most of the residents behave in line with RAITT. For example, Julie acknowledges that the professionalism rating impacted her willingness to voice complaints or critical questions to the faculty because "I want to pass this program." She adds reflectively, "I think morally I should've talked to them more and pushed them more, but I didn't have the energy or courage to do that."

A few of the other residents notably struggle with the professionalism rubric. Stephanie remembers that in December, she and two other elementary residents were told they "were failing RAITT and we needed to do XYZ" to improve. She further explains, "They essentially were like, 'You're failing in professionalism because you make a lot of people really uncomfortable with the things that you say.'" At various points in the fall (like those discussed in Chapters 1 and 2), I observed Stephanie voicing challenging questions to coursework related to teacher–student relationships. But what I do not realize until the end of the year is that she faces consequences for these expressions, as they pose challenges to NETR's approach.

Alina recalls receiving very similar feedback. She explains, "My feedback from NETR was, 'You sometimes ask questions in a way that is aggressive and halts conversations instead of in a way that is moving them forward and is solution oriented.'" However, she tells me she had a hard time voicing her comments in a "solution-oriented" manner because she could not see a productive path forward with NETR strategies she viewed as inherently "wrong."

As mentioned in Chapter 2, Stephanie, Alina, and Edgar posed normative challenges to some of the core practices emphasized by NETR—such as uncritically teaching students to adopt behavior from the culture of power or the relentlessly strict approach to class discipline—without proposing solutions. Therefore, faculty labeled them as failing RAITT, particularly the Affect and Appearance strand of the rubric that deals with how residents engage in coursework. If they failed RAITT, NETR would be unable to recommend them for a job next year because, as faculty explained, "you can't talk to your principal this way" in no excuses schools.

Naturally, this feedback was originally challenging for these residents to hear. Stephanie explains, "I initially felt very angry and I felt like, 'Well, if they don't want me, I should quit.'" In this response, Stephanie explores her options in a way that harkens back to Hirschman's *Exit, Voice, and Loyalty* framework, which suggests that members or consumers of a business have three choices when they encounter undesirable circumstances or products: they can leave or stop consuming said product (exit), they can express their discontent (voice), or they can quietly accept the changes (loyalty).[5] As Stephanie discovers, voice is not an option at NETR. Instead, she can either exit the program or display loyalty to it, which she is initially hesitant to do because this loyalty feels inauthentic to her. But exit also seems risky to these dedicated teachers. Alina acknowledges the high-stakes consequences of failing RAITT as not only having to "quit" the program but possibly also being "blacklist[ed]" from many local charter schools.

While these three residents feel "very frustrated" over the feedback they received, none of them quits. Instead, they draw upon the meaningful supportive relationships they have developed with each other to persevere. Alina explains, "We got through it together." But to remain, these residents ultimately had to change their behavior by displaying loyalty. As Stephanie explains, they did so by becoming "a lot less vocal" in coursework. Alina adds that they decided to "just bide our time, just try to get through this program, get what we can out of it, and move on and maybe address it later when we're more powerful." The effect of this decision, at least in ongoing coursework, is that these residents stop expressing challenges to NETR. And in doing so, they fulfill the professionalism standard for implementing the feedback they received from faculty. While these residents continue to hold internal beliefs that conflict with NETR's values, they outwardly "row in the same direction" as their peers and instructors.

Overall, NETR's standards notably shape residents' behavior in the program, the field, and beyond. The Kraken has a great impact on residents' instructional practice, as those who do not measure up to these instructional standards are not able to continue the program. Meanwhile, the Professionalism Handbook (which includes RAITT) serves as a powerful program structure in the shaping of residents' relational behavior.

The Professionalism Handbook effectively constrains residents' autonomy within the scope of program coursework and activities; they can only interact with one another and with faculty in ways that are deemed "professional" by NETR. If they don't like it, they can exit; but this, too, might feel risky to some because they could get "blacklisted" from other nearby charter schools by doing so. Moreover, RAITT is explicitly intended to prepare residents to form "professional relationships" with various stakeholders once they leave the program and enter schools; and it effectively socializes residents into a certain manner of interacting with students, parents, and colleagues. But without the free use of their voice, the authenticity of these relationships is questionable. Finally, there is a great deal of symmetry here—residents are essentially treated like their no excuses students, who must behave in line with strict behavioral norms and demonstrate particular character traits to make it through the school.

NETR's code of conduct shapes residents' relationships with various stakeholders, but the fieldwork itself also likely teaches residents new and different lessons about interacting with students. I explore this interplay in Tutorial and student teaching below.

MEETING FACE-TO-FACE

On a brisk February afternoon, I return to NETR's Big Hall to observe Julie conducting one of her daily hour-long Tutorial sessions. Julie appears to be the quintessential NETR resident: she is young, recently graduated from a top-tier college, and could be described as "Type A." She is also one of two residents who I will follow into the field next year. Although Julie originally pursued premed in college, her experiences as a camp counselor for children with chronic illnesses and later for "inner city kids" compelled her to teach those who seemed to have greater needs. While she was accepted to Teach for America (TfA) to teach special education, she felt she needed more than 5 weeks of training to serve this population; so, she chose NETR's yearlong residency program instead.

Slowly, I approach the table where I see blonde-haired Julie in her professional attire and three young women of color with hair in shades of chestnut, toffee, and ebony; all three wearing school uniforms. When the bell rings, Julie reminds the students to begin their "Do Now," which is a math problem. Although Julie is a secondary English resident, she tutors students in math because EPHS is short on math tutors and NETR figured her premed background would enable her to tutor on this subject. As the students work on this problem, they begin to chat softly with one another and Julie.

"What are you doing tomorrow?" a student named Doris asks Julie.

"I am student teaching," Julie replies cheerfully. "What are you doing?" Doris shrugs.

Another student, Lana, admits to Julie that she didn't do very well on an assignment.

"Why? Is this the poetry one?" Julie asks, her eyes wide. Lana nods. "That is your thing!" Julie insists.

A moment later, Lana pulls out a long poem and Julie looks it over. "You are reading this? This is deep stuff." Lana responds by telling Julie that her grandmother has all of Maya Angelou's books and that she likes the poetry. Later, Lana pulls out another poem and says she is going to perform it aloud in class.

"You are going to do great!" Julie tells her. Lana beams. "We can practice at the end of Tutorial," Julie adds.

During this exchange, the other two young women are working on the day's math assignment. Lana, too, returns to her work, humming a tune as she does. Then she says to Julie and her peers, "You know why I hate it when I cry? My eyes get so red. My mom is all, were you crying? And I am all, no, allergies man. But we don't even have cats. So I can't even claim that." I interpret this statement as a call for attention or an expressed desire for someone to listen to her concerns, as Lana perhaps expects Julie to ask what made her cry.

But instead of encouraging this conversation, which from Julie's perspective would likely distract from the work at hand, Julie smiles and responds softly, "Can we do, like, two problems without talking?"

"She told you!" Doris chides Lana in reference to Julie's response.

"Yeah, but she did it nicely," Lana says in a matter-of-fact tone.

After a few minutes more of work, Doris asks Julie, "Do you ever get frustrated?" I suspect that this question has been fomenting in her mind since Julie calmly redirected Lana to return to her work.

"Oh my gosh, so much," replies Julie.

"It doesn't seem like it," Doris observes.

"I don't get frustrated at you guys, but everyone gets frustrated sometimes," Julie says.

"I see you in the hall and then all I hear is 'Hi!!'" Doris says with a grin.

Lana smiles and adds, "I just see you and you say, 'Hi!' and it, like, makes my day."

Julie smiles at the praise and explains, "I go to kickboxing and I hit things and then I go to yoga and calm down." The students giggle at this explanation. And then Julie signals for them to continue working on their assignment.

In this exchange, Julie upholds many of NETR's standards for instruction and professionalism. She maintains a compelling teacher presence, redirects students when they get off task, and emphasizes their skills practice, but she is also responsible, undeniably positive in her affect, professional in her appearance, and timely. Additionally, Julie seems to embody one of NETR's favored ideals from relationship coursework: "warm/strict." In this case, Julie smiles, affirms students' academic capacity, and shares short relatable anecdotes, but also insists that students quickly return to the required work if divergences occur.

"Warm/strict" is a term that Julie latches onto because she feels it reflects the way her strict but loving parents raised her and her two sisters in Cincinnati, Ohio. But as she herself acknowledges, the "warm" part is more natural for her to enact than the "strict" part. It is also possible that because students here have become so accustomed to the strict intensity of the EPHS environment, Julie's small gestures of warmth—like smiling and saying hi to students in the hallways—seem more meaningful than they would be in another context.

Tutorial provides residents with time and space to connect with "actual" students (a point residents emphasize because they pretend to be students in teaching simulations). With only a few students at a time, residents can learn about individual students, most of whom come from very different backgrounds than the residents. While residents get to practice lesson planning, instructional moves, and classroom management through coursework and teaching simulations, Tutorial gives them the opportunity to practice building relationships. But while this particular observation of Julie seems to reflect some of her NETR training, many residents tell me that they acquire new and different knowledge about connecting with students in these experiences.

When I ask residents about the aspect of the program that best prepares them to connect with students, most of them cite Tutorial over the prescriptive Relationships coursework or teaching simulations. For example, Alina tells me that Tutorial is "where it happened. It wasn't through NETR, it was through my actual work with the kids this year." In Tutorial, there is only a minimal curriculum that must be covered, resulting in less urgency. There is also very little oversight, which means the residents and students can have unstructured interactions. Rachel tells me, "You have opportunities to sit down and chat with them for a while, which you don't in the classroom." Additionally, many of the residents who are placed at school sites for tutorial also assist with activities like bus duty, where they have opportunities to informally chat with students before or after school. A couple of the residents even tell me that they *had to* form relationships with students in Tutorial because of the less structured nature of the experience; those who failed to do so ended up having challenging Tutorial experiences throughout the year.

Moreover, Tutorial seems to be a unique source of information about connecting with students across racial cultural differences. For example, Julie acknowledges NETR's attempts at promoting culturally affirmative teaching (CAT) (as discussed in Chapter 2), but feels she learned more about how to connect with students from different backgrounds just by "working with kids" in Tutorial. She adds that learning by connecting with students is important because she feels that "empathy or understanding [for] these kids" isn't something that can be taught in coursework.

When I ask Casey (the other resident I will follow into the field) this question, he provides a couple specific examples of how Tutorial helped prepare him to work with students from different backgrounds:

> One of my students for a period this fall wasn't living at home. Thankfully, he very quickly returned. But that's a big conversation to have. I had another student who opened up to me about her past and some of the things [she] experienced as a child. I literally didn't know, just stared at her, I didn't know what to say. Just jaw open, stare. Things I couldn't even . . . There's no way for me to be empathetic about it 'cause it's just so far removed from the way that I grew up in my life. So in that way, it's prepared me, it showed me a world that I have very little experience with . . . And one of my students, we were having a conversation the other day. He's got something going on. He won't really tell me what it is. Drove the point home, so I said, "Even in the worst-case scenario, I think you should still be able to handle your class load right now." And he's like, "We didn't grow up the same way. Your worst-case scenario was probably not the same as mine." And just reminding me sometimes that, I've gotta be careful not to assume and to remember that these kids have had a different life than I have.

Through Tutorial, where students have the opportunity to teach the residents about their lives, Casey feels he has developed more understanding for his students than he would have in the more structured and controlled relationships that are formed through classroom teaching in no excuses settings. Tutorial interactions also seem to allow the residents to begin seeing students from different backgrounds as human beings, with life experiences and needs that might in fact contradict the notion that students have no excuses for late work or behavior violations.

While this Tutorial experience seems integral to residents' preparation in forming relationships across racial cultural differences, it is not well connected to the Relationships coursework or RAITT. As Jose observes, "One of the interesting things to me about the program is the way that there is this really weird wall between your tutor role and your NETR role." While the Relationships course offers many "moves" that can be applied in a teaching setting and some general thoughts about teaching students of color in CAT, faculty rarely make explicit references to utilizing these in Tutorial, which is rarely observed or evaluated by NETR staff. Joe acknowledges this disconnect, suggesting that faculty know Tutorial is "a huge driver of their [residents'] success" with students "across cultural lines," but the connection between coursework and Tutorial is not yet "coherent" and must be better "coordinated."

The salience of Tutorial for residents echoes some of the teacher education literature that suggests that meaningful fieldwork with racially diverse students seems to powerfully impact preservice teacher learning.[6] In working with "actual students," new teachers might begin to see the human beings behind the uniform, reducing the fear or misconceptions they might hold about the students they will serve.[7] This is likely more powerful than teaching moves and professional handbooks.

Unencumbered by rubrics, evaluations, or rigid structures, residents have space in Tutorial to form relationships with students face-to-face. NETR coursework and ideals—like warm/strict and RAITT—likely inform some of their behavior as tutors; but residents also seem to acquire new and different knowledge about forming relationships by working with actual students. In fact, these less structured human interactions might complicate the uniform, distanced, and instrumental approach to forming relationships that residents learn in coursework. But it is uncertain how transferable the relational skills residents learn here will be to their no excuses classroom. It is possible that when they stand at the front of a classroom, what residents learn in coursework and student teaching could take precedence. In fact, when I observe Julie and Casey in student teaching, I see a lot less warmth and a lot more discipline.

MOVING THE NEEDLE THROUGH TRIAL AND FEEDBACK

Student teaching is a very different experience for NETR residents than tutoring. Under the support of a teacher of record who also serves as a coach, each resident works as a student teacher in one class at a partner school on Fridays; this goes on for several weeks in the spring. Concurrently, residents serve as teachers of Saturday academy classes at a no excuses school. Because no excuses schools often require additional instructional time, school days are longer than at traditional public schools, many schools provide instruction on Saturday for students who seem to need extra support, and some have summer academies to help students transition into the model. Saturday academy allows NETR residents an opportunity to teach a different group of students on their own while being observed by a circulating NETR coach. Because they receive structured coaching on both Fridays and Saturdays, student teaching is more coherently connected to coursework, possibly enabling residents to practice the relationship building strategies they have learned in NETR (even though this is not evaluated by the Kraken).

However, when residents begin student teaching in the spring, many of them find that it is hard to form meaningful relationships with students they only see for an hour or two once a week for several weeks. Alina explains, "The way that student teaching was designed this year, it was kind of disruptive. It wasn't consistent. Whereas Tutorial, you were working with a kid for months and months. . . . That more realistically replicates the relationship that you'll have with students as a full-time teacher." Jose's comments reaffirm this idea: "Yeah, with my classes, especially Saturday academy, I definitely don't feel like I know them nearly as well as I want to. With the Saturday academy kids there's just literally . . . no time to really get to know them." Naturally, forming relationships with students takes time and space. And because NETR's spring student teaching is conducted in limited once-a-week sessions where residents must cover copious academic material, residents don't feel they can get to know their students well in this context.

On a weekend in April, I drive over to another local charter school that hosts one of the NETR-affiliated Saturday academies. Soon after entering the building, I observe how this particular foray into student teaching makes it challenging for residents to form connections with students. The class sessions are short, and all the interactions I observe between the residents and students are strictly related to the academic content being presented. There is no time for extended one-on-one conversations and no evidence that these teachers know much about the students who sit before them. Later, when the whole group of residents from this academy debriefs that day's teaching experiences with Joe, the conversation focuses on classroom management and lesson quality, not relationships. The feedback is limited.

When I observe Julie on a Friday in student teaching at another no excuses school, I see this pattern replicated. Julie's instruction here is efficient; she moves through questions and responses quickly. She also issues merits and demerits smoothly but continues to smile, possibly to infuse some warmth into the lesson. Her interactions with students in this setting are much more formal and reserved than those in Tutorial, and there is little evidence that she has been able to forge meaningful relationships with individuals. But this makes sense. With a different group of students on Fridays and Saturdays, and only for part of a semester, residents have to work hard just to learn all the students' names. While some research suggests that field placements might be the most fertile site for learning to form teacher–student relationships,[8] that does not seem to be the case in NETR's spring student teaching because it is too short and too structured.

In their constant pursuit of program improvement through feedback, NETR faculty have recognized the shortcomings of this particular approach to student teaching and have already made plans to change it. Angela tells me that they have redesigned the program schedule to enable teachers to "ramp" up responsibility in the same classroom every Friday over the course of the year. However, she adds that they will use trained coaches to provide feedback to the residents on this experience, to retain "control over . . . the quality of the coaching," instead of relying on the teachers of record in the class for feedback. In this redesigned iteration of student teaching, residents will likely have a great deal more time to form relationships with students before they take over the class. Much like the residents, NETR engages in single-loop learning through trial, receiving feedback, and continuing to evolve in line with their program vision.

The final student teaching experience in July is one that will not change anytime soon, though. In this summer academy experience, residents teach the same group of students every day for a month without any mentor teacher present. Todd explains, "We find that to be a really valuable capstone experience for the residency year. Because it gives you a chance to build a classroom culture, community, set expectations, run the whole show. It's a full dress rehearsal before they begin the actual performance in September." In this "dress rehearsal," residents teach students who are receiving an additional month of school because they either need to make up coursework or because they are new to the no excuses model and are thus required to attend summer academy to adjust to their new setting. As such, summer academy serves as one last time to practice teaching before residents are responsible for a year's worth of learning for a whole group of students.

On a sunny July day, I enter a well-respected charter school where many of the residents are teaching summer academy. I stroll down the hall to find Casey's class. Casey is the other NETR resident I will follow into the field next year. And unlike Julie, Casey acknowledges that he does not quite fit the mold of the average NETR resident. Instead of coming to the program right out of college, exuding exuberance and Type A organization, Casey is nearly 30, has already pursued two different professions—one in sales and one in insurance—and displays a more laid-back attitude to coursework and teaching. When I first interview him, I find his self-effacing humor and self-reflective comments refreshing. Casey is a first-generation college student who majored in political science at a local university. But when his other jobs did not pan out, he found himself drawn to serve those who he feels do not have access to the same kind of excellent education he had. He wants to be part of the solution and acknowledges that he has been convinced by NETR that the no excuses world is it.

Casey is just concluding his first period when I enter the room. His tall, bearded frame stands near the chalkboard, and he flashes me a gregarious smile that alights his blue eyes. All the sixth and seventh graders here—who are grouped by reading level, not age—are students of color, silently sitting in their red collared shirts and khaki pants or shorts.

When Casey dismisses them for the brief 5-minute break between periods, most of the students choose to remain in the classroom. Some of the students dance around the room; others joke with one another or play games of imagination. In these minutes, the class is loud and chaotic but also feels oddly appropriate; this is how one would expect this age group to act.

Casey does not seem to mind the noise for the moment, as this 5 minutes for passing period is not one he is required to structure. He uses the time to call individual students over to his desk to briefly touch base about their work. Meanwhile, the break time begins to tick away on a digital clock being projected on the screen up front.

Soon, Casey reminds students to sit down, his voice becoming firmer: "Folks, you have 30 seconds. . . ." Most quiet down, but a few still talk with one another.

"In your seats; don't play games with me." Casey says, an even harder edge to his tone. When a couple students continue to talk to one another, seemingly confused, he issues them each a demerit.

"Get to work," he tells the class, expecting they know by this point—2 weeks into summer academy—what they are supposed to do when they start each class period. The students attempt to work on the Do Now, but there still appears to be some confusion about what the Do Now question is. Casey soon notices this, looks over the assignment, and announces, "I know what happened now. The Do Now is on the other side of the first [period] handout; who still has that on their desk?" Most of the hands go up. "So get to work on that in the space below, or if you have questions, raise your hand," he continues. A few soft student voices rumble in the background. "Do Nows are silent; there is far too much murmuring," he reminds them.

The remaining class time is fast paced and quite regimented. Casey issues a series of demerits for periodic chatter. Discussion remains on the content at hand, which is English. And throughout most of this period, Casey remains serious, which is unusual for the often-humorous man. I don't see much teacher–student interaction worth noting.

When period 2 ends and it is time for snack—a 15-minute structured time between class periods—Casey once again has nonacademic time to connect with individual students, something he admittedly values. He approaches one young man in the back of the class who is drinking a Yoo-hoo and eating Oreo cookies. Casey jokes with the student about his own love of unhealthy food and talks about a place that has a fried burger. The student smiles at the interaction. Then Casey grows aware of the noise in the room, which has certainly ratcheted up from silent.

"We're not shouting across the class during class; talk with your shoulder partner." Casey tells the students in a loud tone.

The student sitting directly in front of me, who had previously attempted to shout across the class, now begins to practice a version of patty-cake with his shoulder partner, a shy young man who smiles widely during this bonding activity with his peer. But before long, Casey calls out both of their names, demanding they stop making noise. The shy young man appears especially chagrinned.

Casey then counts down to silence and announces to the class: "Snack is a time for remaining in our seats and chatting quietly with one another. It is not a time for clapping or shouting. So because we were so loud, we are going to spend the next 3 minutes of snack silently." The class sits in a tense silence for at least a minute before Casey relieves the tension by stating, "Much better. You have a minute and half. You can quietly talk to the people around you."

Having interacted with and observed Casey before, I am surprised by the serious, strict, and efficient teacher who stands before me. I know Casey to be a relaxed and playful man, who admittedly loves sarcasm and humor, but only small glimmers of that came through today. His classroom was certainly orderly, and his students seemed eager to remain on task, but there was very little space for students to find joy in the lesson. Even the snack period was constrained by teacher control. I find myself baffled by the change and seek to understand more by talking with Casey's NETR coach, Tessa.

Tessa begins by explaining that overall, Casey is a "pleasure to coach." She continues, "He is eager, he is receptive, he incorporates feedback immediately. He also comes to debriefs prepared. He's read my notes, he's generally made notes on my notes. He's very reflective." This indicates that he has successfully embodied RAITT standards in the field. And when I ask her about how he interacts with students more casually, Tessa tells me she thinks he is "strong overall" in this area, often making self-effacing jokes with students and attempting to help those who need additional supports. This description sounds more like the Casey I have seen before: thoughtful, self-effacing, and funny.

However, this description also seems inconsistent with the teacher I observed today. Regarding Casey's class management, Tessa tells me that she has found he can sometimes be "a little heavy handed" with demerits and his tone can sometimes be "a little bit negative." She adds that part of this seems to be a result of judging student behavior as "noncompliance" when it is really just "confusion," and correcting all student behavior "publicly" instead of individually. Nonetheless, she assures me "this is something that we're actively working on right now, so we'll talk about [it in] his debrief." In terms of the Kraken, Casey seems to have gone a bit overboard with "reactive management."

A week later, I meet Casey for coffee and we talk about this experience. He admits he has "been getting a lot of feedback this summer from my coach" about his tone, which has been very different from the feedback he received in the spring. In spring student teaching, he felt like "a visitor . . . helping out" so he was able to "be myself and be this big joyful personality." However, this summer Casey feels overwhelmed by reality of his responsibility, which has caused him to shift his tone entirely. He tells me, "It feels like I'm playing with live ammunition. These kids, some of them are grade levels behind, they're coming into a completely new school. . . . They don't understand the behavioral expectations." Because he believes that his students lack the academic and behavioral skills to succeed in their new no excuses school, Casey's tone has become urgent, his class "all work, no play, no fun."

Casey later acknowledges that this tone can impact the relationships he forms with students because "they don't feel you really are invested and care about the work they're doing, 'cause all you're ever doing is telling them how to make it better, which is what I'm doing." But he also expresses a commitment to changing that, to "relearning and reremembering" who he wants to be as a teacher. And in the last week of summer academy, he reports that he has already begun implementing changes and trying to "celebrate" students more. This would be a promising advancement before he assumes his first real teaching job. And perhaps this was NETR's plan all along: provide sufficient opportunities for trial and error with supportive feedback to move the needle on residents' teaching.

As I reflect upon the fieldwork experiences of Casey and Julie, along with Stephanie and Alina's experiences with RAITT, I realize how much iterating and negotiating it must take to achieve the ideal NETR teacher: one who is obedient to the program or school but simultaneously authentic and authoritative with students, one who is able to balance "warm" with "strict." The program provides coaches to help facilitate the residents' progress toward a specified ideal, offering specific feedback to help them get back on track when they veer too far in one direction.

But I continue to wonder whether NETR teachers will ever be able to feel true to themselves, "undivided" in essence and practice when they teach in settings that so clearly dictate certain behaviors.[9] Both Casey and Julie are naturally more warm than strict, as Alina and Stephanie are inclined to readily voice their concerns; but this no excuses context requires all of them to alter the way they interact with others. And if they feel they cannot truly express who they are here, will the relationships they form with students really be authentic?

REPRESENTING THE NETR BRAND

At the end of July, I drive through warm summer rain in the city to attend NETR's end-of-the-year picnic. When I park my car and walk toward the grassy side yard of the middle school hosting this event, I find most of the faculty and residents huddled under the small green tent that sits in the center and shelters a small barbecue feast. Residents and faculty, many dressed more casually than usual—some even wearing jeans—eat and talk with ease; it is almost as if they have become peers with the faculty today, connecting without RAITT or the Gateway hanging over their heads. In this moment, there is no longer a need for the urgent, instrumental, authoritative tone that shaped content and relationships throughout the program.

As I walk into the action, I meet the two new staff members that NETR has hired for the upcoming year; they are both women of color and both from Southern California. The three of us fall easily into conversation, perhaps because of our California connection, or perhaps because like me, they are still NETR outsiders. Even after a year of observing in this program, I still do not know most of the residents and even those who I connected with in individual interviews do not approach me, nor I them, for I acknowledge they might not want me to identify them as having participated in my study. So I do my best to find an inconspicuous place to set up my laptop, which is not easy at a picnic in the rain.

From my new vantage point, I notice that the cohort has definitely shrunk from the first day. Only 48 of the original 74 residents will now matriculate to schools. In our earlier interview, Angela told me, "We're really proud of our 35% attrition rate in our program. This year nine people failed the Gateway; that's like 15% of our program failed out in January. There were a number of people who exited because they were pretty sure they weren't gonna pass. And I think that's good." This is not unlike the attrition rate of students at many no excuses schools, who voluntarily leave when they find it does not suit them, or are expelled for different reasons. But again, it suggests that not everyone is deserving of the program's—or school's—commitment. The relationship is conditional.

This makes me think about something Casey said about NETR in an interview: "They throw flies in the face of a lot of establishments, which is always a scary thing, and someone is always coming after you and always looking for fault. So I imagine on their end, they're obsessed with only producing people who are gonna represent the NETR brand to the best of their ability." Truly, NETR has established a very unconventional approach to teacher preparation, and to teacher–student relationships, too. Unlike many teacher education programs, NETR has systematically thought about teacher–student relationship development, devoting an entire course toward this end and prioritizing both formal and informal fieldwork with "actual" students. In doing so, they have acknowledged that academic rigor and inter-personal relationships are not antagonistic, but in fact complementary facets of effective education.

But it is also worth noting that they leave very little up to chance or individual preference. By establishing explicit standards and rubrics—like the Kraken and RAITT—and employing trained coaches and faculty to eval-uate residents on these, NETR relentlessly pursues its mission of preparing effective no excuses teachers. The faculty periodically joke about critics who assume they prepare teacher "robots," but residents do emerge ready to "rep-resent the NETR brand," to "row in the same direction" as their colleagues in other no excuses schools. As Todd affirms, "What is expected of you in those schools as a teacher is much more defined than what you might find in a traditionally structured school where teachers are still largely autonomous and are able to close the door and practice the way that they think is best." This NETR brand undeniably shapes how residents learn to teach and inter-act with students behind doors that are rarely closed to instructional oversight (which is another essential ingredient in the formula of no excuses educa-tion).

But today, on the final day of the residency year, the tone is different, more casual, more focused on the human beings moving on to their own classrooms. When the rain dissipates, Todd steps up to a clearing in the grass to address the whole cohort. He recognizes the "remarkable thing" residents have done in completing NETR, and the even more remarkable task that lies before them in teaching. Then he offers "two pieces of advice" for their work ahead. He begins with "Stay humble," which he is confident residents are prepared to do after their intensive and feedback-heavy training. But then he adds, "Stay mindful." And ends with a somewhat playful, self-aware aside: "If there is something you haven't learned here, maybe it is that mindfulness piece."

Many teacher education programs promote self-reflection and self-knowl-edge, or "mindfulness," with the idea that teachers cannot really understand students, or interact with them authentically, until they understand them-selves. But NETR does not operate on this assumption, perhaps because self-knowledge and mindfulness are hard to prescribe. Nonetheless, this mention of mindfulness reminds me that teaching in general—and perhaps especially in a no excuses context—is indeed "fraught with emotion," with internal conflicts between "authority" and "authenticity," between following school rules and behaving in line with a personal code that might conflict with such rules. If teachers are to reconcile two different iterations of themselves, they might *need* to practice mindfulness. And because "the divided self will al-ways try to distance itself from others,"[10] becoming mindful of this precari-ous balancing act might be essential to the development of relationships with students in no excuses schools.

As faculty conduct this graduation, I watch residents individually walk to the front of the gathering to receive their "prize": an NETR sweatshirt, a symbol of their branding. After residents collect these, everyone progresses to the middle school gym to watch a video that features K–12 students responding to questions about their particular tutors. My ears perk up when I hear the question "Why do you think your tutor will be a great teacher next year?"

A few of the students respond to this question by focusing on teachers' relational abilities. I see Casey's name on the screen as one of his older students says, "He does build relationships with students very quickly, actually, it's crazy how quickly he did. He is able to be laid back and strict at the same time, which is important for a teacher." This suggests that Casey found a way to balance authority and authenticity, warm and strict, in Tutorial.

One of Julie's students says something similar, suggesting Julie will be a good teacher "because she can relate to the students a lot and she is really fun. And if you have a problem and you talk to her, she will give you really good advice." Even though these student responses are curated for this video, this student's description of Julie is not very NETR in that she is "fun" and gives students "advice" (presumably about their lives outside of school). This suggests that while NETR training shapes some of their tutorial behavior, residents also likely have more space in tutorial to draw upon innate qualities, like warmth.

This video concludes with students giving "last words or advice" to their tutors. Some of the students provide words of gratitude, others offer small pieces of advice like "make jokes," but the most moving statements come from the little kids. One little boy, a student of Stephanie's, says in a soft shy voice, "Thank you, Ms. S, I love you." This comment moves me because it reminds me of my experiences with my former students, and I remember that the teacher–student relationship often compels reciprocity and flouts instrumentalism. For while the teacher likely impacts the students, as NETR continuously emphasizes, each student relationship may also leave indelible fingerprints upon the heart of the teacher, an invisible brand of sorts. And in this way, the least "coordinated" and most human part of NETR—Tutorial—could leave its own mark on residents. In fact, I suspect that all the NETR teachers here today will carry these fingerprints into their first year of teaching, informing the way they connect with their new students as much as NETR's brand of rubrics and coursework.

NOTES

1. Clift, R. T., & Brady, P. (2005). Research on methods courses and field experiences. In M. Cochran-Smith & K. M. Zeichner (Eds.), *Studying teacher education: The report of the AERA panel on research and teacher education* (pp. 309–424). Mahwah, NJ: Erlbaum; Co-

chran-Smith, Marilyn, Villegas, Ana María, Abrams, Linda, Chavez-Moreno, Laura, Mills, Tammy, & Stern, Rebecca. (2015). Critiquing teacher preparation research: An overview of the field, part II. *Journal of Teacher Education, 66*(2), 109–121.

2. Levine, Arthur. (2006). *Educating school teachers*. Washington, DC: Education Schools Project. Retrieved from http://www.edschools.org/pdf/Educating_Teachers_Report.pdf

3. Lortie, Dan C. (1975). *Schoolteacher: A sociological study*. Chicago, IL: University of Chicago Press.

4. Whitman, David. (2008). *Sweating the small stuff: Inner-city schools and the new paternalism*. Washington, DC: Thomas B. Fordham Institute.

5. Hirschman, Albert O. (1970). *Exit, voice, and loyalty: Responses to decline in firms, organizations, and states* (Vol. 25). Cambridge, MA: Harvard University Press.

6. Cochran-Smith et al., Critiquing teacher preparation research; Hollins, Etta, & Torres Guzman, Maria. (2005). Research on preparing teachers for diverse populations. In M. Cochran-Smith & K. M. Zeichner (Eds.), *Studying teacher education: The report of the AERA panel on research and teacher education* (pp. 477–548). Mahwah, NJ: Erlbaum.

7. Sleeter, Christine. (2008). Preparing white teachers for diverse students. *Handbook of Research on Teacher Education: Enduring Questions in Changing Contexts, 3*, 559–582.

8. McDonald, Morva A., Bowman, Michael, & Brayko, Kate. (2013, April). Learning to see students: Opportunities to develop relational practices of teaching through community based placements in teacher education. *Teachers College Record, 115*, 1–35.

9. Palmer, Parker. (1998). *The courage to teach: Exploring the inner landscape of a teacher's life*. San Francisco, CA: Jossey-Bass.

10. Palmer, *Courage to teach*, pp. 15–16.

Part II

Progressive Teacher Residency

Chapter Four

Cultivating Reciprocal Relationships

This seems so obvious, but just treating students as humans before treating them as students. So thinking of them as whole beings who are forming and . . . are fragile no matter what they may show us.—Mary, assistant director of PTR

PLANTING THE SEEDS

I first walk the cobblestone path of the Xanadu Community School campus in September of 2014. Old-growth trees dot the trail, and I consider with excitement the explosion of color they will produce as I continue to visit this place in coming months. I move on to admire a large expansive sports field, a woodchip-lined playground featuring wooden jungle gym equipment, a greenhouse, and a wild garden filled with plants and flowers. It is this garden that gives me pause, as I notice a sort of ordered chaos here: the tall sunflowers shoot above a jumbled mess of wildflowers, beside a neatly weeded plot of vegetables; a lattice stands empty, waiting to support the fruits of a seed I cannot see; while a few stalks of corn have begun to sprout honey-colored braids at the top. Each plant is unique, and each has support to grow at its own pace and in its own direction, a trend that I will soon find seems to extend to way residents are supported to grow within Progressive Teacher Residency (PTR).

After passing several of the school's characteristic one-story buildings, I wind my way back around to the central meeting room where the first class for PTR will take place. I follow a few wayward teacher residents into the small intimate room, which sits in an unassuming building at the front of the school. It is illuminated by natural sunlight streaming in from the windows at the back of the room. The arched ceiling is painted sea green and the program's "through-lines" are pasted on brightly colored construction paper adorning the walls. They read: "Who am I as a teacher?" "Whom do I teach?" "Why do I teach?" "What will I teach?" "How will I know what my students know?"

Symbols of student identity and creativity characterize the space. Pictures line the large whiteboard at the front, and craft supplies stacked high in baskets rest in the adjacent closet. Inspirational quotes on simple white paper slips are taped on the beige sliding door of one of the closets; the content of these quotes seems to urge students toward their own creative outlets. Student work graces the bulletin board at the back. One of the pieces has macaroni around the edges and displays photographs of a young boy running and playing and relaxing. It is blue and bright, and the name JUSTIN emerges in bold letters from the center.

I am drawn to the freshly brewed coffee and tea sitting invitingly at the back of the room, a staple provided by PTR at every meeting. Meanwhile, the residents this year have taken initiative to organize snacks for each session, a departure from the past when Taylor and Mary (the program's director and assistant director, respectively) provided all the snacks. This is the first indication that despite its advanced age, PTR is not wedded to every tradition but readily adjusts to the needs and desires of the residents each year. As the director, Taylor holds the most sway over the content of the program. She tells me, "As you can imagine, every year and every group requires you to modify the curriculum that you are teaching."

The central meeting room's long wooden tables form a large square in the center, such that every one of the 16 residents will face each other. I sit in a lone chair in between a boxy television set and the snack table. Even though I am not a member of this resident cohort, nor do I know any of them yet, I find this humble space comfortable and familiar.

The residents chat excitedly with one another as they get food and drinks from the back and others find seats at the table. Their jovial tones and easy gaits convey a sense of congeniality. A few of the residents have strands of gray hair; others appear fresh out of college. Fourteen of the 16 residents are female, and 15 of the residents appear white. One resident is Black; and I later learn that one of the white-appearing residents identifies as Latina. The racial homogeneity of the residents strikes a contrast to the three PTR faculty members standing up front: Taylor, the director, identifies as African American; Mary, the assistant director, is white; and Emma, a teacher at Xanadu and a faculty member at PTR, identifies as Latina.

I also notice the residents' clothing. The young women wear long, flowing skirts, casual dresses, or slacks/jeans and loose tops, most of which are quite colorful: pinks, purples, blues, reds. The two men in the group are equally casual, in jeans or khakis and running shoes. This is at odds with what I remember of "dressing to the nines" with my colleagues in my teacher education program, as we tried to project a sense of maturity and professionalism to hide our insecurities. It is also at odds with what No Excuses Teacher Residency (NETR) requires of its residents (as described in Chapter 3). And immediately, I get the sense that PTR will be quite different from NETR.

Calmly, Taylor gathers the attention of the residents by standing silently at the front of room until they all begin to quiet down. She then introduces the course, "The School Aged Child." It will address child and adolescent development from developmental, sociological, and cultural perspectives. Taylor explains that the purpose of the course is to help residents understand themselves and their students, who will range from preschool to middle school age.

She then reads a quote by renowned educator Parker Palmer: "If I am willing to look into the mirror and not run from what I see, I have a good chance to gain self-knowledge—knowing myself is as crucial to good teaching as knowing my students and my subject." Taylor asks residents to consider what this means for them "as a person, a student, and a teacher" in writing for 5 minutes; after this, they will exchange papers with the person next to them, taking time to respond to their peer's journal entry before passing it back.

Taylor walks around the room in metallic blue ballet flats, observing the residents with a coffee cup in her hand, reading glasses and a pen dangling from the round collar of her black dress. Her thick salt-and-pepper hair, styled straight and falling just below her ears, contrasts with her chestnut-toned skin. Taylor is the only person of color in a director-level position at Xanadu; Emma also tells me that Taylor is by far the best-dressed person on campus, perhaps feeling that she is held to a higher standard than her white colleagues. From the beginning, I sense her uncompromising passion for this program, which shines through her every comment. And now, as she walks around the room with a subtle smile on her face, her pride in this work is evident.

After the residents finish writing brief responses on each other's papers, Taylor asks them to begin sharing some of their thoughts about this activity. She reads Palmer's quote again and then opens the floor for discussion. All around me, I watch as residents, whose names I do not yet know, eagerly jump in to volunteer their responses. And the conversation flows freely on the first day:

"I found it so refreshing how reflective this [program is] and how much my guiding teacher is reflecting. Constantly thinking about your self-knowledge is exhausting in a way, but is also really refreshing in that everyone is doing it."

"I think that extends to you as a teacher, what's going to work for you in terms of your style, if you are funnier, or stricter."

"I think it's about self-confidence; knowing myself as a teacher is about knowing my students and my subject. When students see how much you care, it pushes them to go beyond their limit."

Taylor interjects at this point, pushing the residents to go deeper: "How do students know you care?" Again, residents begin to offer responses without first raising their hands:

"To really listen to them and respond, and I think if they think you are really responding, then they respond in turn."

"Following up on other interests they have outside of the classroom, like a soccer game, so they see we care about things outside of the classroom, too."

This initial discussion on the first official day of coursework at PTR centers around the teacher–student relationship, planting the seeds for what is to be a primary theme of the program. Residents touch upon ideas that I find are interwoven throughout PTR coursework: self-knowledge and reflection are critical to adequately serving your students; it is important to be yourself as a student and teacher; students need to know you care; and you can demonstrate this personal care in a variety of ways, including encouraging students, really listening and responding to them, and valuing them for who they are both in and out of the classroom.

At PTR, the teacher–student relationship is considered fundamental to the entire educational enterprise. As Taylor later tells me, "Teaching starts with relationship. Children will care about learning when they know their teachers care about them." Although the residents have only just begun their foray into learning at Xanadu, it seems they have already absorbed the basic tenets of the school's educational philosophy. This is partly because PTR is very much a creature of the school that sprouted it; the residents are treated like the students at Xanadu and they learn to teach like the teachers at the school. But Xanadu is a unique and privileged place, and I soon begin to wonder whether training in this insulated garden—a cocoon of sorts—can possibly translate to the world beyond it.

THE GARDEN OF XANADU

Xanadu Community School stands apart from the rest of the world, both physically and pedagogically. This century-old independent school, serving students in kindergarten through eighth grade, is renowned for its unfailing dedication to progressive education. Resisting the educational pressures of standardization and direct instruction—a luxury afforded private schools that are not beholden to state standards or Common Core—faculty here pride themselves on upholding a constructivist approach to teaching. The secluded campus itself, woven into the top of a verdant hill in an affluent part of town, also represents a notable departure from the traditional image of a school.

Xanadu is but an assembly of modest gray wooden buildings arranged like a village to establish a more communal atmosphere.

Surrounded by large classic homes with perfectly manicured yards, and primarily serving the students of wealthy, well-educated parents, the campus is also far removed from many public school realities. Only 17% of the 500 students in preschool through eighth grade receive any financial aid to offset the steep yearly tuition. Moreover, only a third of the students identify as people of color and almost all the students are native English speakers. Consistent with national trends for teachers, 82% of the 70-person Xanadu faculty is white; but most also hold bachelor's and/or advanced degrees from top-tier universities, which is not the norm among public school teachers. The school also has plentiful resources and a powerful parent association that is quick to advocate for and support the school. In these ways, Xanadu reflects the privileged history of progressive education (which I will discuss more in the next chapter).

Although there are no gates or bars guarding the school's entrance, my early interactions with the faculty at the school suggest that they are quite protective of the revered campus and those who populate it. Before I can conduct extensive observations on campus, I have to be vetted by the school psychologist, who seems to be the unofficial school designee for all matters of research. He asks me many questions about the intentions and methods of my study. I am also asked not to videotape anything.

Taylor, too, seems warm but guarded, admittedly supportive of my research but initially careful not to reveal too much to me as an outside researcher. For example, she did not want me to audio record our interviews. And she seems to feel as though she must set some limits upon my presence on campus, asking me not to attend the orientation for PTR, where guiding teachers and their resident mentees bond over a scavenger hunt across campus and beyond. Outsiders are simply not allowed unencumbered access to this privileged space.

While restrictions are initially placed on my activities here, I am struck by the freedom afforded students. I watch as students run around the campus during recess, skipping on the cobblestone path, heading in and out of buildings, playing with one of the dogs that a teacher has brought to campus. As I begin to observe classes, I notice that classroom doors are rarely locked and students come and go during class without having to ask permission to go to the bathroom or get a drink of water. There is no place on campus where students are not permitted.

This free and flexible environment strikes a distinct contrast to the school where I used to teach in Los Angeles, where security guards fortified gates during the school day, classrooms remained locked, and students were relegated to a narrow, concrete, first-floor courtyard throughout lunchtime (their only break from class). It is also distinctly different from the no excuses schools served by NETR, where students must abide by strict rules and policies that limit their mobility and access to different areas of the school. Again, Xanadu feels like another world entirely.

At Xanadu, students spend most of their class time in homerooms of no more than 16 people. Homeroom teachers spend the first 6 weeks of school establishing a classroom community through introductory bonding activities that only roughly touch upon academic subjects. Then teachers and students jointly construct a "classroom contract" to ensure that every student can feel safe. Once a safe and intimate community is established, homeroom teachers facilitate constructivist project-based learning experiences, provide extensive personalized feedback on students' work, institute individualized supports for each student, and meet with every parent at least twice a year.

The extensive individualized attention and responsive instruction conveys to students that they are at the center of the learning experience here. This is consistent with progressive education more generally, as John Dewey similarly characterized students as "the sun about which the appliances of learning revolve."[1] Emma, who has taught at Xanadu for 6 years, explains that students here understand their centrality: "The kids know that they are . . . and you can see it in their interactions with adults. It's not that they're being rude, it's that we have communicated to them that they're at the center of everything." She describes how she expects students to walk into her classroom at any moment without being invited simply because they know that she is always there for them. Teacher–student relationships here are more equal and reciprocal and less hierarchical than the norm, as students own their agency to shape their relationships and their learning.

Taylor echoes this idea. She tells me that students at Xanadu understand their powerful position: "When you listen to some of the questions children ask here, [it shows] they understand their power, when challenged." She adds that she recently overheard a student who "questioned his grade" tell a teacher, "My parents pay for you to teach." Then, perhaps feeling the need to justify the behavior of some students at the school, Taylor adds, "They are comfortable with self-advocacy. In part because our teachers are comfortable with self-advocacy themselves and teach it."

While Taylor ends up framing students as possessing "self-advocacy," her comments suggest that some of the students at Xanadu also have a sense of blossoming narcissism or entitlement. As Jean Anyon observed at an "affluent professional" school dominated by narcissism (which she defines as a focus on personal development and individual expression like that present at Xanadu), students learn to focus extensively on advancing their own personal goals, sometimes at the expense of more collective endeavors.[2] And while this narcissism or entitlement might be a product of students' home lives—or simply their existence in a society that indicates wealthy and/or white students are worth more than others—it might be further nourished by the school's intensive individual focus.

While students, and their individual needs, interests, and personal development, serve as the central focus of Xanadu, teachers at the school are also clearly valued and respected by the administration. Nancy, an elementary resident who attended Xanadu when she was a student, tells me she can tell teachers feel valued here because "at least half the teachers I had" are still at Xanadu. She suggests some of this has to do with the "autonomy" afforded teachers at the independent school. Moreover, Emma tells me that teachers at the school are paid more than most of their public school counterparts and receive excellent health benefits. And they also receive daily free lunches prepared by the chef at the school—a perk that extends to the residents, but not the students, who must provide their own food.

The school also seems to respect teachers' personal time. Emma explains, "I will say [for] putting the kid at the center, Xanadu is really good about helping teachers know where that boundary is. I'm not expected to make sure every single kid has my cellphone number, I'm not expected to be here till 6:00 every night, I'm not expected to drive kids around." Presumably, the school's elite clientele would not require such extensive support anyway. Still, teachers appreciate the ability to achieve work–life balance at Xanadu, something that is not guaranteed to most teachers.

Throughout my year here, the unique context strikes me as a special garden reserved for a privileged few. In its distinctiveness, Xanadu serves as an influential foundation in learning and teaching for each of the residents who sets foot on campus. And because progressive education seems to have a unique take on the relational side of teaching, this stands out to residents. Meredith, an elementary resident who also attended this school when she was a student here over 40 years ago, observes, "I always wondered what the magic is [here] and . . . I realized the magic is the affective piece." Xanadu is special, in part because the relationships between teachers and students, and among teachers and students, are meaningful.

PTR AS THE "PEARL" IN THE GARDEN

Since its establishment over a century ago, Xanadu has sought to recruit teachers who adapt well to the "Xanadu way." The original director of the program described the ideal Xanadu teacher as one who would not only teach a subject and help students advance academically, but would spread passion, nurture the whole child, teach and learn in communion with their students, and elicit recognition of the beauty in life and humanity in the process. These ambitious ideas about teaching informed the construction of PTR more than 85 years ago to cultivate teachers who embrace the progressive and humanis-

tic pedagogy upon which Xanadu was founded. Like NETR, PTR was originally founded to equip teachers for a specific type of mission-driven school:
their progressive independent school.[3]

Xanadu's original philosophy about teaching continues to permeate the
coursework and activities that PTR promotes. For example, Taylor explains,
"We continue to value collaboration, questioning, empathy, the importance
of strong communication skills, the ability to think outside the box. We are
deep thinkers and doers. . . . The learning that happens between children and
adults is a reciprocal and symbiotic process." When it comes to the substance
and methods of learning, PTR remains devoted to the humanistic ideals that
informed its inception. Throughout the program, Taylor emphasizes the importance of teaching "the whole human," not just the student. And Mary
echoes this idea: "This seems so obvious, but just treating students as humans
before treating them as students. So thinking of them as whole beings who
are forming and . . . are fragile no matter what they may show us."

As is reflected at Xanadu, PTR views the relationship between the teacher
and student as reciprocal and fundamental to teaching and learning. And
Taylor tells me the program even screens residents for relational competency
prior to admission: "We place high value on relationships. And during the
interviewing process and application process, we actually have a recommen-
dation form that requires references to rate an applicant's experience with
children and the ability to connect with them." Once admitted to the program, PTR faculty work to help residents develop further knowledge about
themselves and their students. Mary explains that the program has "a focus
on knowing self and kids in order to develop curriculum that is authentic,
meaningful and relevant to teachers and to kids." While NETR views relationships as a means of getting students to buy into predetermined coursework and behavioral norms, PTR views relationships with students as a
valuable reciprocal experience that enables teachers to design curriculum and
instructional experiences that honor both parties.

While the philosophy of teaching has not deviated much from its roots at
Xanadu, PTR's mission has shifted. Today, the school very rarely hires anyone right out of PTR, a fact that residents often lament. Instead, graduates are
encouraged to go on to other independent schools, public schools, or even
charter schools with a range of different philosophical underpinnings. As a
result, PTR offers teacher licensure in the state, and most of the residents
concurrently complete their master's in education (a requirement for local
public schools) through evening classes at a local university that partners
with PTR.

In the fall, residents student teach at Xanadu, which becomes like a second home. Donna explains, "We are fully included at Xanadu, but I think in a
way that's so thoughtfully done and so well supported . . . I feel like that
holistic experience has been really valuable." Residents spend 8–10 hours a

day on campus, participating in every aspect of teaching life, including faculty meetings, recess duty, parent–teacher conferences, and field trips. Then on Tuesdays and Thursdays, residents attend PTR courses, which meet from 3:30 to 5:30 p.m. The two fall courses at PTR are The School Aged Child (a course in child and adolescent development) and History and Social Studies Education.

In the spring, residents are placed with a new guiding teacher (GT). The year that I observe, 10 of the 16 residents have opted to be placed at public schools in the spring, a higher proportion than ever before. Meanwhile, the residents complete two spring classes at Xanadu: English Instruction, Curriculum, & Assessment and Issues of Equity in Education. Taylor and Mary design the curricula for both the fall and spring courses, which change every year, depending on the cohort of residents that enrolls.

However, finances seem to impact who enrolls in PTR. Residents must pay approximately $11,000 for teacher certification through PTR, which Taylor tells me does not even fully cover the costs of training a resident (Xanadu makes up the difference). Most then pay another $37,000 to a local university to concurrently work toward their master's. The year I observe, one person of color who was accepted was ultimately unable to enroll because of this hefty price tag. Still, PTR is more of a financial drain for Xanadu than a "cash cow."[4] Because PTR no longer primarily serves to supply teachers for the school, I initially wonder why the school continues to support the teacher training program.

Leaders at Xanadu seem to view their work in equipping teachers with the tools of student-centered thinking, relational competency, and responsive project-based pedagogy as doing good for the society that receives PTR graduates. For example, Taylor tells me, "It is clear that in 2015, teachers have much work to do to develop children who are empathic, culturally competent, ethical, humane, and kind. I have a personal commitment to disrupt oppression and institutionalized racism by preparing a different kind of teacher. I believe teachers can be powerful agents for change in their classrooms." This commitment extends to preparing teachers to serve a range of students, including privileged and historically marginalized students alike, at independent and public/charter schools (which I discuss more in Chapter 5).

However, PTR is not merely a service for the wider world, as it does in fact serve Xanadu in meaningful ways. Mary explains, "Part of it is self-interest in that it [PTR] keeps things fresh and alive at the school." She further describes the way that residents provide "new blood" each year that "keeps [Xanadu] teachers on their toes" because they design new curriculum, ask incisive questions, and spark new conversations. Guiding teachers whom I interview also tell me that they get ideas about curriculum and instruction from their student teachers. Moreover, some PTR graduates do eventually return to teach at the school, as several members of the current faculty are PTR alumni.

Mary thus calls PTR "the pearl in the shell" of Xanadu. She adds, "I think without this program, the school would feel really, really different." For several decades, and before teacher residencies became the reform du jour in education, PTR set Xanadu apart from the many other progressive independent schools across the country that lacked a means of training teachers in their philosophy.

Today, PTR not only keeps Xanadu's progressive spirit alive, but also provides the school with fresh perspective, future employees, and a purpose that extends beyond it. Meanwhile, Xanadu provides PTR with the resources to holistically cultivate residents' teaching identities. Throughout the program, I observe how the residents indeed seem to absorb the philosophy, pedagogy, and community displayed for them at Xanadu. On the surface, it does almost seem like a "magic[al]" place. But it is also a place that is sheltered from many schooling realities, accountable only to itself and focused more on the ecosphere within its walls than the world beyond it. All of these factors influence the residents' early perceptions of teaching in ways that might inhibit their ability to teach elsewhere.

POLLINATED BY PROGRESSIVE PEDAGOGY

On a sunny Thursday in September, I follow a couple residents whom I recognize across the sprawling pastoral campus to a small conference room enclosed by glass walls and large windows. As we settle into the small chairs that are arranged in a circle, Mary welcomes the residents to her social studies course. A warm smile stretches behind her glasses to illuminate her light eyes as she pauses and glances around the room. Before she even introduces the course, she tells the residents with compassion, "Before we get into this, I want to take a moment to transition, because I can't even begin to imagine how many decisions you made today and how tired you must be today." She says with a chuckle, "Try not to fall asleep," before she begins to read aloud from a book called *A Little History of the World*. I feel myself relax as she reads in a melodic tone, noticing the utter lack of urgency here.

When she finishes reading, Mary stands and informs the residents that they will be engaging a silent gallery walk activity. She gestures to 12 different artifacts produced by students at Xanadu—maps, posters, photographs, a statue of a man, a video ready to play on a computer screen—many of which have been taped to an area on one of the glass walls. Each artifact is accompanied by a caption consisting of a message or a question, in addition to a blank piece of paper reserved for residents' responses to the artifact and this prompt. She tells the residents, "Take some time to respond to the image, quote, or question that is in front of you and feel free to respond to those who wrote before you."

Residents slowly stand up and make their way over toward one of the artifacts to commence their gallery exploration. The poster closest to me says: "As we investigate the cultures of the past, how do we find out the truth? *Can* we find out the truth?" Meredith, the program's most seasoned resident, glances up from the video she has been watching. The video that flashes on the computer screen features a number of powerful images of war and propaganda and history in quick succession. I can hear the faint sound of dramatic music echoing from the headphones attached to the computer. Meredith looks over to the young resident beside her and softly breaks the silence: "Wow. You have to listen to this." I then notice Leah, a young secondary humanities resident, regarding comments that have accumulated on one of the posters. She considers these with pen in hand before adding additional notes of her own. As the residents continue their progression throughout the intimate space, the posters fill up with various colors from residents' writing implements. Meanwhile, Mary strolls around the room, periodically stepping up to posters to read residents' responses.

In the group debrief that follows the 20-minute activity, residents express enthusiastic appreciation for the gallery walk experience. In response to the question, "What was this activity like for you?" I write down the following resident comments:

"That kind of activity works for me because I feel like I learn better when I am emotionally involved in it."

"With different media—questions, interactive responses, images—I had to think differently."

"Yes, some demanded an interrogative response, some were more narrative, emotional or analytical."

"This was kind of like going to the MFA [Museum of Fine Art]: two pictures can be completely different. The gallery style was really cool for history."

"I appreciate the efficiency of this activity; we are all able to read each other's responses of peers in a short period of time."

"I was trying to think what kind of thing I could [do to] try to apply this to science."

The gallery walk, though silent, requires residents to interact with student work, respond to one another's comments on this work, and make connections to their own experiences. It is "social" and interactive, causing them to feel "emotionally involved" in the process. And it seems to germinate instructional ideas for their varied classrooms. Residents shape their own experience of and takeaways from this activity while Mary stands at the margins and observes.

* * *

The symmetry between the way residents learn in PTR and the way students learn at Xanadu serves as a powerful form of modeling.[5] It is similar to NETR in this way, but the pedagogy modeled could not be more different. Throughout my observations at PTR, I notice that faculty employ various forms of constructivist pedagogy in coursework for the residents. Instead of presenting residents with top-down objectives and specific takeaways for each session, faculty facilitate educational experiences that allow residents to construct their own meaning, learn from the reflections of their colleagues, and consider how they might apply all of this to their teaching. Taylor tells me that she intentionally models "pedagogical approaches we would want them to try in their own classrooms."

In other sessions I observe, residents largely guide the learning for the day. For example, residents sometimes present on strategies or activities they have found useful in their student teaching. On one of these occasions, Meredith discusses how she and her GT asked students to write "praise poems"[6] about a character in a story; students then performed these wearing masks they made. At another point, residents bring in articles about issues that they feel are important and relevant to their experiences in the classroom and they share these in a circle. Taylor deliberately allows residents such "latitude" so they can co-construct their own learning.

Not all of these lessons seem to reach their desired target, though. For example, some residents characterize one of Taylor's courses as "disorganized," and others say they wish for more "structure" in PTR coursework so that they can cover more content or go "deeper" in their discussions. Occasionally, and especially when the topic of the day extends beyond their personal comfort zone—for example, when mostly white residents are tasked with discussing race (which I will discuss more in Chapter 5)—they do not seem equipped to step into the role of knowledge co-constructor. And it occurs to me that for certain topics, residents may in fact need a bit more hand-holding.

Still, residents generally voice appreciation for the coursework, and the way in which they can guide their own learning within it. For example, Ashley, the only Black resident, explains: "One thing that I really like are seminars because they're so discussion based, and we have our norms. You're really being able to listen and really understand where someone's coming from and their views, and to be able to do it in like a safe space." And Donna calls the PTR classes "extremely helpful" for her teaching.

Residents do not, however, express similar appreciation for the local university coursework they complete for their master's degree. Jackie rolls her eyes whenever she talks about this coursework. Donna calls it "frustrating" because she feels like she is "paying a lot" but has been "quite disappointed with just the quality of the courses." And Meredith similarly questions the value of the university coursework. While these residents are not terribly specific about what they do not like about the university courses, I gather from their comments that their primary objection has to do with a didactic pedagogical approach and the way it feels removed from their everyday experiences at Xanadu. This echoes some research on teacher education more broadly, which criticizes overly theoretical or out-of-touch course-work.[7] PTR residents ultimately seem to dismiss much of their university coursework in favor of the more enjoyable and responsive PTR course sessions and their even more salient student teaching experiences.

Residents truly seem to enjoy PTR, a parallel to the way students seem to have fun at Xanadu. For example, Nancy tells me that she feels her alma mater has a mission of "really creating these active, engaged, happy learners. That school should be a fun place to go." Similarly, Mary explains that she feels that good teachers infuse "humor and fun" into their lessons, and that she hopes the residents will learn "how to have a lot of fun with your students." And every time I observe, I see smiles and hear excited chatter among the residents, who seem to be nourished by their learning experiences. But I also realize that unlike NETR, PTR is nestled in a context of abundance, where there is ample room for joy and fun, and little need to attend to the public school realities like standardized test scores or student poverty.

NURTURING EVERY BUD

Xanadu's student-centered philosophy is so ubiquitous throughout PTR that it is almost as if it is in the water, nurturing residents' understanding of the teacher–student relationship. But teachers must learn a great deal about students in order to place them at the center of the educational experience. Taylor explains, "If they want to reach a child, they are going to have to get to know the child." And much of the program is geared toward preparing residents to do just that.

Early in coursework at PTR, Taylor challenges residents to start thinking about the individual students they serve in student teaching. I observe as she invites the residents to complete an activity toward this end. She begins, "Take out a clean sheet of paper, divide the paper in half, create two columns. Then I would like for you to close your eyes." Taylor adds conspiratorially, "If you are closing your eyes, you must be doing something really *special*." She emphasizes this point as it would be done in an elementary school classroom. Then she continues by asking residents to picture all the students in their class(es), with a focus on their general appearance, their "complexions" (a proxy for race), their attitudes, and their apparent feelings about school.

As residents' eyes remain closed, Taylor prompts them, "Now I would like for you to write down all the students whose names you can remember in that one class who are looking at you." Given that residents have only just begun to connect with students, this task seems challenging; but it also sets the expectation that teachers should attempt to "see" students from the beginning.

After a few more minutes have passed, Taylor breaks the silence. She discusses the Pygmalion experiment where teachers were told they had the top students at the school (when in fact students were just randomly assigned to their class); because teachers treated these students like "the cream of the crop," the students achieved more than their peers in other classes. Taylor concludes, "When people believe in us, we rise to their expectations." Then she transitions back to the assignment at hand: "Now look at the names that you have come up with [and add] one strength, something positive, for each child that you have listed. What have you noticed about them in the 2 days you have been with them?"

Residents write quietly, some glancing up at the board and contemplating, brows furrowed. Taylor has just increased the difficulty of this assignment, asking students to not only see the individual students before them, but to consider some of their already visible strengths. By steering resident thinking toward students' positive qualities, Taylor is setting them up to both "see" students and to see the best in them. Instead of focusing on "patrolling" for "broken windows" among students as residents learn at NETR, PTR emphasizes asset-based thinking.

After a few more minutes, Taylor interjects again. This time, she tells a story about a teacher who gave her students personalized notes that included several positive qualities that she saw in each student. Taylor adds that many of these students then held on to their note well into adulthood. She then asks residents to return to their assignment for a few more moments so they can continue to think about what they see in these students and what they might share with them as the year progresses.

Taylor glances around the room, and when she recognizes that most residents have stopped writing, she asks, "What was the experience like for you? Why do you think the children [in my story] kept the note through adulthood? What did the teacher value in her classroom? What did the teacher value in her students? . . . I want you to engage in a turn-and-talk."

Residents turn to the person beside them and excitedly discuss Taylor's questions. I listen as Sam, a secondary humanities resident, describes how he sees some of the students "right off the top of my head," they are fresh in his mind, but admits others completely escape his memory.

Taylor circulates as the residents talk with one another for a few more moments, and then she asks again, "Okay, so, what did the teacher value in her students?"

One of the residents replies, "She valued them as individuals who were each worthy of attention and respect and care." Taylor smiles. This response seems to encapsulate the way that PTR wants residents to value their own students.

Later, when I interview Mary, she reflects upon the value of this experience. She notes that when residents remember some of their students but not others during this early assignment, she and Taylor ask them to think about why this is the case. Mary tells me she and Taylor encourage residents to seek out meaningful knowledge about students from their "files" and "former teachers," but most importantly, from the students themselves. Mary adds that residents should "really listen" to their students: "I mean listen to what is it that interests them, what is it that compels them, who are their friends, what are their families like, what is their life like outside of school, not just in school. I think a good teacher who builds relationships tries to understand their student outside of their particular classroom, too." At PTR, faculty believe teachers should acquire complex knowledge about students—their interests, their previous learning experiences, "what scares them," their families, and more—so teachers can value them as people in and out of the classroom.

The idea of listening to students to learn about them seems to resonate with the residents. Donna tells me, "I think, for me, the biggest thing is just listening to kids. . . . In the morning, and at snack, but often, kids want to talk about something 'off topic,' and I think there's value in listening to those . . . that's how I learned one of my students is an avid swimmer, or that a little girl in my class was really nervous about a dentist appointment in the afternoon." Several other residents tell me they learn about their students by simply asking questions of them, as students are often willing to share quite a bit about themselves.

Taylor takes this a step further, suggesting that teachers not only need to get to know students, but also need to develop empathy for them and their families. She explains, "When a resident begins the program, the seed of empathy is within them. For some, this environment feels familiar. Other settings, less so. I aim to develop teachers who are introspective, empathic, and strengths based in their thinking, approach, and relationship with children who are similar and different from them." Taylor acknowledges that empathy might be easier to practice in the "familiar" Xanadu garden, with students who look like residents. However, Taylor also wants residents to be able to develop empathy for students who are "different from them," which is perhaps a more challenging endeavor, particularly within the socioeconomically and racially homogenous walls of Xanadu.

One of the ways that PTR aims to help residents foster deeper knowledge and empathy for students is through a shadowing assignment. Each resident is asked to select a student who is "struggling" in both their fall and spring classes. In the fall, the assignment requires the resident to follow the student over the course of one full day and then write a short paper about the experience. In the spring, residents complete a similar but much more detailed shadowing assignment over the course of a month, for which they observe their new student for 15–20 minutes at a time in multiple different settings. The goal of each assignment is to consider how a particular student might behave in different settings, and how they could possibly be better supported within the resident's class.

Most of the residents I interview tell me both shadowing assignments influence the way they look at students. Of the first assignment, Sam explains, "I can't overstate the value of following . . . the kids around for a day and shadowing. That kid, still to this day, I feel like I know her better than I know some of the other kids." Similarly, Anna describes the way that she watched a student who was silent in her humanities class light up in physics class, and how this helped her to see a student as "a whole different person." While this seems incredibly valuable, it is also possible that extensively observing one student might lead residents to think they understand that student better than they actually do, leading to what Rosenberg called a "false sense of involvement" when only "superficial understanding" is present.[8] However, many of the PTR residents seem to realize that there is still so much they do not know about the students they observe.

I have the opportunity to read Elisabeth's spring assignment. Elisabeth is one of the two PTR residents whom I will follow into the field next year. Her tall, thin frame seems to take up as little space as possible in the classroom, and her contributions to coursework seem soft and unassuming. As I observe her further, I notice that she listens intently to her colleagues and asks earnest questions, here to learn rather than to be affirmed by others. When she enrolled in PTR, she requested a public school placement in the spring, and became one of two residents placed at City Middle School, a racially diverse public school for spring student teaching.

For her spring shadowing assignment, she chooses to focus on an eighth-grade Black student named Devontaye who has an individualized education program (IEP) for reading comprehension and often presents behavioral challenges for Elisabeth and her GT. In the beginning of the paper, Elisabeth describes Devontaye as "complex and, at times, challenging," as well as "inquisitive, gregarious, and creative." When she watches him work on a comic strip depicting the five pillars of Islam, she is impressed by his artistic ability. However, when it comes time to submit the assignment, Devontaye tells her he "threw it away." She later learns that "at this point in the semester Devontaye was homeless, and bouncing around to the homes of relatives," which she acknowledges likely impacted his ability to submit the assignment. Elisabeth also describes observing him behaving in a "positive and productive" manner in his more structured English language arts (ELA) classroom and commenting about a lesson to "no one in particular" in his math class. She adds, "From my observations, it is clear that Devontaye needs to be in classroom environments that are safe, predictable, and allow him to channel his impulse to verbally process information in a constructive manner. I have found that validating his comments during class and small-group discussions helps build his academic confidence." But Elisabeth humbly concludes that she is ultimately left with "more questions than answers" about Devontaye.

Throughout this assignment, Elisabeth seems to extend an empathetic eye toward Devontaye. She considers why he might behave the way he does, and whether circumstances beyond his control might affect his classroom behavior. Elisabeth remains asset based in her thinking about him but acknowledges that he will need particular supports from her and her GT to succeed. But in this public school setting, with multiple class periods of 30-plus students to teach at once, shedding such an intensive light on every student seems impossible and Elisabeth is not quite sure what to make of this reality, especially in light of the classroom management challenges she faces here (I will discuss this more in Chapter 6).

The limited coursework focused on classroom management in PTR focuses on nurturing interactions with individual students. Residents primarily learn how to enact this by working with their GTs at Xanadu, but Taylor does hold one session on classroom management in the spring titled the "Nurtured Heart Approach" to teaching. A visiting facilitator, Josh Hope, introduces this approach, in which teachers learn to "calibrate" their reactions to children's behavior to shape better responses in the future.

Throughout the presentation, Mr. Hope emphasizes the importance of rewarding positive behavior with attention—"the relationship is the reward"—but ignoring negative behavior. He further suggests that "punitive models" of classroom management give energy to student misbehavior, and thus reinforce this. Instead, he feels teachers should "build the relationship first" with students, then make their rules and requests clear and "give [students] recognition for the power and control it takes to follow the rules." If a student misbehaves anyway, Mr. Hope tells residents that they should offer "resets with as little energy and interaction as possible to prevent students with disruptive behaviors from hijacking the class" and adds that they should avoid arguing with students in class, but offer to come back to an issue in an individual conversation later if the student wants.

These ideas correspond with what I have seen on campus, but they also feel overly general, offering little guidance on specific language, routines, or procedures teachers could use in different situations. When I later ask residents if there is anything they wish they were learning more about in PTR, Leah tells me, "What comes to mind is classroom management techniques." But then she acknowledges that it might be difficult for PTR to teach this because Xanadu and PTR do not ascribe to any behavioral strategy or disciplinary system and instead emphasize the individuality of every teacher's approach to this. And she concludes, "So I think as I say that, I also don't think I would want a 2-hour course every week on techniques. So that is what it is."[9]

Ashley and Donna similarly express a desire for a greater focus on classroom management. Donna specifies she would like guidance on "interactional subtleties, and noticing behavior, and having conversations with children about sensitive topics or difficult situations, or if a child is upset, mediating conflicts." While the relational approach they learn in PTR coursework seems to work well at Xanadu, residents' requests for more concrete strategies indicate that they question how well they are prepared to manage classrooms outside of the garden.

At PTR, residents come to understand that learning about the students they teach is not a quick or superficial process, but one that requires concerted effort and reflection on behalf of the resident. It also requires the development of empathy, of learning to understand the student as a multifaceted human being that is more than he or she projects in the classroom. Knowing students is also not constructed as an end goal at PTR, but rather as the critical fuel they need to provide a more responsive learning experience for those entrusted in their care. While the efficient and directive pedagogy advocated by NETR requires only general knowledge of students and a firm grasp of the rules they all must obey, progressive pedagogy depends on deep and complex knowledge of individual students and the ability to differentiate for their individual needs and interests. PTR indicates that this deep knowledge of students allows residents to construct a space that is nurturing for them all.

However, coming to know and deeply understand every student—and to draw upon this relationship to develop coursework and implement classroom management—may be a tall order in most schools, where teachers might lead multiple different groups of students a day and/or serve 30 or more students simultaneously. Sheltered from the "real world," PTR does not have to interrogate the plausibility of applying its tenets in other settings. Nonetheless, the approach seems powerful at Xanadu, for both the students and the residents.

BLOOMING FROM WITHIN

Much like the Xanadu garden I noticed on my first day on campus, PTR supports all residents to blossom in their own ways, to embrace their own teaching style in line with who they feel they are as unique human beings. To facilitate the process of teacher identity development, residents are supported by the whole Xanadu community. Anna explains, "They really work to integrate the residents and they treat us as members of the Xanadu community." I find that the word "community" is used throughout most of my interviews in reference to the school and the network of supportive relationships residents form with the directors of PTR, their advisors and GTs at Xanadu, their cohort colleagues, and even their students. If raising a child "takes a village," then PTR believes learning to teach children requires a "community."

Similar to homerooms at Xanadu, PTR's yearly resident cohort is never larger than 18. Mary explains that this small size allows her and Taylor to provide individualized attention for each of the residents and to "focus on who they are as human beings, in addition to teachers." It also allows directors to provide residents with a great deal of personalized support.

Mary and Taylor each take a caseload of residents, whom they observe in the classroom and meet with multiple times throughout the year. While the directors provide copious feedback on each residents' teaching—offering "two plusses and a wish" for residents after each observation—they also offer support for residents "as human beings" who have personal issues and concerns that exceed the classroom (such as familial or financial issues). A few of the residents tell me this support is quite helpful and feel like they can stop by either director's office at any time and "really talk to them about anything."

Moreover, residents are supported by one advisor at Xanadu. Advisors do not oversee residents' teaching (that's the job of the GT), nor do they serve to evaluate residents in any way, though residents can ask them to observe their teaching if they want. Instead, advisors serve as impartial mentors, another experienced teacher there to listen to one particular resident and offer advice or encouragement. Ashley emphasizes the importance of "mentorship" to her experience at PTR and adds, "I'm really close to my advisor. I'm really close to Taylor. Everybody at Xanadu." Residents have concentrated access to several experienced educators who can support them at Xanadu, including those who have no vested interest in their classroom behavior.

Furthermore, residents voice great appreciation for the support they receive from their cohort mates. Jackie explains, "I think that the cohort is a huge part of why I did this . . . you have that built in." Ashley builds on this, describing how close she feels to everyone in the cohort, the way they eat together, and how they have established a group Facebook message that they will continue even after they graduate. She adds, "So, the cohort's good. And I think that's not only reflective of like us, in the program, but also the environment that we're in [that] has allowed us to do that." Indeed, PTR screens for residents who have some relational competency, but the intimate cohort and the collaborative school environment also nurtures the formation of deep and meaningful bonds among residents, who are encouraged to work together throughout coursework. However, the most salient relationships residents form to support their teaching are those with their guiding teachers at Xanadu (which I will discuss more in Chapter 6).

While residents develop a strong sense of self as a teacher through these collegial relationships, PTR coursework also supports the development of individual residents through intensive self-reflection. This is evidenced in two of the central program through-lines: "Who am I as a teacher? Why do I teach?" Taylor explains, "I think, too, it is important for teachers to understand and know themselves—to be honest with themselves about why they are coming into this work." Faculty also seem to operate on the premise emphasized in Palmer's quote from opening day, that residents cannot adequately understand students if they don't first understand themselves. As such, much of the coursework is tailored around activities that help residents reflect upon their life experiences and beliefs and help them begin to develop a sense of themselves teachers.

I observe self-reflective activities on numerous occasions. For example, early in coursework, Taylor asks residents to draw a Cultural Identity Wheel surrounded by five circles. In the center of this wheel, residents place their name, and then in three of the five surrounding circles, Taylor asks residents to "write a word that captures some aspect of your identity that has informed the 'calling' to teach children." She adds that in the remaining two circles, they should "write a word that describes an aspect of your identity that cannot be seen but you value deeply." Afterward, Taylor asks them to share their wheel and discuss what inspired them to pursue teaching with another resident whom they have not gotten to know yet.

This self-reflective activity seems to fulfill multiple purposes. It challenges residents to identify core aspects of their identity, including those that are not visible to the naked eye. It prompts them to reflect upon how aspects of their identity inform their "calling" to teach. Finally, it encourages them to share these essential aspects of self with a member of the cohort whom they do not yet know very well, likely forging new connections among the residents.

Through interviews, I learn about other opportunities that residents have for personal reflection. This begins in orientation. Mary explains, "One of the ways we start when people come for orientation is to have them think about their own experience and to have residents tap into what was effective for them when they were students and children." Later in the year, residents continue to reflect upon their past experiences and use this to explore their deep-seated thinking about education. One of these activities requires residents to explore their "family tree of education," how their family has valued education in different ways over generations, which Taylor calls "deeply personal."

The directors feel these reflections prompt a deeper understanding among residents of how they "learned best," which often relates back to their relationship with their teachers. Mary explains, "They will say they learned best when they felt like the adults in their life listened to them, cared about them, respected them, knew how to have fun with them, [and] set clear limits for them." This reflection seems indicative of their own learning experience at Xanadu, and it informs how residents thus want to teach and form relationships with their own students.

Residents also feel they benefit from the extensive opportunity to self-reflect in the program. Jackie tells me, "The fall was just like this whole whirlwind of just like self-analysis and I learned so much about myself in a way that I never really knew before, and loved every second of it." Nancy, too, explains that what she "enjoy[s] so much about the program is how reflective it is," which she feels "makes for good teachers." Elisabeth adds that this self-reflective focus also causes her to explore, "What is my philosophy as a teacher?" In exploring deep personal questions, many of which relate to their path to teaching, residents gain clarity over their own educational philosophy.

While NETR residents must learn to balance authenticity with authority, PTR residents are tasked only with finding and living their authenticity, what Palmer might call their "undivided self."[10] To achieve this, they are surrounded by a supportive community that allows them space to reflect extensively on their past, their educational interests, their motivations for teaching, and what they want in their future teaching experiences. They get to do a lot of iterating, but on their own terms and toward their own goals. The "appliances of learning" within PTR revolve around each resident.

However, it is possible that this resident-centeredness could contribute to a sense of narcissism. In this space, residents and students learn to focus extensively on their own personal development, gazing intently at their own reflection in much the same way that Xanadu's gaze remains inwardly focused. For example, Emma shares that Sam sometimes comes across as "very self-centered in terms of his awareness of the community." She adds, "I cannot come up with a more accurate term than he seems entitled." To illustrate this point, Emma recalls that during Xanadu faculty meetings, Sam has gotten up and gotten a snack whenever he wanted, taken off his shoes midmeeting, or volunteered to share first when the middle school director asked for teachers' reflections (and not necessarily residents' reflections). Sam's behavior with teachers here (behavior that would never fly in NETR) conveys a sense of comfort in the space that Emma does not feel he has earned yet. However, Emma tells me that Sam does not seem self-centered when it comes to the students, with whom "he's very much responsive, and he sees them, and he's very compassionate, and he takes care of them." While he has learned to value himself, he has learned to value students, too.

But it is also possible that Sam displays idiosyncratic behavior. When I talk to other GTs, I do not hear anything negative about residents' interactions with adults in the Xanadu community. This causes me to conclude that like the mythological figure Narcissus, residents—and Xanadu students—

who are already predisposed to gazing excessively at themselves might find their narcissism is nourished by the attention they receive at Xanadu. But for others, the idyllic conditions might instead contribute to increased confidence as a teacher, deeper teacher–student relationships, and the ability to advocate for self and students.

CULTIVATED IN THE GREENHOUSE

At Xanadu, reciprocal teacher–student relationships are fundamental to teaching and learning. There is no instrumentalism. And here, Buber's concept of an I–Thou teacher–student relationship truly seems to thrive for the residents and for the students. PTR constructs relationships as responsive, fluid, and dialogical. Students are viewed as whole people with the agency to co-construct their learning alongside the teacher. The resulting relationship is not akin to that of friendship or family, but a different kind of meaningful relationship, one centered around learning and personal growth for both parties.

PTR approaches the development of these relationships in a holistic way, embedding residents in the Xanadu community and modeling progressive pedagogy throughout coursework. The coursework itself emphasizes a variety of relational forms of knowledge and dispositions: residents learn to develop knowledge about themselves and their students, cultivate empathy and what Noddings would call "caring as relation."[11] They also acquire knowledge about societal forces like institutionalized racism, but the depth of their conversations around this seem limited by the demographics of the cohort (which I will address in Chapter 5).

PTR coursework focuses much less on relational actions than NETR, though, with the idea that residents will establish their own unique ways of being in the classroom. Thus, the program generally relies upon the guiding teachers to model specific strategies and actions. GTs offer residents two different views (one in the fall and one in the spring) of how they might go about implementing progressive approaches to teaching and interacting with students, and truly much of their learning takes place through these apprenticeships (which I discuss more in Chapter 6). So residents do not acquire specific tools in coursework to manage classrooms, provide extra support students who might not be performing at grade level, or connect with parents; it is simply not necessary to learn these actions at Xanadu where parents all attend conferences twice a year, students generally behave in class, and few students need any kind of remediation.

To be sure, Xanadu Community School is not like most school environments. The students here are exceptionally privileged, as most pay a great deal to attend the school. Xanadu also draws a unique crop of parents, who are all strongly supportive of progressive education and select the school because it places their children at the center of the learning experience. Class sizes are very small and built around homeroom. Teachers have the space and latitude to truly get to know students, to design coursework for and with these students, to manage classrooms through these relationships. In many ways, it does feel idyllic. But it is the kind of school that is often reserved for children of the elite, who learn to critically think and self-advocate because they feel worthy of the respect and attention of their adult authority figures.

This causes me to consider that perhaps Xanadu, and PTR as an extension of this, is more like a greenhouse than an open-air garden. While gardens are exposed to the elements, greenhouses are sheltered. Xanadu does not mirror the rest of the world, nor does it really attend to the rest of the world, but instead directs its gaze inward—and in many ways encourages residents to do the same. Shielded from limited school budgets, standardized tests, large class sizes, and the host of challenges that come along with serving students in poverty (or even middle class), or those who have been disproportionately assigned to special education, and/or those who have not yet mastered the English language, residents might not be well prepared for what lies beyond this greenhouse. So how will they feel when they encounter schools that are not able to consistently support progressive education? Will they feel comfortable serving students from different racial and socioeconomic backgrounds? I address these issues in the following two chapters.

NOTES

1. Dewey, John. (1900). *The school and society*. Chicago, IL: University of Chicago Press.

2. Anyon, Jean. (1981). Social class and school knowledge. *Curriculum Inquiry, 11*(1), 3–42.

3. Feiman-Nemser, Sharon, Tamir, Eran, & Hammerness, Karen. (2015). *Inspiring teaching: Preparing teachers to succeed in mission-driven schools*. Cambridge, MA: Harvard Education Press.

4. "Cash cow" is a term that is commonly used to refer to teacher education programs within universities because they train so many teachers who each pay a great deal for their education.

5. Grossman, P. (2005). Research on pedagogical approaches in teacher education. In M. Cochran-Smith & K. M. Zeichner (Eds.), *Studying teacher education: The report of the AERA panel on research and teacher education* (pp. 425–476). Mahwah, NJ: Erlbaum.

6. Praise poems follow a particular format, beginning with "I am the son/daughter of" and include descriptive details and figurative language, and end with a powerful line that sums up the person's identity.

7. For example, Levine, Arthur. (2006). *Educating school teachers*. Washington, DC: Education Schools Project. Retrieved from http://www.edschools.org/pdf/Educating_Teachers_Report.pdf

8. As cited in McAllister, Gretchen, & Irvine, Jacqueline Jordan. (2002). The role of empathy in teaching culturally diverse students. *Journal of Teacher Education, 53*(5), 433–443.

9. Interestingly, the local university coursework that most of the residents (including Leah) complete toward their master's degree actually includes an entire course devoted to classroom management; but because residents generally dismiss this coursework as perfunctory, low

quality, and divorced from their teaching practice, they do not consider it meaningful, or part of PTR at all.

10. Palmer, Parker. (1998). *The courage to teach: Exploring the inner landscape of a teacher's life.* San Francisco, CA: Jossey-Bass.

11. Noddings, Nel. (1984). *Caring: A feminine approach to ethics & moral education.* Berkeley: University of California Press.

Chapter Five

Below the Surface

Who do we teach self-advocacy and who do we teach to walk in a line? I want the residents to think about that.—Taylor, director of PTR

Progressive Teacher Residency (PTR) has an obvious focus on teacher–student relationships, one that jumps from the pages of the program's website and promotional material; but there is no mention of racism or social justice in outward-facing program documents. When I meet Taylor (PTR's director), though, I realize that the program actually has a discreet vision for social transformation, one that operates below the surface.

Taylor's identity as an African American woman directly influences this vision. She explains, "I have a personal commitment to disrupt oppression and institutionalized racism by preparing a different kind of teacher. I believe teachers can be powerful agents for change in their classrooms." Although Taylor does not initially classify this vision as one of "social justice," she recalls discussing her mission at conferences with other educators and realizing that "social justice" is in fact an apt term for what she aims to achieve here. I soon discover that conversations about racism, police brutality, and other forms of systemic injustice begin early and occur often within the bounds of PTR coursework.

Taylor's vision for social change involves teachers engaging students from a variety of racial and cultural backgrounds in education that challenges the status quo. She recalls how she told the residents to think about the Ferguson case, in that the officer who shot Michael Brown was once a student, spending several hours every day, 5 days a week, for most of the year in classrooms. She explains, "We usually blame the parents, thinking that something went wrong at home, but something was also missing from school."

In Taylor's mind, what was missing from this officer's education were teachers who shed light on the realities of institutional racism, prepared students with critical thinking skills and taught an antibias curriculum. She later reflects, "I wanted residents to understand that they have a lot of power to impact future police officers, state attorneys; they have the potential to impact children from different socioeconomic strata, genders, races, in the same way." She believes that PTR graduates can effect change in their service to a range of different students, including white and affluent students like those predominantly served by Xanadu.

However, Taylor also hopes that many PTR graduates will go on to serve historically marginalized students; and this, too, seems essential to her vision of social justice. She tells me that students of color deserve to have teachers who "honor the multiple lenses and rich cultural backgrounds they bring to school" even if the teachers do "not look like them." And she adds, "While many of these students may not have access to schools like Xanadu, they should have access to the kind of teachers Xanadu, and schools like it, want to hire."

Taylor maintains that graduates of her program, who are trained in student-focused and asset-based teaching, should spread this kind of teaching to areas where it is often lacking; she adds, "Who do we teach self-advocacy and who do we teach to walk in a line? I want residents to think about that. You don't just teach that here at Xanadu, but also teach children who don't look like the kids here to ask questions of you." Again, though, Taylor's passionate vision for social change through PTR is not obvious from an outsider's perspective; and it might not even be obvious to the faculty at Xanadu, the progressive independent school that houses PTR.

Progressive education has a complicated history with racism and social change. In the early 1900s, it was upheld as a panacea for all social ills, but historians of education have criticized progressive education for failing to deliver social advancement across contexts. This is partially because it was "a movement aimed exclusively at white, middle-class students"[1] whose parents wanted to provide them a "superior" and less rigid form of education.[2]

Progressive schools, most of which were established as private or independent institutions, allowed white students to escape from urban public schools, as a form of legal segregation. And the progressive model worked well for most of these white students, who already had a firm grounding in dominant cultural and social capital. However, when progressive education began to spread to public schools around this same time, the effect was not as desirable, perhaps because it was not well supported in lower-resourced areas.[3]

Progressive education might also have historically underserved students of color because of the assumptions progressive educators made about these students. For example, some early progressive educators (who were all white and mostly male), believed in the "theory of recapitulation," which suggested that people of color were "sociologically deficient" and needed to be "civilized" and/or "sort[ed] into their appropriate social roles" through education.[4] As a result, most progressive schools either attempted to assimilate students of color into the majority—thereby suppressing the home cultures of these students—or simply allowed students to pursue topics and activities that educators perceived were of interest to students, without providing them with the tools to be successful in the dominant culture. Neither of these approaches resulted in consistently better academic outcomes for students, and progressive education largely fell out of favor in public schools.[5]

A century-old independent school founded by early progressive educators, Xanadu is subject to the same history of exclusion and prejudice as other well-established progressive institutions. But over time, Xanadu sought to shed the vestiges of this history, and by the 1980s, the school seemed to be "on the cutting edge of progressive education, and diversity and inclusion," according to one teacher. However, this same teacher acknowledges that the school has not made much progress on antiracist practice and inclusion since that point, instead "resting on their laurels" and becoming "complacent."

Symbolically, Xanadu still seems committed to racial awareness and various forms of diversity. Signs designate the school as a "safe space" for all. Moreover, the school itself (though not PTR) has a "Diversity Mission Statement" that calls Xanadu an inclusive institution with a "multicultural" curriculum. And goes onto claim that its "diversity"—in terms of everything from race and socioeconomic status to gender identity and sexual orientation—contributes to "a wiser and stronger community."

In practice, Xanadu is visibly committed to LGBT awareness and support, sponsoring clubs, hosting after-school LGBT speakers, offering professional development (PD) on the subject, eliminating gendered bathrooms, and supporting faculty who openly identify as LGBT (including the head of the school). One transgender student's parents even paid for the Xanadu faculty to complete a training on how to better support transgender students. The mostly white progressive educators at Xanadu generally feel comfortable discussing and advocating for LGBT issues. But especially when compared to the school's loud and comprehensive approach to this, discourse on race seems muffled, as if it is occurring under water.

Xanadu serves a mostly white and largely upper-income population. While the website reports that 34% of the students identify as people of color, only one or two (of 16) students in each class I observe appear Black or Latinx. Meanwhile, 82% of the faculty identify as white. And many of the teachers of color who came to work here in the last several years chose not to remain. By some accounts, eight teachers of color left in the last 5 years because they did not feel Xanadu was "a great fit" for them. And one teacher suggests this is because faculty at the school do not value the experiences of people of color as much as they should. For example, this same teacher remembered a PD session at the school on race that made many white teachers so uncomfortable that "they didn't come to school the next day." When the school proposed another PD session on race, a white teacher responded, "Haven't we already done race?"

However, a handful of vocal educators—most of them teachers of color—continue to advocate for the confrontation and discussion of race and racism on campus; and they openly address these issues in their own classrooms and sometimes at grade-level faculty meetings, too. For example, Leah (a secondary PTR resident) tells me that the sixth-grade team centralizes issues of race in curriculum (assigning *Roll of Thunder, Hear My Cry*) and in their discussions about how best to serve their few students of color in the classroom.

The school also attempts to better support its population of students of color by sponsoring "student affinity groups." These intimate groups meet monthly behind closed doors during lunch, are facilitated by a volunteer faculty advisor, and provide a "safe space" to discuss issues that are relevant and responsive to the students they serve. One teacher characterized these meetings as essential for students of color on campus, but the voices that feel safe speaking in these intimate meetings do not seem to carry throughout the school.

While discussion of LGBT issues is widely embraced at Xanadu, discourse around race seems to be more muffled: occurring in small groups or grade-level teams, isolated to particular classrooms with teachers who initiate these conversations, or relegated to discrete PD sessions from the past. It is not quite what scholar Mica Pollock would call "color mute," in which people carelessly use racial terminology or do not talk about race at all, but the tenor and resonance of conversations about race are softer than many topics of injustice on the progressive campus.

It is within this well-established context that Taylor undertakes a precarious journey. Unlike Xanadu's administration, she does not feel complacent, continuously reinventing the PTR curricula to better illuminate the realities of structural racism and oppression, as well as the potentially transformative ways teachers can work to address these with their students. But in an environment where conversations of race are muffled, and the student population is largely white and privileged, supporting PTR's transformative vision must feel like swimming upstream.

TREADING WATER IN CONVERSATIONS OF RACE

Issues of racism, privilege, equity, and multiculturalism pervade PTR course-work. But unlike NETR, the ways in which PTR approaches this work are complex and layered, implicit and varied. Mary, PTR's white assistant direc-tor, observes, "Racial tension has come up naturally in our seminars, but it hasn't felt like a one-off; it's come up because of the issues we're talking about anyway." Mary's course focuses on how to plan, teach, and assess social studies lessons, including a session on using "Facing History and Ourselves" as a framework for history; while the word "race" is not on the syllabus, residents often bring it up in her class. Mary adds that many of these conversations have "naturally bubbled up" because of "Ferguson." Be-cause the residents have so much authority in their own learning process here, they shape the coursework around race in consequential ways.

In the year I observe, Taylor assigns residents the book *White Like Me: Reflections from a Privileged Son* by Tim Wise for the residents' summer reading. This text—part memoir, part essay—explores how structural racism allows white people like Wise to benefit from a kind of privilege that begins at birth and influences all aspects of people's lives; it also implores white people to work alongside people of color to advance systemic change, in part through education. In assigning this book, Taylor implicitly sets the expecta-tion that residents will enter PTR more racially aware than they perhaps would have otherwise.

However, none of the PTR coursework has designated time to discuss or debrief this text, nor does the fieldwork at Xanadu enable residents to work with students of color who likely have experience with the racism Wise explores. This leaves residents to make sense of their responses to this work on their own. That is, until they bring the book up in Emma's Middle School Cultures class, which only the seven secondary residents take, all of whom are white.

Emma's Middle School Cultures class is a space where residents seem to feel comfortable volunteering thoughts about race. This is in part because Emma is a skillful practicing teacher who readily creates an inclusive and intimate environment for discussion. Her classroom is colorful and eclectic, with sofas in the back and student artwork adorning the walls; meanwhile, Emma herself is warm, approachable, and open minded. She has also de-signed a curriculum geared around exploring the impact of students' identity factors—including class, gender identity, sexual orientation, and race—on their experiences in school. Emma, who self-identifies as Latina and gay, has done a lot of thinking about these topics and exudes knowledge and passion on the subject matter. All of this contributes to residents' sense of comfort in her classroom, but Emma also acknowledges that she is probably less threat-ening to residents she teaches in this course than some people of color because she represents "stealth diversity," in that she comes across as white and her sexual orientation is not visible. Again, faculty seem to feel that messages about race and racism at Xanadu must be cloaked in subtlety.

In one October session, Emma invites one of her colleagues—an African American teacher at the school—to coteach a session on the "Facets of Student Identities." The day's lesson focuses on racial microaggressions: indirect or subtle slights directed at historically marginalized people. Throughout this lesson, most of the residents seem eager to participate and learn; none of them voices any resistance to the idea that microaggressions could be well intentioned but inflict real harm on individual students. Although conveyed through a narrow lens, this lesson seems to communicate the importance of maintaining awareness of cultural norms and racial stereotypes and remaining sensitive to the experience of individuals. However, I do notice that Courtney, a secondary science resident who graduated from a prestigious university prior to attending PTR, says nothing throughout this session.

After this seemingly instructive lesson, with 10 minutes left of class, residents initiate the first conversation I have seen about *White Like Me.*

Sam, a secondary humanities resident, asks, "Can we discuss this? I really like this book."

Courtney jumps in, complaining, "I was really irritated by the way the author wrote the book; there were a lot of assumptions about white people that made me angry. The way he framed a lot of things really irritated me."

Emma's response is gentle. "You are not the first person to tell me that."

Courtney continues, perhaps emboldened by Emma's seemingly understanding response; she refers to what she calls the author's "racism against whites," and adds that the author made her feel, "like, I just want to punch you right now."

Emma's eyes briefly widen, but then she offers sympathetically, "It could be generational." She concedes that the forms of racism Wise describes might not seem as obvious today as they did a generation ago.

Courtney allows, "Maybe that was true for my parents, but that's not how I experienced it."

"His intent is to provoke," Leah says.

Emma confirms this. "Absolutely. Look at his YouTube videos."

Then Sam laments, "He provoked, but there was no one there to have a discussion about it."

Courtney continues, passionately, "He provoked too far. . . . I was like, I am done with this."

At this point, the time for the day's session is up, without any resolution or even time to really discuss this book or Courtney's vehement response to it. But Emma reassures the residents, "Don't worry, I won't drop this conversation."

Throughout most of the coursework she leads, Emma seems to take pains to help residents feel comfortable. While this allows space for residents to bring up conversations about uncomfortable topics like the racism and privilege discussed in their summer reading, it does not push residents like Courtney to reflect upon why she might be having such an intense reaction to Tim Wise's words. And despite the fact that the existence of microaggressions implies that racism is related to power, Courtney still asserts that Wise's book represents "racism against whites." This reveals a distinct misunderstanding of what racism actually means, that it cannot in fact be used against white people because structurally and institutionally, those with white skin have always had power over people of color in the United States.[6] As such, Courtney's comment suggests that while the lesson on microaggressions was perhaps illustrative on one level—in that it communicated a more sensitive approach to individual students, something PTR emphasizes throughout—it might not have challenged all residents' innate assumptions about broader issues of racism.

A month later, Emma makes space in her course to return to Tim Wise's work, as promised. With 35 minutes left of class time, Emma opens the second installment of their discussion of *White Like Me.* She writes three phrases on the board—"Our students, cultural capital, multiple identities"—but allows the residents space to carry the discussion.

Instead of responding to these cues, residents begin by sharing their discomfort with reading this text. Jackie, an outspoken secondary science resident, is one of the first to speak up, seemingly from the perspective of a Xanadu Community School faculty member. She notes that trying to engage in a discussion of race during a 90-minute afternoon faculty meeting "can shut some people down. . . . You shouldn't be opening this conversation unless you have 3 hours." Although it does not feel like Jackie is attempting to criticize Emma here for devoting only a half hour to this discussion, she makes a point about the importance of having time to engage in extended dialogue about race and racism.

Sam chimes in that *White Like Me* is not a good book to read on public transportation and still have a good day because it made him hyperaware about how he was interacting with other human beings.

Leah nods and says she read it last year as she was commuting to or from work, and she just had to "sit down and write a lot of things down, because it's a lot of big ideas." She notes that it made her uncomfortable, and wonders aloud, "Am I upset or am I uncomfortable in a good way? Or am I upset because I know this is true?" Emma asks her for an example. Leah says that he puts the onus on white readers to make dramatic changes, adding, "It's not just an idea; at some point there needs to be action."

Emma affirms this comment, suggesting, "It's not the extent of your ideas, but your actions." No one specifies what kinds of actions or changes the book recommends, and this abstract idea passes without resolution.

Emma then asks the group, "Who covered up the book when you were reading in public?"

A few of the residents raise a tentative hand. But Leah asserts that she was proud of it: "I am reading this book!"

Emma admits to the group that when she was rereading it in preparation for this class, she covered it up on Xanadu's campus, because she didn't want anyone to come over and start a potentially hostile conversation about it; she didn't have energy to engage with that. In this comment, Emma implies that some of the faculty at Xanadu are resistant to the ideas presented in this book, that they likely do not even realize Taylor has assigned the text. The residents, who generally hold a rosy view of Xanadu and its faculty, do not respond to her admission.

Sam then brings the discussion back to his own experience reading the text, suggesting, "Anything that I do on the [train], I kind of think about it as performance art." Everyone laughs and the focus of the conversation returns to Sam, and away from their discomfort.

Emma again tries to bring the discussion back to focus on the issues presented in the text: "The reason I bring it up is because in my first diversity training, the group defined racism as having ever taken advantage of white privilege, knowingly or unknowingly."

Although Emma has not asked a question or demanded any personal admissions, Leah responds to this from a personal perspective. She explains matter-of-factly that she is guilty of racism by this definition because she has fully taken advantage of her white privilege, attending a private school and college that her parents were able to pay for, and was able to have assistance to apply for a federally funded grant, and she never had any doubt about her right to "be here or apply for a grant." There is no bitterness or anxiety in her voice; Leah simply acknowledges the myriad ways in which her white privilege has served her, indicating that she has spent time thinking about this, perhaps in response to reading *White Like Me*.

Emma nods in response to Leah and then transitions to a document she wants to share with the residents. She asks, "Who is familiar with Peggy McIntosh's backpack of white privilege?" A few of the residents raise their hands. "This is a seminal work, part of the canon of diversity work. Basically, she says that these are assumptions that white people can make based on their race that people of color, specifically Black people, cannot make," Emma finishes and then uses the projector to display McIntosh's 26-item list. "It's a long list!"

As residents regard and seemingly process this list, Emma continues, "Is there a list of things that gives students privilege in schools? That is the issue of cultural capital, as members of the dominant group we belong to. I belong to a lot of the power groups. I am able bodied, look white, was raised Christian. You have to decode in order to code-switch. How do you take your white identity and leverage that to help your students?" There is a lot here, and any one of these ideas seems ample fodder for a fruitful conversation.

Instead of responding, Gia, a secondary math resident, looks bewildered. "How can you achieve that without social change [from the] outside?" she asks.

Sam responds that he has been reading Delpit's *Other People's Children* in his spare time, which prompted a discussion between him and his girl-friend about how to teach students with less access to dominant cultural capital. While his girlfriend expressed a wish that the "social situation" was different so students could just learn what they want, Sam insists that students from nondominant groups do need to learn the culture of power "so they can be taken more seriously."

This reminds me of the narrative around the importance of navigation presented in NETR. And indeed, Emma has just prompted residents to consider how people of color may feel the need to "code-switch" along these lines to advance socially. But this is one of the only times I hear mention of considering how to teach students from nondominant groups how to access the culture of power, perhaps because most of the students at Xanadu already have such access. And it seems that many of the residents and teachers at Xanadu prefer to imagine a better world than confront the injustices rampant in the current one.

Then Jackie wonders aloud, her tone colored by passion and frustration, "How do we go out in this world; we will be standing in front of a room that is 97% not white . . . and you look nothing like the children sitting in your class, except that you are female, even though some don't identify as that. How do we reduce [that divide?] . . . [If] I am going to come into your classroom, why should you care?" This indicates to me that Jackie has been considering teaching in schools unlike Xanadu but does not feel prepared to teach students who do not look like her.

Emma responds to Jackie's difficult question about a "cultural mismatch" between teachers and students by sharing a brief anecdote about how her few students of color at Xanadu are eager to acquire cultural capital, which she can provide. And then she poses some broader questions for the residents to consider: "How do you as a white teacher get the investment of your class? And do you as a white teacher begin to scratch the surface of how to help students develop cultural capital? . . . And the other question is, does helping students feel valued in an inclusive classroom necessitate devaluing the cultural capital that some students have inherently?"

No one seeks to directly respond to any of these critical questions. Instead, a couple of the PTR residents again share some of their own personal thoughts and experiences, which seem to focus more on socioeconomic disparities than race, in part because that is what residents feel they must deal with most at Xanadu. For example, Jackie discusses a harmful belief among many of her students that it is "normal that everyone gets an Audi for their 16th birthday," when others are here on scholarships. Xanadu does not offer residents an opportunity to work extensively with people of color, so they conflate racial inequality with socioeconomic inequality.

But it also seems that poverty, homophobia, and gender discrimination are easier to discuss for most people than racism. Emma acknowledges this as part of white privilege: "From my perspective as a Mexican American woman, part of that privilege is that you don't have to talk about race." But she suggests that if residents want to create "change in our schools," they need to start "pushing the white leaders . . . to have these conversations."

Elisabeth, a secondary humanities resident, immediately asks, "How do you create a curriculum to help facilitate those kinds of conversations?"

Jackie quickly builds off this. "How do you tie it into every single day at Xanadu?" to which Emma responds, "To make it part of the fabric of the school instead of an add-on. But we are out of time."

Sam observes, "But there is never enough time!" The residents hesitantly pack up their bags, many of them continuing this discussion as they slowly progress out of the room. Courtney is one of the first residents out the door, and I realize that despite her active condemnation of Tim Wise a month before, she has not contributed once to today's discussion. While some of the other residents seem eager to acknowledge their privilege and engage with ideas of racial injustice, even after class, Courtney does not. I wonder if her silence is a form of resistance.

In this conversation of race, racism, and privilege, some trends emerge that seem common to PTR coursework. First, the conversation is not very directed. While the pretext for having the discussion is a debrief of Tim Wise's book *White Like Me*, the ideas Emma poses at the beginning do not in fact anchor the discussion. Instead, residents carry the discussion in various directions, occasionally prompted by Emma to connect their thoughts to ideas of privilege or cultural capital, terms that residents seem to generally understand but that are not collectively defined.

Additionally, many of the residents' comments seem to be a means of processing their own experiences with reading a text like this, as they attempt to explore their own racial identity and sense of privilege. This is useful, and their personalized reflections (a hallmark of PTR coursework) reveal their comfort with the facilitator, perhaps in part because of her "stealth diversity." Leah, for example, remembers this conversation as "pretty frank and rich" and "safe." However, most comments do not seem particularly deep or profound, nor do residents seem to really push one another's thinking, which might be partially because of the white homogeneity of the group.

Emma interjects with several critical questions, but residents do not appear to know how to address these or seem overwhelmed by the enormity of the social problems revealed by these questions. In response, they sometimes ask important related questions about engaging and effectively teaching students who come from such vastly different backgrounds or integrating issues of race into the everyday discussions at the school. Emma relays insights from her personal experience, but she does not have the time or a set of tools to offer in response to complex questions like this. Such tools might be missing in PTR because they do not seem necessary on the affluent and mostly white Xanadu campus, where conversations of LGBT issues are part of the obvious "fabric of the school" but conversations of race are not. Ultimately, the uncoordinated discussion ends prematurely, without any consensus or sense of how to move forward regarding residents' own racial awareness or the potential "action[s]" that such competence might stimulate. Incapacitated by the lack of time and direction, these conversations sometimes feel like treading water.

WAVES OF RACIAL DISCOMFORT

The PTR course that seems to have the most potential to provide residents with a strong foundation in racial competence is the "Issues of Equity in Education" course. This spring course, which is led by Taylor, features a powerful syllabus with readings from antiracist and sociopolitical texts like *Can We Talk About Race?* by Tatum and Perry, and *Con Respeto: Bridging the Distances Between Culturally Diverse Families and Schools* by Valdes. The course description suggests that classes will focus on "educational issues, policies and trends, which currently impact children, teachers, families, schools and communities," including "issues of equity and inequity in schools" and "the historical foundations for the achievement gap and teaching gap." Course assignments include visits to a variety of school types and presentations on these visits, personal reflections on "Issues in Education and Equity in the News," and a pro/con paper about a "topic of current educational significance and controversy." But the words "race" and "racism" are absent from the body of the syllabus, appearing only in the titles of required readings. Even in this course, content on race is kept under the surface.

Residents generally express excitement in anticipation of this course. For example, Sam explains, "I'm interested to see what they do with that [course]. I think a couple of us have been talking to Taylor about wanting more focus on that, and I think she got the message and I'm excited about what she's got for us." A couple other residents also tell me that they wish they were learning more about issues of race, culture, and equity and voice excitement about the syllabus. However, a series of unprecedented snowstorms steal precious classroom hours from PTR and delay the start of this course by 3 weeks.

When the course finally does begin, Taylor asks residents to help her continue to "shape the syllabus" by bringing in articles about issues of equity that are important to them. While residents bring forward several different education-related justice issues, no one explicitly brings up racial injustice. Taylor remembers, "They didn't realize how much they had shared without sharing. Only one person used the word 'privilege'—I think it was Leah—and I was waiting. And I don't think anyone joined the words 'white' and 'privilege' together." Taylor expresses disappointment by this omission, but I notice the irony here, as the syllabus for this course similarly avoids naming "race" as a focus of the course.

Some of the residents—who are accustomed to feeling "cozy" in sheltered Xanadu—seem to feel more discomfort than they would like in this spring class. Leah, who explored her discomfort while reading *White Like Me*, reflects that she sometimes felt like "I need this [class] to be over because I am very uncomfortable with how this feels right now." And she adds that "more often than not" she did not feel this discomfort was the productive type. She clarifies that this seemed to result from Taylor's demeanor: "Sometimes she has an air that is alienating to people, or intimidating is probably a better word." When I ask her why she feels "intimidated" by Taylor, she explains it has to do with "little ways of how she carries herself sometimes in seminar of really striving in with a point to prove" and "putting them on the spot" if people didn't say the right thing.

Taylor's conspicuous racial identity seems to play a role in residents' discomfort. Jackie explains, "She definitely, at times, is like, 'I am a Black woman,' I don't mean to say this quite the way it's going to come, but like, 'Hear me roar.'" This suggests that some of the residents perceive Taylor's racial identity to be a loud force in the way she facilitates her coursework, unlike Emma whose identity is "stealth." Leah reinforces this idea: "In such an obvious, overwhelmingly white group of students, I think her opinions on race hold an even stronger resonance or force or power and I think that people are still able to have good conversations and real conversations sometimes, but I think other times the force of her opinions made it hard for other people to hear theirs, whether in agreeing or disagreeing." This might have been why Leah connected the words "white" and "privilege" in Emma's class, but not here.

While residents at PTR have become accustomed to feeling like their own opinions and experiences are just as valuable as those of the instructors, even in coursework on race, Taylor seems to exert more obvious "force" or "power" in directing this spring course. This sometimes feels uncomfortable to the white residents in particular, likely because they have limited experience with Black leaders. As a contrast, Ashley—the only Black resident—feels "really close" to Taylor, and reports that she feels "safe" in seminar discussions.

In March, I have the opportunity to observe a session of this course, focused on a chapter from Lisa Delpit's book *Multiplication Is for White People*.[7] This chapter centers the importance of teachers becoming "warm demanders," the idea of holding students to high academic expectations in a caring and culturally competent way.

Although the session does not touch upon teaching across cultural differences as much as I expect it will, I note two moments where Taylor asserts slightly more authority than usual to push residents to consider how race functions in different spaces. In the first instance, she actually brings up no excuses schools, suggesting that teachers in these schools often think they are being warm demanders because they are holding students to high academic and behavioral expectations, but that they are actually behaving like "prison guards." She lets out a laugh that sounds almost cynical and then continues, "I'm going there! . . . [When] someone who is not African American, but European, starts yelling but has no cultural competence or care behind this, but just exercises power because they supposedly have it, it is not going to be perceived the way it was intended."

These passionate comments may cause residents to consider how their racial power over students of color might influence the way their classroom management strategies are perceived. These comments also serve to distinguish "warm demanders" from NETR's idea of "warm/strict,"[8] in which teachers balance their responsibility to uphold the school's behavior management system with small infusions of warmth like smiling and displays of positive reinforcement. PTR's use of Delpit is very different from NETR's.

Taylor's second attempt to push residents' thinking on issues of race occurs later in the class, when a white resident attempts to make a point about how curriculum seems to be even more important than responsive management: "In order for kids to be engaged and care, you have to have a curriculum that facilitates that. At Xanadu, the curriculum is so interesting." Taylor responds to this comment by challenging the overly rosy view of Xanadu and its curriculum. She explains that an African American student at the school complained to her because his Xanadu homeroom teacher "didn't want to touch slavery" in the curriculum; as a white male, the teacher was "not comfortable teaching [it]." Taylor then responds more directly, "I agree with you that we have a great curriculum and great teachers, but I don't know everything that's going on in classrooms. I have heard throughout the years that there are teachers who are not comfortable teaching certain things. The children are aware of this." I have never heard Taylor express a critical word about Xanadu in coursework, but here she implies to all the residents that Xanadu is not the perfect place they think it is; teachers here are just as susceptible to racism and white fragility as they are anywhere else. Taylor concludes that residents have a "responsibility" to help their colleagues move past racial discomfort like this.

In both instances, Taylor exerts a more authoritative tone and inserts a little more of her own perspective than usual. Neither interaction feels uncomfortable to me as the observer, but I do notice that her comments are laced with a critical tone that might cause residents discomfort. Emma later tells me that in an environment where conversations of race are not "part of the fabric of what's happening every day," being pushed by the only person of color in power in the school to have explicit conversations about race, to become more culturally competent, and to speak up when colleagues prioritize their own comfort on issues of race could feel like "too much, too soon."

While most people of color face the realities of this institutional racism on a daily basis, one of the many privileges granted to white people in our current system is the ability to be "color blind" or maintain "racial isolation." As such, white people often exhibit forms of what scholar Robin DiAngelo calls "white fragility" when forced to confront glaring evidence of racism or the benefits afforded to individuals based on white skin.[9] Common white responses include denial, defensiveness, guilt, self-righteousness, and complacence. Courtney's response to *White Like Me* is a clear example of this, but other residents' responses to Taylor in the Equity course also seem to fall in line with this definition. Such responses allow individuals to remove themselves from the conversation, to turn inward in escape. Taylor sometimes challenges residents to move beyond these responses; but at other times, she might not "push" residents enough.

Although I do not observe the afternoon session on white privilege because Taylor thinks residents might feel too vulnerable for observers, I later hear about it. Taylor tells me, "We eased into the Peggy McIntosh piece and I was surprised by how superficial [the conversations were], how we weren't able to go much deeper and I didn't want to push too hard." While Taylor does occasionally assert her expertise, and believes "discomfort is productive," she also intentionally tries to "create a space where the residents feel safe" (hence "eas[ing]" into the piece and asking me not to observe this session). This balance between productive discomfort and safety proves precarious when discussing race.

Elisabeth similarly remembers this discussion of white privilege feeling somewhat superficial, but she attributes this to a lack of time (which she recalls as approximately 20 minutes) and "structure" for the discussion of a "sensitive topic." This causes me to wonder about the limits of the constructivist resident-led pedagogy often employed in PTR. When Ashley speaks up in PTR coursework about her own perspectives and experiences, it feels powerful and important. For example, when she discloses her fears about her brother entering public spaces where he could be threatened with racial violence, the room grows heavy with realization about the human toll racism takes. However, one resident alone cannot be expected to carry the entire conversation, and Ashley does not always choose to speak. As Taylor observes of progressive environments, "Who you surround yourself with, it does matter. Who is around the table does deepen, push, strengthen, affirm the thinking about a variety of issues. The more difference, the richer, even if it is uncomfortable at times." The sea of white faces influences the direction of residents' journey in coursework on race, and when Taylor overtly exerts her positional authority, it is as if she must paddle alone against the tide.

However, it is possible that the Equity course was not as productive as it could have been because it lacked structure or organization in general. Both Leah and Elisabeth suggest that while they were both excited about the syllabus and the potential of the course, it did not live up to their expectations in execution. Leah suggests that this is partially because Taylor is "so disorganized" and struggles to "stick to a syllabus." Elisabeth echoes this, suggesting, "I feel like the syllabus was sort of. . . . It was there, but a lot of it changed . . . we didn't really cover everything I thought we would." However, Elisabeth acknowledges that the snow days disrupted a few sessions.

But some of the seeming disorganization of the course, or lack of structure in discussions, could stem from the absence of an overarching framework, a set of tools, or a guiding mission around the education of students of color or advancement of social justice more generally. In some ways, it seems that residents acquire pieces of a puzzle without an underlying reference point for how to link these pieces together in their practice. It is all implicit; it is mostly "stealth." Leah later reflects that she does feel compelled to "become an agent of change in your classroom," a part of Taylor's vision that transferred to the residents. But Leah adds, "I didn't have a sense of how hard that is in the context of adults in big schools. I didn't feel I had a sense of how to do so." Thus, while their views on progressive pedagogy have been anchored at Xanadu, residents' thinking around race is still in flux, possibly because the program lacks explicit scaffolds to support this.

In the end, Taylor reflects that she would probably give this class "a C" grade for implementation. Nonetheless, the texts residents read, the ideas presented throughout the course, and even Taylor's insistent points about the importance of racial competence seem to have some influence on the residents. Leah, too, acknowledges that there was value in "reading and talking about" race regularly with the cohort in this setting, and admits that "even if I wish that she [Taylor] taught it differently, I think I am glad of the syllabus and glad of the idea[s]." Confronting racism and privilege through reading and discussion is a helpful first step in grappling with white fragility,[10] but as Leah realized by reading *White Like Me*, combatting racism is not "just an idea . . . at some point there needs to be action."

DIPPING A TOE INTO CLASSROOM DISCUSSIONS

PTR's coursework—including the Issues of Equity course—ends up preparing residents to have some conversations about race, racism, and privilege in schools. Just as many of the residents tell me they feel comfortable having such conversations with Mary, Emma (who represents "stealth diversity"), and each other, most also end up feeling comfortable and confident enough to broach these kinds of conversations while student teaching mostly white classes at Xanadu. As Sam explains, "There [are] some things that it's better for me to be talking about with a group of adults before I try to deal with it with a group of kids." So while conversations of race sometimes feel superficial or stagnant in PTR sessions, they seemingly prepare residents to initiate similar discussions with their students.

Throughout the winter and spring, I observe or hear about residents leading discussions about race in their own student teaching placements. For example, during a December solo teaching day, I see Leah holding an impromptu Socratic discussion about police brutality in the cases of Eric Garner and Michael Brown (I discuss this episode more in Chapter 6). Moreover, Elisabeth tells me that during her Xanadu solo week in December, she and her students also discussed "Ferguson . . . and Eric Garner," because the students "were really feeling these current events very acutely in their lives, and so we were able to make a very clear connection between the idea of othering people in Salem and how the Puritans treated people who were perceived as outsiders, and then the way today, we still sometimes treat people as outsiders or other." In the spring, I also watch Sam teach a lesson at Xanadu on the Civil War novel *Lola LeRoy*, considering the advantages and disadvantages that characters are afforded because of their racial appearance. When Sam later connects this to the abolition movement, students identify how white abolitionists were more readily able to advance the cause because of the color of their skin.

However, just as is the case in PTR, these critical conversations in Xanadu classrooms might be limited by the homogeneity of the student population. Anna, a white secondary humanities resident, explains:

> I think that the discussions of structural and institutionalized racism, as much as one might try to prevent it, the eyes do fall on the one kid of African American descent in the room to say, "Speak to the Black experience with racism." So, it's been hard to really foster an open dynamic where one person isn't speaking for the experience of their race but also that's open to hearing their one experience and hearing the experiences and opinions of kids who have never thought about racism.

Although PTR residents push their students to consider issues like structural racism, police brutality, and other forms of oppression, these conversations may only go so deep when so few students have personal experience with these issues.

PTR does end up supporting residents to have critical discussions about racism and unjust social structures with students, or at least with students who look like them. Unsurprisingly, it is easier for white people to have conversations about race with other white people. This is nontrivial, especially at a school where some teachers avoid the topic of race altogether. And in a sense, this might fulfill part of Taylor's vision: PTR residents can go on to teach primarily white students to become more critically conscious and racially aware. However, this does not mean the residents feel equally empowered to teach students of color.

In the spring, residents begin expressing hesitation about teaching in an urban and/or public school. Part of this likely stems from the way residents become inculcated in the "cozy" garden of Xanadu and wish to find a similar place to teach. But it also might be because their fieldwork has not prepared them for the realities of teaching in other schools. As Elisabeth acknowledges, "Xanadu is a little sheltered" and residents on campus do not learn about the realities of standardized test pressures, differentiating curriculum for students with disabilities or English language learners, or explicitly teaching about the culture of power.

Moreover, the lack of fieldwork with racially diverse students is essentially a comment upon what the program considers "quality student teaching placements." By placing residents with predominantly white students, the program unintentionally perpetuates notions of white supremacy.[11] If PTR does not emphasize work with students of color, why would residents feel it necessary to seek out positions that serve nonwhite students?

Later, when I ask Leah if she feels PTR prepared her to teach students who come from different backgrounds than her own, she acknowledges, "I don't know, is the short version. Probably the more honest answer is, not really. . . . I feel like I wish I could say yes and I think PTR wishes they could say yes, but I think also does acknowledge that while they talk about it sometimes they do not really provide experiences [in] preparation." Thus, while PTR equips residents to have critical discussions of race and racism with white students, the white residents graduating from the program in this cohort do not seem to feel comfortable bringing their progressive pedagogical approach to schools that primarily serve students of color. In a program that relies heavily on the power of teaching through modeling, it is unsurprising that the residents do not feel comfortable teaching a population of students with whom they have very little experience.

RIPPLES IN THE WATER

Taylor envisions preparing "change agents" through PTR to address oppressive forces through curriculum and pedagogy that actively confronts current events and historical legacies. She hopes that residents will bring their transformative pedagogy to both white students and students of color, affluent students and those from low-income backgrounds. But this vision, like much of the discussion of race on Xanadu's campus, is muffled or conducted below the surface.

PTR is nested in an institutional context with a legacy of white supremacy. Serving students of elite white families for generations—as an escape from the racially diverse urban center—Xanadu has long been isolated from the realities of racism and oppression. As such, white teachers at Xanadu feel entitled to avoid critical conversations of race. But they proudly confront LGBT issues. This discrepancy seems to reflect white fragility, for while straight privilege is a pertinent issue, it is less visible, less threatening to white people, and less palpable at a school where the preeminent leader is openly gay. LGBT issues also seem to have recent social momentum with the legalization of gay marriage. In contrast, the battle for racial equity has been visibly waged for centuries, but institutional racism persists. So while Xanadu might have once been on the forefront of civil rights issues, the fight against racism here has fallen below the surface. Taylor is the only school leader who still perceives racism to be a real threat, as she knows from experience that it is. But she, too, feels the need to be sensitive to the white fragility of the residents and the school faculty.

PTR—which emphasizes residents' comfort, safety, and personal experiences—is heavily focused on sensitivity in discussions of race. Taylor uses coded language in program documents, and Emma avoids discussing course texts with Xanadu teachers. Emma tries to make residents feel comfortable by listening without challenging residents' white fragility, as exemplified in Courtney's outburst against *White Like Me*. Taylor, too, tries to avoid "push[ing] too hard" with residents; and when she occasionally challenges them to think deeper, they react defensively. But in the process of this sensitivity, this careful "push[ing]" with extensive opportunities for self-reflection (as discussed in Chapter 4), residents do learn about racism on both institutional and individual levels.

In PTR coursework, residents have space to share their own experiences and opinions around race and privilege, which is a helpful first step in grappling with white fragility.[12] These conversations sometimes feel fragmented or stagnant, in that they are not oriented around any explicit mission, grounded with concrete strategies for culturally responsive instruction, or enriched by a racially diverse cohort. But just as treading water is a demanding form of exercise requiring much work under the surface, these conversations on race seem to help residents develop their muscles of racial competence and leave ripples of change in their thinking. Some residents end up feeling comfortable discussing racism and police brutality in student teaching with their mostly white students, which is no trivial feat, especially at a place like Xanadu. This suggests that open conversations about race and privilege, regardless of how messy they seem to be, may be influential for new teachers' proficiency in initiating difficult conversations with their future students.

One recent study found that progressive schools today effectively teach students to think critically and "analyze the causes of racial inequality," but that these institutions may not provide adequate opportunities for students to transform this learning into actions that challenge such inequality.[13] This finding seems to extend to the residents from PTR, as their newfound awareness about and comfort discussing race does not translate into a desire to confront systems of oppression by working with students of color. Residents complete their most influential fieldwork at Xanadu, with a population of students that is largely affluent and white. Here, they do not learn about the necessity of teaching skills of navigation—which are still important for students of color who must learn the "dominant language" in order to change it[14]—likely because the privileged students they student teach already possess such skills. There are no overarching frameworks, no explicit vision for serving students of color, nor do they have opportunities to practice this work in student teaching. This preserves residents' racial isolation and dissuades them from working in more racially diverse schools.

Ultimately, PTR challenges residents to consider their own privilege, discuss institutional racism and police brutality, and advance the critical consciousness of their mostly white students through similar means. Because of this, PTR graduates might end up changing the way that some privileged students think about the world; and this could fulfill part of Taylor's social justice vision, as residents might positively "impact future police officers, state attorneys" and other influential figures to change their racist thoughts and behaviors. Nonetheless, this cohort of PTR graduates may not change who has *access* to the student-centered, asset-based, critical progressive pedagogy espoused by PTR because of where they ultimately choose to teach (as I will discuss more in the next chapter). And in the end, PTR and its graduates seem poised to primarily advance the educational and life outcomes of already privileged students.

NOTES

1. Fallace, Thomas. (2015). *Race and the origins of progressive education, 1880–1929.* New York, NY: Teachers College Press, p. 125.

2. Graham, Patricia A. (2005). *Schooling America.* New York, NY: Oxford University Press, p. 53.

3. Graham, *Schooling America.*

4. Fallace, *Race and the origins of progressive education*, p. 125.

5. Fallace, *Race and the origins of progressive education*; Graham, *Schooling America.*

6. Bonilla-Silva, Eduardo. (2014). *Racism without racists: Color-blind racism and the persistence of racial inequality in America.* Lanham, MD: Rowman & Littlefield.

7. Delpit, Lisa. (2012). *Multiplication is for white people.* New York, NY: New Press.

8. Lemov, Doug. (2010). *Teach like a champion: 49 techniques that put students on the path to college.* San Francisco, CA: Jossey-Bass.

9. DiAngelo, Robin. (2011). White fragility. *International Journal of Critical Pedagogy, 3*(3), 54–70.

10. DiAngelo, White fragility.

11. Souto-Manning, Mariana. (2018). Toward praxically-just transformations: Interrupting racism in teacher education. *Journal of Education for Teaching, 45*(1), 97–113.

12. DiAngelo, White fragility.

13. Seider, Scott, Jennett, Pauline, Graves, Daren, Gramigna, Kathryn, El-Amin, Aaliyah, Yung, Jennifer, Clark, Shelby, Kenslea, Megan, Soutter, Madora, Sklarwitz, Sherri, & Tamerat, Jalene. (2016). Preparing adolescents attending progressive and no excuses urban charter schools to analyze, navigate, and challenge race & class inequality. *Teachers College Record, 118.*

14. El-Amin, A. (2015). *"Until justice rolls down like water": Revisiting emancipatory schooling for African Americans—A theoretical exploration of concepts for liberation* (Unpublished doctoral dissertation). Harvard University, Cambridge, MA.

Chapter Six

Learning the Ropes

Keeping in mind that just the slightest shift in the direction of the bow (or front) of a ship will set its course for the many miles ahead, imagine the impact you can have in just 1 year, in 1 week, in 1 day, and even sometimes in one moment to help set the ship's or child's course .—Mary, PTR assistant director

Many teacher education programs throw mentor teachers and novices together without much help or instruction.[1] This results in inconsistent student teaching placements: some preservice teachers have great experiences with mentors who model excellent teaching practices and support them to develop instructional acumen, while others may have neglectful, authoritarian, or generally ineffective mentors. No Excuses Teacher Residency avoids this pitfall by removing the mentor teacher entirely and relying instead on trained instructional coaches who enter classes at scheduled times and provide prescribed feedback (as described in Chapter 3). But Progressive Teacher Residency (PTR) takes a different tact: carefully matching, training, observing, and supporting the pairings of guiding teachers (GTs) and residents at Xanadu Community School. The residents who elect for a spring placement in a public school, though, experience something a bit different.

PTR relies on a model of supportive mentorship because faculty believe that new teachers should learn the ropes of this challenging profession from experienced educators. Residents at PTR have a range of mentors—the program directors, their advisors, and each other—but their most profound mentors are undeniably their GTs. Each resident has the opportunity to learn from two different GTs over the course of the year. In the fall semester, all the residents are placed with GTs at Xanadu; in the spring, residents have the opportunity to select a placement with a GT at a local public school or continue at Xanadu. Both GTs serve as mentors who model effective teaching practices and support residents to take on increasingly more responsibil-

113

ity until they reach "solo week," where they teach by themselves for a whole week at the end of the semester.

Mary (PTR's assistant director) emphasizes the importance of being supported throughout this experience: "It's a program that focuses a lot on the importance of mentorship. And I think most people who leave this program know that they need to continue to find mentors in their lives, and continue to ask for feedback 10 years down the road." Instead of ascribing to the individualistic "sink or swim" method of preparing teachers, PTR believes that growing as an educator requires intensive support and feedback from others throughout a career. Residents become accustomed to this at Xanadu in the fall, and perhaps even learn to rely upon it.

Because Xanadu is a relatively small school, and PTR only has 16 residents to support at a time, the directors are able to keep a close eye on all the resident–GT pairings on campus. Teachers at the school are expected to support residents at some point in their career, and many welcome it as a chance to learn from "new blood." GTs are not financially compensated for their mentorship, but they are supported. This begins with a large notebook for GTs that provides instructions on how to best support PTR residents. The PTR directors also "watch over" and provide "constant feedback" on the partnership in the fall, ensuring that it is functioning well in terms of planning, coteaching, and debriefing lessons. PTR also holds course sessions where GTs and residents work together to improve their coteaching experiences. The resulting partnership they create becomes the lynchpin of residents' educational evolution at PTR: learning the ropes of teaching by practicing under the guidance of experts.

Most residents cite their fall student teaching at Xanadu as the most influential experience for their developing practice. Donna (an elementary resident) describes why:

> I'd say for me, what was most helpful this year was really my fall placement. . . . The learning curve was probably much steeper for me in the fall, but I also clicked really well with the woman I was working with, in terms of her sense of humor, even her voice level, but really her style and personality aligned with mine; so in that regard, everything she was doing, I can see myself emulating: the way she listened to kids, the way she problem solved, her classroom management style. . . . So for me really being able to watch her, and her too, forcing me to start those conversations [about practice].

What Donna describes is an immersive apprenticeship with a well-selected mentor who supports her progress through modeling and feedback. This is the pairing that Xanadu aspires to create for every resident in every placement, but such a standard is not easy to achieve.

Taylor is quite intentional about establishing these resident–GT pairings at Xanadu, carefully considering what she knows of their personalities and experiences before placing them together. She is able to do this in the fall because she has relationships with all of the Xanadu teachers and has sought out extensive information about the residents. And most of the residents I interview say they are pleased with their fall GTs. For example, Jackie (an elementary resident) asserts, "I had the best 4 months of my life, I think in the fall, and Taylor will say it too, that [my GT] and I are the best matched resident–mentor teacher ever."

But these pairings are not always ideal. Emma (a PTR faculty member and Xanadu teacher) tells me about the first resident she was paired with: an older woman who had had a high-powered career and raised two daughters. The resident's identity factors caused Emma to assume that she would be able to manage Emma's classroom of middle school students, but Emma soon found that "my students walked all over her." While Emma tried to help this resident learn to effectively manage a class, she describes the mentoring experience as "hard."

While not all the resident–GT pairings result in close personal relationships, every resident I interview in this cohort credits their fall GT as helping them develop as a teacher and person. And the recipe for this successful pairing seems to boil down to a careful balance between what Emma calls "freedom and feedback." Residents talk about the incredible "feedback" they receive on their teaching, lesson planning, student interactions, and general thinking about teaching. This is not directive feedback, but the kind of feedback that inspires self-reflection. Nancy (an elementary resident) explains,

> It's so nice coming into a program where every day, you're asked to question yourself, your GTs are questioning [you], also offering suggestions, they're also questioning themselves. I mean, kinda like, "I wonder why I taught a lesson that way," or "I should have done this differently," or "This really worked for these kids but not for these other ones."

Elisabeth (a secondary humanities resident) says that she ends up discussing "philosophical questions about approaches to teaching, but also really concrete things" with her GT. She adds that she really values the "reflection" she engages in through these conversations, which occur "about twice a week, once to talk about curriculum for the week and then once to talk about my personal and professional growth in the program." In these exchanges, GTs do not seem to uphold themselves as the ultimate authority in all things teaching but instead seem to pose questions to the residents that facilitate their own personal understanding and growth, as is consistent with progressive education more generally.

On the other hand, GTs grant residents a great deal of freedom to play, to make mistakes, and try again, particularly during solo teaching. GTs may help residents plan for these moments, but residents are given the freedom to design their own curriculum and instructional strategies for solo time. And then GTs leave the classroom and residents have complete freedom as the only adult around for a week or more (a structure that might not be possible in public schools where a teacher of record legally must remain in the room). Meredith explains, "I think the fun thing with Xanadu, they let you play. . . . If you fall flat on your face, that's okay. You'll have another class." There is not a sense of urgency or a need for perfection during solo week, even though they are working with actual students. Elisabeth feels this freedom helps residents to develop their own unique approach to teaching because in PTR, "there's not one way to be a teacher."

The unique nature of the Xanadu student teaching placement makes these clinical placements what they are. Residents become immersed in the classroom: they observe, they support instruction, they coteach, they discuss educational philosophies, and receive extensive feedback. Then they reflect on their experiences with GTs, in writing, in coursework, and with each other. Finally, they get to solo teach in the moments, days, and a full week where the GT leaves the room and allows the resident to take the helm. In these ways, GTs at Xanadu deploy the various forms of expertise that McDonald, Bowman, and Brayko identify to support new teachers' relational learning: "knowledge, modeling practice, articulating practice, inviting candidates into practice, and providing guided assistance."[2] And the residents tell me that this experience is the most influential in their learning about how to connect with individual students.

But can learning to teach in this unusual and privileged setting truly prepare residents to teach in other schools? And what about those who elect to student teach at a public school in the spring?

BEGINNING IN SAFE HARBOR

Time and again, I hear residents tell me that Xanadu is "safe." As I have discussed in Chapter 5, Xanadu seems to feel safer for the LGBT students and faculty than for the students and faculty of color. But in many ways, the school does work toward establishing a supportive community for students and residents that sets it apart from other schools.

Leah, a secondary humanities resident, explains, "There's a wider school culture that's very explicit about being kind and being inclusive. And that it's sort of the Xanadu way." I identify this as a common refrain. The focus on kindness and inclusivity begins within the classroom, from preschool onward; but the school also consistently reinforces these ideas through assemblies, field trips, and community-building events. Students learn to work together and accept one another: it's the Xanadu way.

Because of this unique culture, Xanadu has not felt the need to set up explicit structures for behavior management or discipline. Instead, how well the classroom and school community functions largely relies upon relationships between teachers and students. John, Leah's fall GT at Xanadu, says, "We don't have a real formal disciplinary system here at Xanadu, so a lot of the ways that you assuage . . . problematic behavior . . . [are by] having a conversation [with students] rather than exacting punishment."

Leah tells me that she has learned a great deal from watching John engage in this kind of relational management: "I think what strikes me about him is the way he is really good at noticing that something needs to be said, and taking a student aside and saying it in a really thoughtful way that they will . . . respect and hear." She adds that his classroom management often consists of establishing "a partnership" with students toward better behavior, which starts with individual conversations with them where he says, "I know you can do better and I know you want to do better than this." And "I'm not angry at you. But we're working together on this." For John, and seemingly many other teachers at Xanadu, classroom management is a function and extension of teacher–student relationships, a philosophy Leah absorbs both in PTR coursework and through her experiences with John.

Leah is one of the residents whom I follow into student teaching, and later into her first year of full-time practice. She initially strikes me as laid back and confident. She often wears flowing bohemian skirts with her hair in a long dark French braid. When she speaks in PTR coursework, which she does economically, her voice is loud and poised, her contributions incisive and critical. The eldest child of two lawyers, a graduate of an Ivy League university, and a Fulbright scholar who served in Tajikistan, Leah comes to this program with an impressive pedigree. But she in no way reads as an elitist. She makes easy friendships with everyone in the cohort and engages others with self-effacing humor. Leah also admits to being hard on herself, especially when it comes to classroom management; but John tells me she just needs to develop more "confidence."

To understand more about their teaching partnership and the way classroom management functions in the "safe" Xanadu classroom, I observe the pair on a day in which John leads the sixth-grade class. John is a tall man in his 30s who has the look of an outdoorsman, wearing a red-, white-, and blue-plaid long-sleeved collared shirt, khaki-colored Carhartt pants, and brown hiking shoes. His stance is laid back; his gait conveys self-assurance and ease in this setting. The students have just finished a test, and John picks up an African hand drum and pats on it a few times to secure their attention. One girl shouts to her peers in an assertive tone, "Be quiet!" As students quiet down, a boy observes, "That was like 3 seconds," in reference to how long it took for everyone to focus up front. These comments seem to indicate that at least some of the students are invested in supporting John's management, allowing him to exert minimal effort to capture their attention.

When the students are all quiet, John tells them that today they will be discussing the book they are reading together: *Home of the Brave*, in which a Sudanese refugee recounts his journey to America through verse. John's voice is calm, low, and melodic, easy to listen to. He asks the students, "What is the point of reading a book together?" Several hands go up and John calls on them one by one.

"To hear other people's experiences with the book," one student offers.

"To share [the] experience. Discuss different points of view," another student adds.

John initially scribbles these responses on the whiteboard, his back to the students, who wait patiently for the next person to be called upon to share. Leah notices this and gets up from her seat to take John's place as scribe; no verbal communication needed. Relieved of his scribing duties, John walks over to a side table and grabs a small carton of orange juice, presumably left over from student snack, to sip while he walks around the room. He calls on another student. As the discussion continues, John casually moves over to an unoccupied desk and sits down. I smile at the spectacle of the large man in a tiny desk sipping his small carton of orange juice like a student. But neither the students nor Leah seem to view John's behavior as unusual, and he continues to facilitate the discussion from his new location.

Later, after having returned to the front of the classroom, John introduces the next activity, where students will analyze similes from the book. A student raises a hand and asks if she can share a random coincidence with the class. John signals that she can. She proceeds to offer an anecdote about a song she sang at a recital that is unrelated to the content at hand. John does not dismiss her off-topic remarks, which seem to feel important to her; instead, he nods and quickly moves on without further comment. Two boys then move over to the whiteboard and climb on chairs so they can serve as scribes for this next activity.

Throughout the remainder of the lesson, I notice the freedom students have to move around. A student jumps out of her seat to help another read the next simile/metaphor. Then another student walks in from outside, presumably having grabbed water or gone to the restroom without asking permission (which is not required here). And another student stands near the side desk where the leftover snack sits and shovels saltine crackers into his mouth. One of the scribes on the chair up front plays with the refrigerator poetry that is scattered across the board while he is waiting to record the next connotation. John and Leah ignore these movements, just as students pay no heed to John's idiosyncratic behaviors, and the lesson continues uninterrupted. Most students continue to follow the discussion without pause, referencing their books and taking notes. And those who step away for a moment soon return.

Again, I cannot help but notice the stark difference between the freedom afforded children here and the control imposed upon students in no excuses schools.

As a teacher, John remains assertive but calm. He models patience with students, ignores most of the off-task behavior, casually reminds students to return to the task at hand or raise their hands to contribute to class discussion, but never alters the tenor of his own relaxed voice. Leah circulates in a supportive role, pointing to the work at hand or placing her hand on a student's shoulder as a soft reminder to focus to the lesson. The classroom resembles an ordered freedom: students in and out of seats, moving around, fidgeting and eating, but never interrupting the lesson. And when John directly requests a behavior, students acquiesce.

John's overall classroom management strategy is effective, but subtle. Students clearly respect John and respond to him without question, but their restless preteen energy bubbles just below the surface. Moreover, it occurs to me that this kind of classroom management—one without an explicit set of rules or consequences—is perhaps more readily achievable at Xanadu, where there is an expectation of kindness and no expectation of disciplinary consequences. When I observe Leah during a solo teaching day, I witness how she manages to continue this culture in John's absence.

During the week of resident solo teaching in December, I walk into the sixth-grade classroom where Leah is already involved in facilitating a Socratic discussion of recently publicized police brutality with this same group of students. This strikes me as a brave conversation to be having on her own (for John will not be in the room during solo week) and so early in her teaching career. She later tells me this was an impromptu lesson, one that was not planned but rather initiated by the students. The intended lesson for the day was a discussion about Islam in preparation for their art lesson on the tessellations common in mosques. But before I arrived today, when Leah went to open this discussion, a student raised his hand and conveyed what Leah read as an "urgent need" to discuss the Eric Garner case, as the jury had just delivered its verdict failing to indict the police officer responsible for this man's death. Because John facilitated a discussion about Michael Brown's death by police in Ferguson the previous week, Leah has decided to allow space for students to discuss Eric Garner's case today as a "follow-up."

The class is set up in a messy "fishbowl" shape, with a small group of students in a rough circle at the center in the discussion, and a scattering of students surrounding it. Although this format usually indicates that only the students in the inner circle can speak while the outer circle observes before they switch positions, all students seem eligible to participate in this unscheduled discussion. And many seem eager to contribute, with multiple students jumping in at the same time. Leah reminds them, "We want one person to talk at a time we want to be extra respectful about this." As a couple students continue to speak simultaneously, she adds, "I need everyone to raise hands. This is very important and we want to hear each other."

One student raises a hand and volunteers, "If it was a Black police officer and a white man, they would have punished the Black police offer because people are so biased." Students jump in to respond, some offering comments that are only tangentially related to the Garner case. Leah redirects them, asking them to return to the case, and students begin raising their hands to ask clarifying questions. Leah recounts the facts of the case (such as what happened and whether there was an official trial). She adds thoughtfully, "You can talk to your parents about whether they think it's a good idea to watch the video. But there are a lot of questions about what happened." Then Leah calls upon students to share their opinions; some express frustration with police, some share anecdotes about the possibility of more harmony between police and people of color.

After about 20 minutes, Leah passes around blank note cards to all the students, asking them to write down a number from 1 to 10 to convey their interest in "talking more about Ferguson and/or Eric Garner or policing or protests." Then she asks them to add a few sentences in response to "How are you feeling [about this]?" This allows students an opportunity to voice their feelings in a less public forum and gives the chance to continue the discussion if they would like. As they complete their note cards, Leah tells them "Thank you all for listening to each other. Because it's a difficult subject and people can get really upset. It is our job as a classroom community to listen to each other and to be respectful. That is part of being in the Xanadu community, too." And when students have turned in their note cards, Leah moves on to introduce her scheduled lesson, "geometry in Islamic art," which she created because all PTR residents must design at least one art-related lesson.

When Leah later reflects on her solo teaching more broadly, she focuses on what she perceives were deficits in her teaching. In a PTR course session devoted to reflecting on solo week, Leah wonders aloud, "There were moments where I saw gaps or needs, areas where I don't have disciplinary tools. Is that a gap [in me] as an educator or a gap in me as a person? Where I am just not willing to be strict enough with them." And she later tells me that she also feels like she needs more development in "general classroom management skills," and wishes PTR coursework did more to supplement the implicit management she absorbs from John. Of course, most new teachers also cite "classroom management" as the single topic in which they feel they needed more preparation.[3]

When I consider the above observation of Leah, though, I primarily see strengths. Leah displays willingness to alter her lesson on the spot to honor students' needs and interests in the moment. Many new teachers tend to strictly stick to their planned lessons, as if even slight deviations could derail their entire day. Leah designed a unique and sophisticated lesson—one that brings to bear her previous experiences and education to teach culture, art, religion, and history—but when a profound teachable moment presents itself, she rolls with it, and makes space for students to process publicly disturbing events. Although Leah must remind students multiple times to speak one at a time or raise their hands, students take her redirections and gentle guidance in stride and clearly feel safe enough with her to share their questions and opinions about this volatile case. This says a lot about how well she has been able to build relationships with them over the semester.

Leah's willingness to engage in a discussion of racism and police brutality also speaks of her sense of comfort in this space, and supports the idea that her PTR coursework on race has somewhat enabled her to be open to such conversations in the first place (as mentioned in Chapter 5). To top it off, she manages to return to the meat of her scheduled lesson after 20 minutes without shutting any of the students down, and instead honoring their continuing interest and feelings about this topic with the note card. I am impressed.

The way that John and Leah teach and manage the class in these examples is enabled, at least in part, by Xanadu's unique culture. Here, their efforts are uninhibited by standards for academics or behavior, cushioned by the inherent safety of the culture, and bolstered by the expectation that both teachers and students can construct the learning for the day. They have freedom (and in Leah's case, the preparation in PTR) to entertain digressions, support student movement or requests, and alter lesson plans on the spot. Teachers are seen as facilitators here, not disciplinarians. So at Xanadu, a resident in her first week of solo teaching can alter a lesson she designed on the spot to engage in a respectful conversation about racism and police brutality, without resistance or recourse. But few schools are like Xanadu, and when the residents venture beyond this safe harbor, they may not be prepared for the realities that await them.

COLD AND CHOPPY SEAS

A bitterly cold and historically snowy winter settles upon the city for the spring semester. It cancels several school days, delays multiple course sessions for PTR, and leaves many residents adrift in their placements, separated from the warm Xanadu community to which they have become accustomed. Eight of the residents are placed at Belmoor School, a mostly white K–8 public school in an affluent suburb; meanwhile, two residents are placed at City Middle School (CMS), which serves a racially diverse population of students in a mixed-income urban area. Taylor determined these placements based on residents' expressed interests, assigning the two residents more interested in teaching at urban schools to a placement at CMS.

While Mary and Taylor cruise over to these public schools at least six times throughout the spring to observe residents and their new GTs, they are not able to provide the same amount of support for the pairs that they did at Xanadu. There are no PTR sessions for the public school GTs to attend, nor do these GTs seem to receive any feedback on their mentorship. The residents in public schools also no longer have the opportunity to drop by Taylor's or Mary's office during the day. In some ways, these placements have cut the cord between these residents and Xanadu.

Almost all the residents I interview who opted for a public school placement in the spring characterize it as challenging and disappointing. Jackie tells me, "The transition is hard into the second placement. . . . January was really hard." She goes on to explain that she is struggling to "navigate a less cozy situation" at Belmoor. Because Xanadu is so nurturing and supportive, it is difficult for residents to leave it for a school that is much more traditional.

Donna explains this transition in more detail. She tells me, "It's very clear, both from my own experience, and I think I'm fair in speaking for others, that we aren't integrated or valued or acknowledged in the same way we were at Xanadu. . . . When there was a resident event, like Solo Week . . . the entire community kind of knew it, and you'd hear little snippets of encouragement here and there." And she contrasts this by explaining that at Belmoor—where she feels there is little community or camaraderie among the teachers—the PTR residents seem to be treated as "'others' that are taking up space in the classroom, or kind of getting in the way, or maybe kind of an extra burden on teachers." While residents were treated like valuable additions to the educational experience at Xanadu, they begin to feel like "burdens" at Belmoor.

Most of the residents also tell me that they have been largely disappointed by the pedagogical lessons, guidance, interaction, and/or support they have received from their GTs at their public school placements. Leah tells me that her guiding teacher did not really seem to "want to be a guiding teacher" because she did not offer Leah much guidance at all. She feels they were poorly matched, and that based on what she has heard, many "matches in the spring did not go as well." But Leah, quick to take responsibility, admits, "I think I could have gotten more out of it if I had asked more specifically and directly and adamantly for certain things." At Xanadu, Leah did not have to ask for much support or guidance from John, but this is not forthcoming at Belmoor.

Jackie, who loved her GT at Xanadu, also expresses disappointment in her guiding teacher at Belmoor. She tells me, "We definitely have very different teaching philosophies." Jackie further explains to me that her guiding teacher essentially handed her a binder at the beginning of the spring and told her, "It's your unit!" and she could do what she wanted with it for the classes she would be leading; but she did not feel he offered her much support in this process, nor did he seem to have time to discuss the curriculum with her.

Of course, this observed difference in support between Xanadu and public school teachers is not one that can be solely attributed to the GTs themselves. It takes a lot of time, intention, and support to guide new teachers. While faculty at Xanadu have many resources to support their mentorship—including the fact that mentorship is built into the culture of Xanadu—the teachers in public schools are largely left to their own devices when it comes to mentoring their PTR resident. These public school partnerships are a recent addition to PTR, and Taylor does not seem to have close relationships with the guiding teachers at these other schools. Moreover, these public school teachers have numerous additional drains on their time and energy that Xanadu teachers do not, including up to 80 students to serve at a time, a plethora of standards to cover, various differentiations and accommodations to make for students with disabilities or those whose first language is not English, and classroom management issues brought about by poverty, hunger, or racism. This public school placement thus seems to more closely resemble the student teaching placements characteristic of traditional teacher education programs: they are variable and not well connected to program coursework, but they give preservice teachers a more realistic taste of working in traditional schools.

Some of the residents feel like this experience of teaching in a public school is essential to their ability to move beyond Xanadu. For example, Nancy appreciates that "there's like a different perspective and point of view that I'm seeing [here at Belmoor], and it's raising questions I wouldn't even have thought about had I stayed at Xanadu for the whole year. So curricularly and just professionally, [I'm learning] what it really looks like to teach a class of such diverse learners." Thus, those who venture to teach beyond the walls of Xanadu before they graduate from PTR may be better prepared for other schools than those who stay behind. For even Jackie, who complains a great deal about her spring placement, admits, "I needed to grow and learn and break away from the safeness of [my fall GT's] classroom."

Elisabeth, as one of the two residents placed at CMS, faces a situation that is even more distinctly different from Xanadu. While the eight residents at Belmoor have each other to commiserate with, Elisabeth and Gia are the only two residents at CMS. Additionally, CMS faces challenges that neither Xanadu nor Belmoor must consider; for example, 58% of the students at CMS qualify for free or reduced lunch and 27% have designated disabilities. Student discipline is an issue at the school, and teacher absenteeism is significantly higher than the state average. As a result, Elisabeth faces challenges of classroom management and differentiation for disabilities that most of her peers do not. Toward the end of the spring, Elisabeth tells me, "I felt very isolated for a lot of the semester . . . not feeling like there were other . . . people who I could talk to about what I was going through." Although she ultimately wants to serve a more culturally and socioeconomically diverse student population, the transition from Xanadu to CMS proves trying.

Elisabeth is the other PTR resident I will follow into the classroom after she graduates. When I go to observe Elisabeth in her spring placement, I get a sense of how different it is from Xanadu. Her classroom is illuminated only by long florescent lightbulbs, as the shades on the windows have been tightly closed to shut out sunlight. The gray-and-green-checkered tiled floors reflect the school's construction in the 1960s. Maps and posters—including images of Native Americans and African dancers, the pillars of Islam, and inspirational quotes—line the yellow-tinged walls. Despite the bright posters, the room feels stifling to me.

At the beginning of the day's lesson, Elisabeth takes the lead at the front of the room as students sit in their desks, which are organized in a loose circle. She uses a vivid map of India to display how to search for text features on an atlas. A few students wander in late, finding seats just outside the circle where they proceed to chat with one another; one boy taps repeatedly in a rhythm on his desk.

Elisabeth's guiding teacher, Pam—a casually dressed white woman who seems to wear her years of teaching experience in the wrinkles on her face—stands at the back of the room with a shrewd gaze trained on Elisabeth and the students before her. When Daniel, a student of color, gets out of his chair and begins to wander around, Pam tells him brusquely, "Get over here!" And then, in the middle of Elisabeth's lesson, Pam asks the class, "Who wants to see Daniel do some push-ups?" Several students yell out, "Me!" Pam jokes in a dry tone, "Two hundred thirty-seven push-ups!" Then she tells Daniel with a smirk, "Get back to your seat and quit being a smart-ass." Daniel returns to his seat, and Pam nods before joining the circle. This display seems to overshadow Elisabeth's soft-spoken style, and I cannot imagine a teacher ever saying this to one of the privileged students at Xanadu.

As Elisabeth continues to discuss topography in India so students can understand the geographic challenges of a battle that occurred on this terrain, several students engage in side conversations. Elisabeth pleads with them, "I just need you guys with me for one more minute." A student sharpens a pencil at the back. Two boys sitting next to each other continue to chat. "Does anyone have any idea what maritime means?" Elisabeth asks. "By the ocean," one student responds over the chatter of her peers. "Seriously, guys?" Elisabeth says to the off-topic students. "I know sitting in a circle is exciting; we will break into groups in one moment." She attempts to continue the discussion, but many students remain off task.

Elisabeth relents: "So I think we are going to break up now. I would like you to go to a table, you can choose who you are working with. . . . Groups of three or four." The students noisily move to tables throughout the room. Pam asks Elisabeth which group she would like for Pam to work with, and Elisabeth points to a group of boys, most of whom had engaged in side conversations throughout her lesson. Meanwhile, Elisabeth does her best to circulate around the room. The work at these groups appears variable: some of the students seem to work diligently and finish the task quickly, while others get sidetracked in conversations with their peers and do not complete the task before the bell rings.

When I later ask Elisabeth about this class, she tells me that she has had to deal with classroom management issues "24/7." Elisabeth's fall GT was one of the strictest and most orderly teachers at Xanadu. From him, Elisabeth learned a great deal about forming relations with students at the beginning and then using routines and protocols to manage a class, which worked well in the fall. But at CMS, she has not been able to use much of what she learned from her fall GT because her classes here operate under different rules amidst a different school culture. Additionally, she feels it has been "hard" to get to know all 80 of her students, especially when compared to the 16 she had in the fall.

Elisabeth also notes that the population at CMS is very different from Xanadu, and while some are the children of professors, others come from families with little money and no computer at home on which to complete assignments. Moreover, she acknowledges that Pam's teaching style is "distinctly different" from both her own style and that of her Xanadu GT, Jack (whose pedagogy she largely praises). She says this has caused some problems for her because when Pam gives her feedback, she says things that Elisabeth does not feel are helpful, like "Be bolder" or "Be more theatrical." While these strategies have apparently worked for Pam, they do not suit Elisabeth.

Elisabeth later tells me, "When you are so ensconced in one method, it is hard to code-switch to another place." Having been apprenticed into the importance of forming reciprocal relationships with all her students—as a means of designing lessons, caring for students, and managing a classroom—Elisabeth struggles when school structures and the classroom culture of her GT are not conducive to such connections. And it seems this insight applies to all the residents. Most elected to join PTR because of what they knew of Xanadu. The residents are passionate about progressive education when they enter the program and more passionate about it when they practically live it at Xanadu. And when they are separated from the place that gave them so much inspiration, and must transition to working in a very different environment—on much choppier waters—with dissimilar rules, policies, curricula, and philosophy, residents unsurprisingly find it cold, unsettling, and perhaps even disillusioning.

THE XANADU CURRENT

Later in the spring, at an evening event at Xanadu geared toward exploring new directions for PTR, I listen to Viola Martin talk about her experience with the five PTR graduates she hired in the past. Viola, a Black woman who used to teach at Xanadu, now directs the Douglass School, an urban independent school that serves African American boys from low-income backgrounds. She begins by acknowledging that Douglass School "wouldn't be what it is today" without the help of PTR graduates "who can dream with you." She further praises PTR graduates because "they *get* children; they know you have to be in relationships with children. They are gifted with curriculum . . . and progressive education." But she adds, "There have been challenges."

Some of Viola's challenges with PTR graduates stem from their "short life span" at the school. Viola explains, "One thing that contributes to that is classroom management. They buy into our mission. Some have taught at a traditional private school [first]. Then they are dealing with rambunctious boys, some of whom have issues. When they can't manage the class, they take it personally." She later adds, "One thing I realize having taught here at Xanadu is that you don't have to really manage children. Education is appreciated. When you go into a different situation where children don't know what is expected . . . you have to set up the culture, what your systems are so children can understand it. . . . How are these things going to line up?"

Viola's comments leave me with the sense that PTR graduates are quite relationally adept, that they understand students, care about students, can effectively enact progressive pedagogy, and have big ideas. But that they might initially struggle with classroom management in a dissimilar school, largely because this is so implicit at Xanadu, an extension of school culture, and thus it is not an explicit focus of PTR. Moreover, residents seem to take it personally when their approach to managing a classroom does not work the way they expected, likely because classroom management here is established as a function of the relationships each teacher has established with students.

Taylor works to maintain connections with public schools because she believes that public school teaching experience will help those who want to work in settings unlike Xanadu. Some research also suggests that extended clinical placements in particular contexts help equip teachers to work in similar settings.[4] But to realize this part of Taylor's vision, the residents would ultimately have to set their course toward public and/or urban schools in the end.

When I ask the residents where they are planning to teach the following year, few of them express interest in teaching in public or charter schools after graduation. For example, Donna tells me, "One thing that's been frustrating for me is I feel like while I've learned a lot about being in a public school, I feel like the quality of feedback and confident instruction and, I don't know, real investment in what I'm teaching is quite different, and I feel like what I've learned is that I don't really want to be in a public school." Instead of preparing Donna to teach in public schools, the spring placement dissuaded her from doing so entirely.

Although Elisabeth still voices interest in working in a public school, she is less certain about working in an urban setting. She explains, "When I entered this program, I initially thought that I would want to definitely be in a school similar to the population of students I worked with in City Year, and so, a large urban middle school. But now I feel like I could go a lot of different directions." City Year is a "gap year" service program in which recent college graduates are placed in urban Title-1 schools as "student success coaches" to further support student development. While she felt comfortable supporting students in urban schools through city year, Elisabeth is not confident in her ability to *teach* students in similar urban settings.

It seems that many of the residents' ideals have been challenged by the realities of working in less resourced spaces, made up largely of brick and concrete; in these spaces, instruction is fertilized with standards not the progressivism to which they have become accustomed. But instead of rejecting the program philosophy when it appears inconsonant with their school setting, the residents are rejecting schools that are not like Xanadu. Their preparation is quite influential.

Most of the residents want to teach at a place like Xanadu, where they feel their own needs can be better met. Nancy says she wants to teach at a school that has the kind of "community" she has found at Xanadu. Jackie tells me that the "coziness" that she experienced in the fall is "what I seek in my life going forward." Donna lists more specific requirements: "I think I need to be as an educator, in a place where the curriculum is rich and purposeful, that I can give students a reason why we're practicing certain skills, or meet them with genuine excitement when I launch a topic." She adds that she wants to teach at a school that supports meaningful projects and has "real resources." These residents have seen what is possible at a school with many structural advantages—like a rich history of progressive education, small class sizes, teacher autonomy, and a culture of mentorship—and so most of the residents seek out jobs at similar schools, where they can more readily enact the kind of teaching they learned in PTR. The current brings them back to Xanadu.

Taylor observes this trend and tells me, "Many residents are seeking places where they will have some freedom to develop curriculum, fewer discipline problems, so they can do what they enjoy doing. I heard that time and again '*I* want to be able to teach. . . .' '*I* am looking for a community like Xanadu.' [But] what is good for our students could be very good for other students in places where there is interest and need." When it comes to searching for a job after PTR, most of the residents look for a place that will fulfill *their* needs and desires first; and few of them express a desire to spread progressive pedagogy to areas where it is lacking. The intensive relational and resident-centered focus here—without an explicit collective vision for advancing social change—may have the unintentional side effect of nurturing what Jean Anyon would call "narcissism" in some residents (which I will discuss more in Chapter 7).[5]

Nonetheless, Taylor continues to believe in PTR's broad focus. She tells me, "Our mission is a good one. We are about preparing teachers for independent and public schools with the recognition that Xanadu's foundation and mission and project-based approach is good learning for any teacher to start out with. I believe what we are doing with our residents can be very useful and effective in urban public schools and traditional independent schools if there is an openness to it." Taylor is passionate about supporting residents to move onto public schools; in fact, it is one of the reasons she came to PTR. And while she acknowledges that Viola Martin from Douglass School implied PTR residents are "weak in some areas," Taylor insists, "I am not in the mind of only focusing on suburban public schools." This makes Taylor's job a lot harder, as preparing residents for a range of contexts is much more fraught and challenging than preparing them for one specific context.[6]

Regardless of Taylor's passion for serving students beyond schools like Xanadu, she and Mary seem to be cognizant of the fact that when residents initially leave the program, they might be better off starting at a school that can offer them more support. Elisabeth tells me about how she applied to a few jobs at more urban schools, but Taylor and Mary encouraged her to broaden her search to suburban schools. Elisabeth further explains that when she was offered a job at a suburban public school but was waiting on a more diverse urban school to respond to her interview (because it served a population she was more interested in working with), she asked Taylor for advice. Elisabeth remembers Taylor telling her, "You really want to get some good experience, get a couple years at a more suburban school, and then you can always go back to that [urban school] in the future." When I ask Elisabeth why she feels Taylor (and in some ways Mary, too) encouraged her to pursue the job at the suburban public school, she reflects, "The sense I got is that they just wanted me to feel really supported in my first year of teaching, and they weren't sure I was going to get that support [at the urban school]." So while PTR aims to prepare residents for a variety of school contexts, the directors also seem to acknowledge that some might not be ready to jump into an urban school without support right after graduation.

Institutions that are able to faithfully implement progressive education are beautiful and admirable, but the unique formula that enables them to thrive is complex and requires great resources. Viola Martin sheds light on the challenges of preparing residents within Xanadu for a school outside its walls. What works for Xanadu might not work in other contexts, as different groups of students in different school cultures and contexts have different needs. That is not to say that teachers cannot implement progressive pedagogy at public schools—there are many stories of teachers who have done just that—but it's not as easy as attempting to do so in a school where the whole community powerfully supports progressive education and reciprocal teacher–student relationships. Residents seem to learn this when they move into their public school placements in the spring, and most of them do not like the feeling. Taylor and Mary seem to understand this challenge and, in caring for their residents as human beings, wish for them to find a more supportive and congruent environment in which to begin their career.

SETTING SAIL

On a brisk summer day at the beginning of June, I drive through the gorgeous green neighborhood surrounding Xanadu. Although the clouds have obscured the sky for most of the day, the sun has decided to emerge now, as if gracing this graduation with light. I walk into the large Xanadu event hall that doubles as the teachers' lunchroom, which has deep brown wooden floors and a warm brick fireplace. Today, it is buzzing with excitement and chatter as residents stand by or sit with their families in the rows of chairs that face the front. All the residents who started the program will graduate today.

The residents greet me warmly, and I meet their families, who beam with pride as their children prepare to graduate from this prestigious teaching program. Then I see Taylor, who gives me a hug and tells me she practically considers me "family" at this point. Although I have tried to remain an impartial observer set apart from the group, I have realized that PTR is so close knit and relationship focused that few people would be able to enter this space repeatedly without becoming immersed in the community, which is perhaps why it is so hard for the residents to leave.

Mary steps up to the small podium in front of the fireplace and welcomes the residents and families to the graduation. I find her remarks to be thoughtful and reflective of many of PTR's ideals. She begins:

> Some might say that knowing as much as possible about your students is the
> most important part of the teacher's job. But what if it's just as important to

understand yourself to become an effective teacher? . . . If you aren't aware of who you are and what you have to bring and the things with which you struggle, and what makes you laugh or what questions inspire you, then the heart and soul of what happens in your classroom gets lost somehow.

And a program that began with a focus on the residents ends with this. Self-knowledge and reflection are paramount to teaching and connecting with students in the Xanadu way. And teacher authenticity feeds the "heart and soul" of the classroom.

Mary goes on to discuss the many images residents have evoked when discussing teaching. She says they have compared it to growing up, a sound-track, an airport, mining gold, and various books or movies. But she would like to add "just one more image" for this cohort:

Imagine a large ship in port. Actually, try to picture many, many ships in a port with billowing sails, all ready to head off to multiple destinations. I'd like the residents to imagine that those ships are the students they've already taught and those they will teach, and each ship carries boxes and parcels filled not with things but with the elements that make each child unique. Their triumphs, their failures, their families, their joys, their fears, all their experiences, and even their potential. Keeping in mind that just the slightest shift in the direction of the bow (or front) of a ship will set its course for the many miles ahead, imagine the impact you can have in just 1 year, in 1 week, in 1 day, and even sometimes in one moment to help set the ship's or child's course. It's both a responsibility and a privilege, and you all are ready.

As Mary concludes her opening remarks, I consider the way she has characterized teaching as helping to shape the course of a student's life. She, like Taylor, believes that students come to the classroom with numerous "elements" that make them special, but a teacher can have great influence over their life course. PTR faculty believe the teacher can thus serve as a "change agent" in society, as they send "ships" out from their classrooms and into the world.

Now the residents, too, will all leave this unique place, setting sail to new destinations. In her speech, Mary notes (as I have heard Taylor state before) that "children everywhere deserve" teachers like these residents: teachers who honor the whole child before them, engage them, challenge them to think critically, and design curriculum around them. But in their quest for personal development, support, and comfort, most of the residents pursue schools that serve children like those at Xanadu.

I discover that 12 of the 16 residents will move on to teach at independent schools, while Elisabeth, Courtney, and Leah will teach at nearby suburban public schools, and Ashley will initially venture out to an urban charter school in New York City.[7] This indicates to me that the public school placement might have actually had the opposite effect of the one intended: instead of equipping residents for public and/or urban schools, it dissuaded most of them from teaching in these contexts. The course of residents' lives has been influenced by the strong current of PTR, and I do not blame most of them for wanting to anchor themselves in schools like Xanadu, where they feel better able to live up to their teaching aspirations.

In many preparation programs, teachers focus on survival in their field-work, adopting strategies just to "get the job done," developing a myopic view of what it means to teach. And this can inhibit their advancement in the long run because these teachers may be reluctant to abandon these survival strategies, to grow.[8] But at Xanadu, residents have seen what is possible. It is a place where education revolves around the individual student, or the resident in PTR. A place where learning is active and fun, and the resulting community feels familiar, supportive, and safe. A place where teachers, residents, and students alike can all play, make mistakes, receive thoughtful feedback, reflect, and try again. It is a place where they can discover their authentic, "undivided self."[9]

But it is not a place that is grounded in reality, or at least the realities of most public schools. Like Samuel Taylor Coleridge's opium-induced dream of Xanadu in the poem "Kubla Khan," the world of education residents experience here is elusive, with its pastoral campus, immense resources, highly educated faculty, affluent student population, small class sizes, and pervasive progressive ideals. Residents find it hard to reconcile their fundamental preparation in this space when they enter public schools that are unlike it.

Still, there is something powerful about having the Xanadu experience, because wherever these residents eventually end up, a precedent or an ideal has been established, one they can grow toward. When these teachers form relationships with students in their future schools, they will think about the whole person before them. For they have learned to look for each students' strengths, to try to uncover the challenges that might impact their behavior in class, to offer empathy and personal care, to make learning fun and responsive, all while being true to themselves. They will take this "magic" with them to other places, and though they may find it hard to implement faithfully in settings that are vastly different from Xanadu, it will likely stay "in their blood" (as Mary says).

They will also carry their relationships with each other, their GTs, and the PTR faculty with them. As Elisabeth recalls Taylor and Mary telling her, "Just because the program's over, doesn't mean our relationship's over." Because ultimately, PTR is not about getting to a particular end goal, but about forging fundamental connections with other human beings that inform residents' teaching for years to come.

NOTES

1. Levine, Arthur. (2006). *Educating school teachers*. Washington, DC: Education Schools Project. Retrieved from http://www.edschools.org/pdf/Educating_Teachers_Report.pdf; Mason, Kevin O. (2014). *Preparing for the classroom: What teachers really think about teacher education*. Lanham, MD: Rowman & Littlefield.

2. McDonald, Morva A., Bowman, Michael, & Brayko, Kate. (2013, April). Learning to see students: Opportunities to develop relational practices of teaching through community based placements in teacher education. *Teachers College Record, 115*, 25.

3. Levine, *Educating school teachers*; Mason, *Preparing for the classroom*.

4. Clift, R. T., & Brady, P. (2005). Research on methods courses and field experiences. In M. Cochran-Smith & K. M. Zeichner (Eds.), *Studying teacher education: The report of the AERA panel on research and teacher education* (pp. 309–424). Mahwah, NJ: Erlbaum; Feiman-Nemser, Sharon, Tamir, Eran, & Hammerness, Karen. (2015). *Inspiring teaching: Preparing teachers to succeed in mission-driven schools*. Cambridge, MA: Harvard Education Press.

5. Anyon, Jean. (1981). Social class and school knowledge. *Curriculum Inquiry, 11*(1), 3–42.

6. Feiman-Nemser, Tamir, & Hammerness, *Inspiring teaching*.

7. Ashley leaves this school after 6 months and moves to an independent school.

8. Feiman-Nemser, Sharon. (2012). *Teachers as learners*. Cambridge, MA: Harvard Education Press, p. 41.

9. Palmer, Parker. (1998). *The courage to teach: Exploring the inner landscape of a teacher's life*. San Francisco, CA: Jossey-Bass.

Part III

Into the Field and Beyond

Chapter Seven

From Learning to Teaching

While school conditions often trump teacher preparation, programs that link a broad social mission and vision of teaching with contextualized teaching practices can play a critical role in preparing and retaining strong teachers for hard-to-staff schools.—Sharon Feiman-Nemser, Eran Tamir, and Karen Hammerness, *Inspiring Teaching*[1]

The previous chapters represent two very different approaches to teacher preparation, relationships, race, and education in general. Many of these differences stem from each program's ideological underpinnings, which remain almost at odds despite their location in the same geographical region; for in the United States, the lack of agreement on the purpose of schooling makes space for a wide spectrum of teacher education programs and schools, a spectrum on which No Excuses Teacher Residency (NETR) might seem to sit on one side, and Progressive Teacher Residency (PTR) the other. However, glimmers of each approach can be seen across a variety of schools, due in part to the history of educational reform in the United States.

The no excuses model is largely reflective of the industrial origins of modern-day schooling and "the cult of efficiency" that took over schools in the mid-1900s. This model resurged with a focus on standardized testing after the publication of *A Nation at Risk*, and again with the No Child Left Behind Act.[2] Each of these reforms focused on education for "the masses."

Progressive education, on the other hand, emerged as a countermovement to industrial schooling, refocusing on the needs of the individual child—including their "psychological, social, physical, moral, civic, aesthetic, and even intellectual" development.[3] White affluent parents continue to drive the demand for this type of education, as they desire what they perceive to be a superior educational experience for their children. The historical push and pull between these two educational approaches is evidenced in the smorgasbord of educational options available today, from no excuses charter schools and highly regimented private schools to progressive public or charter options like High Tech High and private Reggio Emilia or Waldorf schools. Therefore, the approaches to both education and relationships represented in this book might be more generalizable than they seem.

Nestled in a no excuses context, NETR privileges efficiency and technique to advance student achievement and "close the achievement gap." Here, teachers are viewed as technicians who can "objective[ly]" implement prescribed moves and strategies and packaged canonical curricula in "the most efficient way possible." A creature of a century-old independent school, PTR begins from an entirely different standpoint, namely, that truly transformative education must be student centered, active, critical, messy, responsive, and joyful. Toward this end, PTR aims to prepare teachers who can employ the tools of constructivist pedagogy to teach students to critically think and self-advocate.

Thus, where NETR is focused heavily on academic achievement (the ends), PTR centralizes the experience of education (the means). In NETR, residents are all expected to "row in the same direction" as their colleagues yet be the "ultimate authority" within their classrooms; in PTR, residents' and students' unique preferences and strengths are celebrated in and out of the classroom. These disparate approaches to education influence each program's vision of teacher–student relationships.

Each program's internal coherence is reflected in the way its relational vision corresponds with its broader philosophy to education. Consistent with its privileging of academic ends, NETR views teacher–student relationships as *instrumental*: teachers acquire "professional relationship capital" with students as a means of improving their behavior and effort, thereby increasing achievement. However, such relationships are not seen as impacting the teacher's behavior or effort (as this is primarily influenced by school structures).

In contrast, PTR establishes relationships with students as *reciprocal*: teachers must get to know students as "whole people" so they can shape their curriculum and instruction around their students. This reflects PTR's commitment to a constructivist process of learning. In the process of advancing these different visions of education and relationships, each program promotes a different set of relational competencies for residents to learn. These competencies provide insight into the various forms of knowledge, dispositions, and actions that teacher education programs may use to prepare teachers for relationships with students.

RELATIONAL COMPETENCIES

In line with their alternate pedagogical and relational visions, NETR and PTR promote different relational competencies in their coursework and field-work. PTR focuses most on the knowledge and dispositions that teachers must develop to foster reciprocal relationships with students. This begins with *self-knowledge*, a deep, reflective understanding of who teachers are personally and professionally. PTR upholds the idea that teachers can only understand their students if they first understand themselves. Likewise, PTR faculty continually emphasize the importance of *knowledge of students*, in-sisting residents must acquire complex information about those they serve, both as students and people, including their interests, families, previous educational experiences, "what scares them," and more. Additionally, Taylor, as the director of PTR, insists that residents cultivate *knowledge of society*, including an understanding of the social and political forces (e.g., institutional racism, homophobia, sexism) that continue to shape the broader culture, education, and individual experiences—including that of the teachers and their students.

Throughout the program, PTR also stresses the importance of teachers' relational dispositions: teachers' mental and emotional stances toward students.[4] The first of these is *authenticity*, which is essentially the dispositional manifestation of self-knowledge. Throughout the program, residents in PTR learned to honor their unique identity, and to design their own curriculum and facilitate instructional experiences that were consistent with this identity. They also develop *empathy*. PTR constructs this as both a cognitive process of intellectually understanding how a student might be thinking or feeling based on what they know about students, and an affective one, where they learn how to identify with a student and their emotional experience.[5] Similarly, PTR focuses on *care*, as both a disposition and action whereby teachers feel and express genuine concern for students and attempt to support them in the fulfillment of both their academic and personal needs.[6]

The development of all these forms of knowledge and dispositions likely informs teachers' relational actions, but PTR does not really prescribe these, believing "there's not one way to be a teacher." Through modeling by guiding teachers and PTR faculty, the program does, however, emphasize one particular action as an extension of relationships: designing *responsive curricula and instruction* in the form of constructivist lessons that responded to students' or residents' needs and interests.

NETR, on the other hand, primarily approaches instrumental teacher–student relationship development through action. For example, the program establishes care not as a feeling, but a series of actions or moves, most of which center around providing or reinforcing academic support for students (e.g., "the high five" and "the private check-in"). NETR also centralizes actions related to *classroom management*, in which teachers interact with students in ways that shape both the classroom culture and their individual relationships with students. Through both proactive and reactive management moves, the program emphasizes a teacher's authority over students, and suggests they should find ways to "authentic[ally]" implement school rules and norms.

Moreover, faculty have systematized a process of *connecting with parents*, providing sample scripts, rubrics, and guidelines to help residents learn to call parents—to inform them of challenges, to praise students, and ultimately to encourage their support for student achievement in their schools. The program has also codified guidance on how teachers should dress, smile, accept feedback positively, interact with colleagues and administrators, and more. NETR even proposes structured conversations with students about the need to navigate the existing culture of power, instead of emphasizing knowledge of society. As faculty are admittedly wary of too much "thinking and feeling," the program advances the motions of relationships far more than it promotes the development of relational knowledge or dispositions.

The two programs in this book also attempt to equip residents with *racial competence*. Ali Michael defines racial competence as "the skills and attitudes required to develop and maintain healthy cross-racial relationships, notice and analyze racial dynamics, and confront racism in the environment and in oneself."[7] This relational disposition may begin to develop from knowledge of self, students, and society but is only realized through meaningful work with people of different races. And it is critical, because when teachers—and particularly white teachers—enter classrooms without having developed racial competence, they often maintain biases against children of color that negatively affect their relationships with them.[8] However, neither program in this book quite succeeds in advancing racial competence because both approach this in line with the way they approach coursework on other subjects: NETR focuses on actions like explicitly teaching students to navigate the culture of power without analyzing it, and PTR embraces "thinking and feeling" about racism without explicit structures or fieldwork to support this work in action.

There is scholarship to support the development of competencies like this for effective teaching practice more generally.[9] In NETR and PTR, 10 central competencies emerge as particularly important in preparing teachers to connect with students. These are summarized in Table 7.1 on the next page.[10]

Although each program focused on a different subset of these competencies, all 10 may be important for teachers to develop in order to meaningfully connect with students, especially across racial and cultural differences. Of course, what teachers learn in their preparation programs might not translate to their beginning practice; thus, it is worth exploring how graduates of

Table 7.1. Relational Competency Table

Relational Competency	Type	Definition
Knowledge of Self	Knowledge	An understanding of one's personal history, thoughts, behavior, culture, identity, and social position
Knowledge of Students	Knowledge	Seeking out information about students (their interests, needs, dreams, family life, cultural background) from a variety of sources
Knowledge of Society	Knowledge	Understanding of social and political forces that shape society, education, personal experiences (including racism, classism, homophobia, etc.)
Authenticity	Disposition	How a teacher brings self-knowledge and sense of personal identity to bear in classroom practice
Empathy	Disposition	Cognitive and affective understanding of students' mental and emotional experiences, as well as behavior that responds to students accordingly
Racial Competence	Disposition	Knowledge, attitudes, and experience required to understand and confront institutional and individual racism and connect with people across lines of race
Care for Students	Disposition and Action	A genuine concern for and an approach to the fulfillment of students' academic and personal needs. Includes advocating for students' interests with other adults.
Connecting with Families	Action	Working with parents/guardians to better understand and support students personally and academically
Designing Responsive Curricula and Instruction	Action	Designing curricula and instruction that intentionally responds to student interests, cultural experiences, and needs
Establishing Safe and Inclusive Class Communities	Action	Includes classroom management, but also involves establishing trust between and among students as an extension of interpersonal relationships

NETR and PTR draw upon their program learning when they step into their first full-time teaching job.

INFLUENCES ON NEW TEACHER BEHAVIOR

Despite their notable differences, the two programs represented in this book also share some striking similarities. Both NETR and PTR are highly coherent programs that employ structures, pedagogy, and curriculum that directly correspond with their own mission and vision. They both acknowledge the importance of teacher–student relationships and uphold clear (yet differing) visions for the purpose of these relationships and how these advance their respective educational agendas. Both also recognize that racial competence is important for connecting with students and employ some coursework in an attempt to support its development. Moreover, each program stresses extensive fieldwork and intentionally supports either guiding teachers or coaches to provide constructive feedback to residents as they practice teaching and interacting with students. Coursework in each program intentionally connects to these practical experiences, as opposed to being overly theoretical, and makes space for the discussion of relationships. These similarities— which are often associated with teacher residency programs [11]—may enable these programs to powerfully impact new teachers' relational practice.

Residents in both programs end the year feeling fairly prepared for their beginning pedagogical and relational practice. And many attribute this to their extensive fieldwork. For example, residents in both programs report that they learn the most about connecting with students by working with them in at least one of their field placements: in NETR, this is Tutorial; in PTR, the placement(s) at Xanadu. However, these self-reported reactions do not necessarily correspond with how these new teachers utilize what they have learned once in the field. As teacher educators may often wonder, will program learning stick with graduates?

For new teachers, their first school site is truly where "the rubber meets the road." And whatever they encounter here might cause them to integrate, adapt, or reject what they have learned from their preparation program. [12] Additionally, new teachers' behavior is likely mediated by their personal values, views, and previous educational experiences. Educational sociologist Dan Lortie would call this "the apprenticeship of observation," [13] in which people enter the teaching profession thinking they already know how to teach because they have observed it as students. Both individual and school factors can influence how and what new teachers carry into the field, and how they interact with their students. [14]

As a result, some research casts doubt upon the influence of teacher education programs on new teachers' practice. [15] But other research paints a more hopeful picture, suggesting that "mission-driven" teacher education programs with supportive fieldwork can improve teacher retention and success. [16] The two residency programs represented in this book are both "mission-driven" residency programs, which may indicate a better chance of successfully preparing teachers for their future schools. But what program graduates encounter at their first teaching site is still likely to influence how they teach, as well as how they form relationships with their students.

What is it about a school site that might shape teacher–student relationships? What could influence new teachers to behave a certain way, or to draw more upon some relational competencies than others, in their interactions with those they serve? School rules govern discipline, and influence which student behaviors teachers should reward or reprimand. School structures like class sizes and the length of class periods affect how much time a teacher can spend with individual students. The population a school serves—including students' racial and cultural backgrounds, English language proficiency, learning disabilities, sexuality and gender identities, poverty, hunger, access to technology outside the classroom, sense of safety in and out of school, and so forth—influences what needs, interests, assets, and challenges teachers will need to address in the classroom. However, as I discover when I follow program graduates into the field, schools with similar profiles on paper may have distinct and subtle cultures that can also powerfully shape teacher–student relationships.

INTERACTIONAL CULTURE

To make sense of the subtle social differences I observe at school sites when I follow residency graduates into practice, I draw upon a seminal article utilized in many schools of education: Jean Anyon's 1981 "Social Class and School Knowledge." Anyon's primary argument in this article is that social class is reproduced through the knowledge that is perpetuated in schools. She observes four different "dominant themes" related to this that characterize "student-teacher interaction" at the different sites: *resistance, possibility, narcissism,* and *excellence.*[17]

I refer to these themes as a school's interactional culture; and though I suspect there are likely other forms of interactional cultures at play in schools today, the four that I observe each fall into one of Anyon's categories by happenstance (which I will describe in Chapter 8). Each teacher residency program also seems to be predominantly shaped by one of these cultures. Therefore, I summarize the four themes Anyon derived from her study as a heuristic for understanding how school and program characteristics around teacher–student interactions might contribute to one of these four interactional cultures.

Resistance

Although Anyon admits to observing "some amount of resistance" in all the schools she studied, this theme dominated interactions between teachers and students at the two urban working-class schools in her study. For their part, the teachers at these schools focused on basic skills, "routine tasks," and discrete classwork without explaining the motivation for this work or inviting students to engage in "decision making of their own." Teachers generally held deficit mindsets about their students and resisted teaching more complex material because, in the words of one teacher from Anyon's study, "they never get it, and they'll never *use* it!"[18] Moreover, teachers at the two working-class schools also prioritized "physical control" over students' behavior through strict classroom management, as opposed to engaging their "hearts and minds."[19]

In response, students exhibited active and passive resistance to instruction. They felt like their teachers were overly punitive and failed to teach meaningful content. Thus, students actively resisted teachers through outward "sabotage" of classwork by losing materials, interrupting the teacher, and exhibiting other forms of distracting behavior. Additionally, students displayed passive forms of resistance through inattention or failing to respond to the teacher's questions. Although Anyon finds some hope in the way students rejected their inadequate education, she acknowledges that the culture of resistance set most students up for failure in school and beyond by undermining positive relationships between teachers and students and inhibiting meaningful learning.

Possibility

At the urban "middle class" school in her study, Anyon documents a sense of possibility or hope among teachers and students regarding the potential of education. At this school, "education in particular seems to be accepted as important, indeed vital, to one's ability to get a job or enter college."[20] Education in this case was largely seen as the acquisition of content generated by "experts," represented in textbooks, and presented in a formulaic fashion. Teachers wanted students to be able to conceptually understand and explain this content (not just retain it); however, knowledge was not related to students' own experiences, nor was it viewed as something students could create themselves. Who they were outside the classroom had no relevance within it.

Therefore, teacher–student relationships at the middle class school were more unidirectional and perfunctory, with teachers "depositing" knowledge in a process that Paulo Freire would call "the banking model" of education.[21] Students accepted the idea that if they "work[ed] *hard*" to learn what teachers taught them, they could be "anything that they wanted" in life, and this reduced their resistance to teachers and content.[22] Despite the positive connotation of the word "possibility," Anyon raises red flags about the potential consequences of this culture, suggesting that it leads to "mystification" or unquestioning compliance to the existing social order without questioning this.

Narcissism

At the suburban "affluent professional school," Anyon identifies narcissism as shaping teacher–student interactions. While this term sounds distinctly negative, in this case, Anyon uses the word "narcissism" to describe a school culture that focuses on personal development and individual expression. She explains:

> This emerges, for example, in the emphasis in the classroom on thinking for oneself, on externalizing, in creative projects of all sorts, what is internal in the attempts to individualize instruction, in the personal discovery intended by the science and math programs, and the principal's and teachers' stated emphasis on personal development and creativity as important goals of education. [23]

To support this instructional vision, teachers sought to "know and nurture every child"[24] and encouraged them to construct their own meaning from curricular material, which often included news media about current events. In general, students responded favorably to this approach, describing lessons as fun. They also felt that their opinions, experiences, and responses to content were valuable, and that they could "make" their own knowledge; thus, they readily engaged in lessons and even wrote and performed plays of their own in which they "hamm[ed] it up." Teacher–student interactions were thus characterized as more reciprocal and holistic here. Additionally, students at this school were taught to be charitable to those less fortunate than themselves because there were "good reasons for social struggle,"[25] but ultimately focused more on their own personal development than collective goals (like social change). While Anyon does not characterize narcissism as negative (and actually seems to view this school more favorably than the others), her use of this value-laden term suggests that such a culture could perpetuate a sense of egoism, selfishness, and/or entitlement among students.

Excellence

In the suburban "executive elite" school, which served students from the wealthiest backgrounds, Anyon observed a theme of excellence, which she describes as "the necessity of preparation for being the best, for top quality performance."[26] The parents served by this school occupied the upper echelons of society and held clear ideas about how their children should live and learn, and they often initiated communication with teachers. In response, teachers felt pressure to prepare the children of these wealthy parents for elite colleges and "important jobs" through "brisk" coursework that did not involve any "narcissistic coddling." In social studies classes, the curriculum was "sophisticated, complex, and analytical" and explicitly addressed issues of social class, making it the "most honest" and the "closest to being socially critical" of all coursework in the study.[27] Students had to actively participate in knowledge development here, and teachers expected a lot of them.

However, the culture of excellence seemed to cause students to focus more intently on "competition and performance" in order to "get into the 'best schools'" and be "the best." As a result, students experienced the stress of individualistic competition, unmediated by teacher nurturance, but supported by teacher expectations that they could and should actively engage with critical and relatable knowledge. Ultimately, this culture fostered mastery of dominant cultural capital and reinforced a quest for superiority that likely helped these students remain in the upper class in society.

While Anyon observed these themes in schools nearly 40 years ago, the four schools where I follow program graduates into beginning practice each happen to correspond with one of these four themes. Moreover, reflective analysis indicates NETR and PTR each perpetuate one of these dominant themes. This may suggest that educators learn some of the interactional patterns represented in these cultures in teacher education (and possibly, principal preparation) programs.

NO EXCUSES TEACHER RESIDENCY: FROM RESISTANCE TO POSSIBILITY

While some of the behavior management in NETR is consistent with resistance culture, the program deliberately promotes an interactional culture of possibility. Faculty stress the urgent need for students to acquire conceptual knowledge and skills so they can get into college. Instead of viewing students as incapable of understanding or applying difficult concepts—as is common in resistance culture—NETR insists all students should be able to fulfill comprehensive standards and acquire all relevant knowledge, without excuses. And this knowledge comes from the canon in the form of prescribed curricula presented in a formulaic and efficient manner. Residents learn strategies to "modify lessons" along these lines. While some of the "reactive" strategies residents learn for managing their classroom are consistent with the physical control of resistance, residents also learn to eliminate the need for reactive management by using "proactive" strategies like issuing "merits," using "positive narration" to affirm desired behaviors, and getting students to "buy in" to class.

The NETR course on teacher–student relationships is centered around the goal of getting students to "invest" in the teacher and course such that they work to meet specific standards. One of the ways teachers are taught to motivate course demands is by deploying the four "loves": love you, love the team, love the journey, love the destination. Residents often draw upon the idea of "love the destination" in coursework and fieldwork, suggesting to students that they can achieve their desired goals if they fulfill the school's academic and behavioral expectations. By getting students to "buy in" to possibility, teachers may proactively suppress both active and passive forms of resistance to school rules and curricula.

The focus on possibility is also consistent with NETR's emphasis on navigating the culture of power. As the program asserts, students must acquire forms of dominant cultural capital to achieve social and economic mobility. Residents are thus explicitly taught to emphasize to students that in order for them to reach their desired "destination"—their American dream—they must work hard in line with the norms promoted by the school. But there is little space to interrogate why this is the case.

Most no excuses schools seem similarly premised on suppressing resistance and promoting possibility. Leaders of these schools often publicize the no excuses model as an alternative to low-income public schools where they suggest that resistance—in the form of disciplinary chaos and low academic standards—is a dominant theme. They justify their focus on physical control over students by insisting this is necessary to reduce visible resistance to keep students safe and help them concentrate on work. In fact, no excuses schools construct "control" as a form of "care."[28] They similarly promote the idea that students can learn to navigate the system and achieve the American dream through this hard work and good behavior.[29]

Being trained in the culture of possibility through NETR is thus likely an advantage for most of the residents who graduate from the program and matriculate to schools with cultures that closely resemble this; this is because residents not only become familiar with the culture of possibility, but they learn to buy into it. But Julie and Casey, the two residents from NETR whom I follow into the field, soon find that no excuses schools that seem similar from the outside can have distinctly different interactional cultures (which I will discuss in the next chapter).

PROGRESSIVE TEACHER RESIDENCY: NARCISSISM DOMINATES

On the other hand, PTR is dominated by an interactional culture of narcissism. This is especially obvious when looking at Xanadu Community School, the context in which residents' most profound learning experiences occur. Some of the teachers talk about parents who stress academic achievement in the form of grades and scores on the high school placement exam that many take to attend private or exam high schools after Xanadu, but teachers generally regard this pressure on students as ill advised. Xanadu simply does not stress quantitative and comparative academic achievement. In fact, students do not even get grades until they reach the middle school classes here. Instead, students and residents at Xanadu focus heavily on personal development and individual expression. For example, students often complete reflective writing assignments, share out memories with the class, pursue projects of interest to them, and work toward individual goals that they have set along with their families.

Highly constructivist, student-centered instruction characterizes teacher–student interactions throughout Xanadu and PTR. Residents learn to know students in and out of the classroom through informal interactions, reflective student assignments, and face-to-face conferences with parents. Although Xanadu features common curricular units across classes, residents are supported to use their knowledge of students to create lessons within these units that respond to students' individual interests and needs. PTR encourages residents to integrate current events and engage in discussions of social inequalities with their classes, promoting critical thinking and an understanding of unjust structures. Students are not simply expected to absorb expert knowledge and skills and then regurgitate this on tests but are instead asked to generate their own understanding through the assignments described above. Through coursework that reflects a progressive philosophy and their semester or yearlong placement at Xanadu, residents are apprenticed into an interactional culture of narcissism.

Narcissism at Xanadu manifests in a few different ways. For students, the focus on their own personal growth and development seems to empower them to take risks and pursue their own interests. For example, numerous Xanadu students voluntarily perform at the annual school fair, and "ham it up."[30] Students also seem willing to "self-advocate" (according to the director) in ways that display they feel entitled to a particular kind of education. For residents, an individualistic focus leads them to develop deeper self-knowledge and hone their teaching style. But it also might lead some to prioritize their own personal needs—like a comfortable work environment—over serving historically marginalized students who do not often have access to progressive education.

While some behaviors associated with narcissism seem desirable (such as the ability to think critically, generate knowledge, and self-advocate), a culture of narcissism might inhibit the desire to work toward advancing what Anyon would call "collective goals." This is likely one of the reasons most of the residents seek out jobs at independent schools similar to Xanadu when they graduate, as they believe in this culture and prioritize their own interests over an effort to spread progressive education to spaces where it is less often available. When Leah and Elisabeth—the two PTR residents who I follow into the field—move into their first teaching jobs, they, too, come to learn that schools can look similar but have very different cultures.

INTERACTIONAL CULTURE IN SCHOOLS

School culture undeniably influences teachers. For example, several scholars have linked school culture to teacher retention and sense of success.[31] Here, I suggest that a certain aspect of a school's broader culture—the interactional culture—could potentially influence how teachers interact with their students, particularly new teachers who do not have much teaching experience. This has implications for teacher–student relationships, and by extension, students' academic outcomes.

When I follow graduates from NETR and PTR into their first full-time teaching job, I observe the influence of interactional culture. As I will illustrate in the next chapter, the teachers who enter school sites characterized by an interactional culture consistent with that of their residency program feel more able and willing to draw upon the relational tools they have acquired in their programs than those who enter schools with inconsistent cultures. However, even in the cases where a school's interactional culture conflicts with that of their residency program, the teachers I follow maintain their strong support for the culture and relational tools of their residency. This finding underscores how very influential these two programs seem to be.

NOTES

1. Feiman-Nemser, Sharon, Tamir, Eran, & Hammerness, Karen. (2015). *Inspiring teaching: Preparing teachers to succeed in mission-driven schools.* Cambridge, MA: Harvard Education Press, p. 15.

2. Mehta, Jal, & Fine, Sarah. (2019). *In search of deeper learning: Inside the effort to remake the American high school.* Cambridge, MA: Harvard University Press.

3. Graham, Patricia A. (2005). *Schooling America.* New York, NY: Oxford University Press.

4. Mercado, Carmen I. (2016). Teaching for critical consciousness: Topics, themes, frameworks, and instructional activities. In A. Valenzuela (Ed.), *Growing critically conscious teachers: A social justice curriculum for educators of Latino/a youth.* New York, NY: Teachers College Press.

5. For more information about the differences between cognitive and affective empathy, see Jolliffe, Darrick, & Farrington, David. (2006). Development and validation of the basic empathy scale. *Journal of Adolescence, 29*(4), 589–611; Pecukonis, E. V. (1990). A cognitive/affective empathy training program as a function of ego development in aggressive adolescent females. *Adolescence, 25*(97), 59–76.

6. Cooper, Kristy, & Miness, A. (2014). The co-creation of caring student/teacher relationships: Does teacher understanding matter? *The High School Journal, 97*(4), 264–290; Noddings, Nel. (1984). *Caring: A feminine approach to ethics & moral education.* Berkeley: University of California Press.

7. This shortened definition comes from a brief article with Ali Michael; see Michael, Ali. (n.d.). Treating racial competence as a skill to be learned. University of Pennsylvania Graduate

School of Education. Retrieved fromhttps://www.gse.upenn.edu/news/educators-playbook/treating-racial-competence-skill-be-learned. But for an extended definition of racial competence, see Michael, Ali. (2015). *Raising race questions: Whiteness and inquiry in education.* New York, NY: Teachers College Press. Also see Milner, Richard. (2003). Reflection, racial competence, and critical pedagogy: How do we prepare pre-service teachers to pose tough questions? *Race Ethnicity and Education, 6*(2), 193–208.

8. Haviland, V. (2008). "Things get glossed over": Rearticulating the silencing power of whiteness in education. *Journal of Teacher Education, 59*(1), 40–54; Hyland, N. (2005). Being a good teacher of black students? White teachers and unintentional racism. *Curriculum Inquiry, 35*(4), 429–459; Picower, B. (2009). The unexamined whiteness of teaching: How white teachers maintain and enact dominant racial ideologies. *Race Ethnicity and Education, 12*(2), 197–215; Sleeter, Christine. (2008). Preparing white teachers for diverse students. *Handbook of Research on Teacher Education: Enduring Questions in Changing Contexts, 3*, 559–582.

9. For self-knowledge, see Brilhart, Dan. (2010). Teacher conceptualization of teaching: Integrating the personal and the professional. *Journal of Ethnographic & Qualitative Research, 4*(4), 168–179; Gomez, Mary Louise, & Lachuk, Amy Johnson. (2015). Teachers learning about themselves through learning about "others." In D. J. Clandinin & J. Husu (Eds.), *The SAGE Handbook of Research on Teacher Education* (pp. 457–472). London, England: Sage. For knowledge of students, see Grossman, Pam. (1990). *The making of a teacher: Teacher knowledge and teacher education.* New York, NY: Teachers College Press; Villegas, Ana María, & Lucas, Tamara. (2002). Preparing culturally responsive teachers: Rethinking the curriculum. *Journal of Teacher Education, 53*(1), 20–32. For knowledge of society, see Darling-Hammond, 2012; Sleeter, Preparing white teachers. For authenticity, see Kreber, Carolin, Klampfleitner, Monika, McCune, Velda, Bayne, Sian, & Knottenbelt, Miesbeth. (2007). What do you mean by "authentic"? A comparative review of the literature on conceptions of authenticity in teaching. *Adult Education Quarterly, 58*(1), 22–43. For empathy, see McAllister, Gretchen, & Irvine, Jacqueline Jordan. (2002). The role of empathy in teaching culturally diverse students. *Journal of Teacher Education, 53*(5), 433–443. For care, see Cooper, Kristy. (2013). Eliciting engagement in the high school classroom: A mixed-methods examination of teaching practices. *American Educational Research Journal, 51*(2), 363–402; Noddings, *Caring.* For connecting with families, see Lawrence-Lightfoot, Sara. (2004). *The essential conversation: What parents and teachers can learn from each other.* New York, NY: Random House. For designing responsive curricula and instruction, see Darling-Hammond, Linda, & Bransford, John. (2007). *Preparing teachers for a changing world: What teachers should learn and be able to do.* San Francisco, CA: Jossey-Bass; Gay, Geneva. (2000). *Culturally responsive teaching: Theory, research, & practice.* New York, NY: Teachers College Press; Villegas & Lucas, Preparing culturally responsive teachers. For classroom management, or rather what I call establishing safe and inclusive classroom communities, see Gay, Geneva. (2006). Connections between classroom management and culturally responsive teaching. In C. M. Everston & C. S. Weinstein (Eds.), *Handbook of classroom management: Research, practice, and contemporary issues* (pp. 343–372). Mahwah, NJ: Erlbaum; Wubbels, Theo, Brekelmans, Mieke, Den Brok, Perry, Wijsman, Lindy, Mainhard, Tim, & Van Tartwijk, Jan. (2015). Teacher–student relationships and classroom management. In E. T. Emmer & E. J. Sabornie (Eds.), *Handbook of Classroom Management.* New York, NY: Routledge. I entered this research expecting to see programs attempting to develop teachers' knowledge of self, students, and society; their care for students; their responsive curricula and instruction; and their classroom management. Competencies like empathy, authenticity, racial competence, and connecting with families are all competencies that emerged that are relevant to teacher–student relationships throughout the research process.

10. A version of this table appears in Theisen-Homer, 2020.

11. Berry, Barnett, Montgomery, Diana, & Snyder, Jon. (2008). *Urban teacher residency models and institutes of higher education: Implications for teacher preparation.* Chapel Hill, NC: Center for Teaching Quality; Guha, R., Hyler, M., & Darling-Hammond, L. (2016). *The teacher residency: An innovative model for preparing teachers.* Palo Alto, CA: Learning Policy Institute.

12. Clift R. T., & Brady, P. (2005). Research on methods courses and field experiences. In M. Cochran-Smith & K. M. Zeichner (Eds.), *Studying teacher education: The report of the AERA panel on research and teacher education* (pp. 309–424). Mahwah, NJ: Erlbaum, p. 331.

13. Lortie, Dan C. (1975). *Schoolteacher: A sociological study*. Chicago, IL: University of Chicago Press.

14. McDonald, Morva A., Bowman, Michael, & Brayko, Kate. (2013, April). Learning to see students: Opportunities to develop relational practices of teaching through community based placements in teacher education. *Teachers College Record, 115*, 1–35.

15. For example, Boyd, Donald, Goldhaber, Daniel D, Lankford, Hamilton, & Wyckoff, James Humphrey. (2007). The effect of certification and preparation on teacher quality. *The Future of Children, 17*(1), 45–68.

16. Feiman-Nemser, Sharon, Tamir, Eran, & Hammerness, Karen. (2015). *Inspiring teaching: Preparing teachers to succeed in mission-driven schools*. Cambridge, MA: Harvard Education Press.

17. These themes are organized by the social class with which they are associated (e.g., resistance is to the working class as excellence is to the executive elite class); however, they are not necessarily hierarchical in appeal, nor do their titles effectively connote the desirability of this type of school culture (e.g., narcissism sounds negative but is potentially the most admirable and transformative of the school cultures, while possibility is the least transformative).

18. Anyon, Jean. (1981). Social class and school knowledge. *Curriculum Inquiry, 11*(1), 10.

19. Anyon, Social class and school knowledge, p. 32.

20. Anyon, Social class and school knowledge, p. 16.

21. Freire, Paulo. (1970). *Pedagogy of the oppressed*. New York, NY: Continuum.

22. Anyon, Social class and school knowledge, p. 16.

23. Anyon, Social class and school knowledge, pp. 21–22.

24. Anyon, Social class and school knowledge, p. 17.

25. Anyon, Social class and school knowledge, p. 22.

26. Anyon, Social class and school knowledge, p. 30.

27. Anyon, Social class and school knowledge, pp. 30, 37.

28. Kershen, Juliana Lopez, Weiner, Jennie Miles, & Torres, Chris. (2019). Control as care: How teachers in "no excuses" charter schools position their students and themselves. *Equity & Excellence in Education, 51*(3–4).

29. Green, Elizabeth. (2014). *Building a better teacher: How teaching works (and how to teach it to everyone)*. New York, NY: Norton; Whitman, David. (2008). *Sweating the small stuff: Inner-city schools and the new paternalism*. Washington, DC: Thomas B. Fordham Institute.

30. Anyon, Social class and school knowledge, p. 21.

31. See, for example, Feiman-Nemser, Emir, & Hammerness, *Inspiring teaching*; Johnson, Susan Moore, & Birkeland, Susan E. (2003). Pursuing a "sense of success": New teachers explain their career decisions. *American Educational Research Journal, 40*(3), 581–617; Kraft, Matthew A., Papay, John P., Charner-Laird, Megin, Johnson, Susan Moore, Ng, Monica, & Reinhorn, Stefanie K. (2012, June). *Committed to their students but in need of support: How school context influences teacher turnover in high-poverty, urban schools*. Paper Presented at the Annual Meeting of the American Educational Research Association, Vancouver, BC, Canada.

Chapter Eight

Contradictions in the Field

The genesis of truly transformative activity is in the contradictions within and between social settings.—Jean Anyon, "Social Class and School Knowledge"[1]

The two mission-driven teacher residency programs represented throughout this book seem to powerfully shape how their residents think about teaching and relationships. But how will this translate to teachers' behavior at their first job site? Will other factors—like their own beliefs or a school's interactional culture (introduced in Chapter 7)—affect how well they are able to use what they learned in their programs?

The following cases document the experiences of Julie and Casey from No Excuses Teacher Residency (NETR), and Elisabeth and Leah from Progressive Teacher Residency (PTR). All four of these teachers reflect the average graduate from each program (and the average beginning teacher in general) in that they are young (under the age of 30) and white. They all teach either English language arts or social studies for seventh- or eighth-grade students at a public or charter school (as opposed to an independent school). Finally, they all seek out schools that appear, at least on paper, to support the kind of education they learned in their residency programs. But under the surface, these four schools are all very different.[2] Contradictions between their residency program and school sites seem to influence what graduates feel able or willing to use from their programs when they teach and connect with students.

JULIE AND RESISTANCE AT PINNACLE ACADEMY

Throughout the program, Julie appears to be the quintessential NETR resident: young, well educated, and "Type A." She is also naturally warm and smiles frequently, demonstrating a "positive affect" in all coursework and fieldwork. Julie receives excellent evaluations in NETR and is distinguished as one of the top residents in the program. As a result, she enters the teaching profession with high expectations for her practice, and her ability to implement all that she has learned in NETR.

Julie gets her first teaching job at Pinnacle Academy Middle School (PAMS). PAMS is located in Brickfield, a small city bisected by a river that was once home to a thriving textile industry. Brickfield is one of the lowest-income areas in the greater metro area that surrounds the central city. Its school district recently entered receivership, leading to a turnaround process that has brought in multiple different charter management organizations (CMOs) to take over district schools. Unlike most no excuses schools, PAMS is not a school of choice, but rather a neighborhood public school operated by a no excuses CMO. This designation is actually one of the reasons Julie applied to PAMS, because she wanted to serve students who might not have parents or guardians with the wherewithal to seek out charter school options.

Just past the city center, near a large brick church, sits the tall red-brick school building that is home to PAMS and another small charter school. At the start of each day, a PAMS administrator stands outside the side entrance to the building and greets students with a handshake before they enter; this allows the administrator to ensure that students' attire complies with the strict dress code. The students then climb two flights of tiled stairs, yellowed with age and use, to arrive at the PAMS-occupied third floor. At the beginning of the year, the hallways and classrooms on the floor feel rather bare, featuring off-white floors, walls with wood paneling, some standard school-issued signage, and little decoration. Classrooms contain desks aligned in rows, with two desks paired together in each row so teachers can assign students to work with a "shoulder partner." The rooms have a few posters, most of which correspond with particular school policies; there is little color.

Like most no excuses schools, PAMS's mission is to close the "achievement gap" and prepare students "to navigate" society. The school serves a little over 300 students; the vast majority are Latinx, with a small percentage of white and African American students. Nearly all the students qualify for free or reduced lunch, nearly 30% are classified as English language learners, and 16% have a disability. All students attend this school because they live in the immediate area and have been assigned here, not because they have elected to do so. When I ask students what they think of the school, they tell me it is "boring" or "not fun" because "we do the same things every time" and "sit all day in the same spot" and they would "rather stay home."

The school day at PAMS is highly structured. Students' physical movement is limited, as they remain in the same classroom all day—except for lunch, which is in the basement—and various content teachers rotate in to teach them. Classes move quickly, instruction relies on teacher directives, and students often complete independent work in silence. Within classrooms, teachers closely monitor student dress, posture, and behavior and issue merits and demerits accordingly. Although the occasional student trickles into the hallway without a chaperone, these spaces are generally empty and quiet. All of this seems consistent with what NETR expects of the schools its residents will join; they "sweat the small stuff" so that students can presumably focus on their academics.

At first, Julie voices excitement about working at PAMS and expresses confidence in the school's leaders. She puts in long hours at the school and enforces school norms without fail, issuing merits and demerits in an efficient manner and noting these on a clipboard she carries with her. Julie justifies this by saying, "You can't be all lovey dovey unless the kids respect you. The only way that's going to happen is if they know that you mean business." However, she worries about becoming "a dictator." And while she sometimes adopts a persona that seems more serious and stern than is natural for her, she regularly affirms desired student behavior (as prescribed by NETR) and her ready smile and natural enthusiasm periodically emerge.

Because all students take a double block of English language arts (ELA) each day, Julie teaches only two different homerooms and sees all her 67 eighth-grade students at least twice a day throughout the year. This structure allows her to quickly learn names and relevant information about each student. The early lessons that I observe seem to run in a coordinated and preplanned way. There is little time or space in each class for drawing upon background knowledge about students, interacting with them about non-academic topics, differentiating assignments for individuals, or for digressions of any kind.

Still, a few of Julie's students test norms of silence and stillness from the get-go, and Julie responds by approaching them individually and asking them in hushed tones to quietly focus on her lesson. If they continue to disobey, she quickly issues a demerit or sends them out of the classroom to the dean and returns to the lesson up front, seemingly unfazed. She and her co-teacher end up having the highest number of "sendouts" at the beginning of the year. But while she wears a mask of indifference during these interactions, Julie admits to feeling distressed when she feels she must remove students from class for resisting her requests. And in line with her training, she acknowledges that ideally "you don't have to be as reactive [in class management]; you can be proactive."

As the year progresses, student resistance to the school's prescribed order becomes increasingly evident, as does the administration's attempts to suppress this through physical control. Throughout my five visits, I often see students being removed from class for various (mostly minor) infractions. The principal, dean, and the director of curriculum pop in and out of classrooms, seemingly frenetic, enforcing the school's discipline policies and often moving through the halls with a rule-breaking student in tow. By the second semester, a couple of Julie's students have stopped attending school altogether.

Julie begins to question what she feels may be an inhumane approach to school discipline; she acknowledges, "I think a lot of the kids sort of feel like it's [the school] run like a jail." As such, she too begins to resist the established order and becomes increasingly laid back in class, wears more casual clothing, refuses to don the characteristic no excuses stopwatch, issues fewer demerits, stops carrying her clipboard, and rarely reminds her students to "tuck in their shirts" or "sit up straight" (despite the fact that her principal notices this and tells Julie to enforce all rules consistently). Julie also increasingly attempts to connect with students in less formal ways in and out of class, organizing occasional activities and games in advisory that have little connection to prescribed content, allowing students to listen to their own music during independent work in class, and using unstructured time like lunch to sit and talk with students about their lives. While Julie's interactions with students begins to digress her training, her pedagogy remains firmly rooted in NETR's formulaic, efficient, and didactic presentation.

When it comes to communicating with parents, Julie follows school protocol more than NETR lessons. According to school structures, each teacher is responsible for calling the parents or guardians of a small group of students in their advisory period with any concern, but they are not expected to reach out to the parents of other students. The advisory teacher is also expected to have short conferences with each of their advisory group's parents at three scheduled times over the year. Julie fulfills these responsibilities and calls her advisory group's parents at other times, acquiring some additional information about each of these students. However, she rarely reaches out to the other parents. Instead, she relies on the school counselor, principal, and other teachers, who relay relevant information to her from the regular communication they have with students' families. This is counter to NETR training, which would suggest that she call all her students' parents, both to offer praise and discuss concerns. However, Julie tells me that there is often a language barrier she has trouble navigating and she finds that some parents cannot "afford a phone."

When I interview students in February, they say they generally like Julie as a person. They tell me she is "nice," "calm," "respectful," "always smiling," "nurturing," and "a good person" who "wants to help everybody." All the students also feel that she cares about them academically, as "she pushes us" and "thinks we are capable of doing the work." The female students feel she shows personal care for them, too. One tells me, "She is just like always asking us like what we do after school, what we do in other classes, and what other things we do." Another girl explains, "She looks us in the eyes like [she is] interested in what we say." And they report feeling that Julie "understands us" more than the other teachers at the school because she is genuinely interested in their lives and gives "good advice." Conversely, the male students feel Julie understands them as students but knows little about who they are outside of the classroom, which suggests she is better able to connect with students of her own gender. Because of her efforts, students generally seem willing to cooperate in Julie's class—as one male student explains, "I mean, nobody is messing [with] her"—even though she begins to rely less and less upon the use of demerits, and by her own account stops "sweating [all the] small stuff" (like posture and tucked-in shirts).

But while most students seem to appreciate Julie as a person, they express feeling underwhelmed by her pedagogical approach. They characterize Julie's class as "a little boring" because they do "the same thing over and over again," which is "the same as other teachers." When I ask the students if any of their work in her class relates to their life outside of school, most are confused by the question and do not know how to answer. But some tell me that they get to do reflective writing on Fridays and that is their "favorite."

Julie notes that her students seem most engaged when she teaches culturally responsive curricula. The director of curriculum, who designed the units Julie modifies, included what she calls "culturally relevant books"—like those about the Dominican Republic from where many students' families originate. When she begins to teach these books, she notices "a huge up in engagement" and feels the students become "more comfortable" with her as a teacher. However, Julie's lessons around this content are still efficient and controlled, students do not have a lot of time to process or respond to this media, and much of the focus remains on the academic skills students should be developing in reading or writing about this. I do not observe any opportunities for them to engage with the work on a personal level, which may be why they do not bring this content up when I ask them if anything in class relates to their lives.

In the second semester, the director of curriculum stops designing units and Julie is forced to design curricula from scratch, which she feels ill prepared to do. NETR's instructional methods course focused on "modifying" lessons, not designing them, and it never addressed teaching culturally responsive content, which Julie now feels was "irresponsible." Thus, she begins to feel increasingly overwhelmed at PAMS.

By April, Julie has become quite critical of the school leadership at PAMS. Weeks of her class end up being occupied by preparation for PARCC (Partnership for Assessment of Readiness for College and Careers) tests, as the school leadership demands that she give students practice test after practice test while they sit silently. She says she hates this because "they are human beings, not testing robots." As a result, Julie believes students have become increasingly frustrated by and resistant to the school, and she notes that referrals to the dean's office skyrocket around this time (upwards of 50 per day). Julie also voices outrage about the school's hiring of ineffective teachers, which she thinks signals low expectations for students.

While Julie increasingly characterizes the school culture as negative, she views the students positively: "They're very smart kids, and they understand that some of our rules are unnecessary, and overly strict, and unempathetic." For a while, she thinks she will remain at the school despite its challenges because "I really love my kids." But when she tells her students this, she recalls them responding, "Why are you staying? This place is terrible." Ultimately, she seems to have formed relationships with many of them, but neither she nor her students seem invested in the school.

As I watch Julie chat with a group of her female students about romantic relationships, family, and social groups when she takes them to the park in May, I realize that Julie traverses the blurry line between teacher and friend—a line that NETR strongly advises teachers eschew. And the "relational capital" she develops with students seems more a product of her warm personality and willingness to resist school policies than the skills she learned in NETR, which include "sweating the small stuff" and "rowing in the same direction" as other teachers and administrators. However, her lesson planning approach and pedagogical style—even when teaching more culturally responsive content—is quite indicative of her training at NETR, which ends up being inadequate when she has to plan units from scratch.

Although Julie was trained in a culture that promoted possibility, she entered a school dominated by resistance. Thus, she ultimately decides that she can no longer morally justify working at PAMS, where students do not seem to be valued as "human beings" in discipline, testing preparation, or teacher hiring. As the year ends, Julie finds a job at a well-regarded preparatory charter school in the central city where a few of her NETR colleagues work. The culture at this school proves to be much more congruent with what she has learned at NETR; she explains, "There's just more buy-in and I feel more comfortable enforcing the rules, since it's a school and system that families and students voluntarily chose versus PAMS, which was forced upon them. There's just a healthier culture so enforcing the discipline system to the extreme happens waaaayyy less often, which is so nice." At this school where no excuses policies are executed with minimal student resistance, Julie again feels comfortable becoming "much more of a disciplinarian," implementing the strategies she learned in NETR. Despite identifying the potential limits of her training, she maintains her belief in NETR's model and seeks out a school where she can better practice what she has learned.

CASEY AND POSSIBILITY AT TRIUMPH ACADEMY

Unlike Julie, Casey is in his late 20s, has already pursued two different professions—one in sales and one in insurance—and displays a more subdued and relaxed attitude to NETR coursework. Although he is white, he is a first-generation college student. Throughout our interviews, he demonstrates self-effacing humor and self-reflective comments. But as noted in Chapter 3, Casey struggled to balance his humorous authenticity with the disciplinary mandate placed on his shoulders in summer student teaching. He ends the residency year feeling less successful than Julie in the program, but remains optimistic for his first teaching job.

After NETR, Casey secures a job at Triumph Academy Middle School (TAMS). TAMS is located in a gentrifying neighborhood in the central city. Because of its proximity to the ocean, it has become an increasingly popular and somewhat affordable settlement for young professionals. This has led to an increase in housing prices. The students who attend TAMS are not generally from the immediate neighborhood, though, as the charter school selects students through a lottery and thus draws students from several different neighborhoods, most of which are in more industrial parts of the city.

TAMS fills a small three-story brick building that used to be a Catholic school and sits across from a tall gray stone church. Although the school has no courtyard or green space of its own, it abuts a small public playground that is made up of concrete basketball courts and features colorful murals and several tall planted trees. The building itself is brightly lit, with polished wood and tile floors, newly painted walls with colorful accents, and consistent signage and décor featuring the school's colors: navy and marigold. The school day at TAMS also begins when a member of the school leadership greets students and checks for dress code violations. Classrooms feature large windows trimmed with dark blue and school-approved posters on the walls. Like at PAMS, students sit in a desk that is placed next to that of one of their peers, and these pairs of desks are organized in rows across the room. On paper, Casey's school site looks almost identical to Julie's because the CMO of PAMS modeled itself after the Triumph network.

TAMS serves a little over 200 students in total, and most of the students are Latinx, with a handful of white, African American, and Asian American students. The school reports that approximately 70% of students qualify for free or reduced lunch, 10% are English language learners, and nearly 20% have a disability. All of the students have elected to attend this school, and most become acclimated to the model in fifth grade. Students at Triumph do not move rooms, not even for lunch. Instead, the teachers move around them and lunch is delivered to each homeroom class.

Some of the students I interview characterize the school as "overly strict" and "stressful." Nonetheless, most students feel safe at the school, and one tells me that at Triumph she is "really part of a team." Moreover, students seem convinced that attending this school is in their best interest, in that it could lead to economic and social advancement. For example, one of Casey's students tells me that at this school, "they set you up for like later in life." Thus, there is a general sense at Triumph that the students are lucky to be here, as parents or guardians have won them entrance through the lottery.

Because of the school's "pedigree," Casey feels pressure to effectively implement the well-established social studies curriculum he is given when he arrives. He teaches two double blocks of social studies each day: eighth-grade Foundations of Government in the fall, and seventh-grade Ancient Civilizations in the spring. He also helps colead one seventh-grade home-room class throughout the year. In total, he serves 56 eighth graders and 56 seventh graders, but he only has to focus on one group per semester. Like Julie, he sees his students twice each day. Each of Casey's courses comes along with preplanned daily lessons, which he must simply modify to better fit his teaching style. He does this by integrating jokes into the lessons and adding a few additional activities. But for the most part, Casey sticks closely to his school's provided curriculum and maintains efficiency through a timer he projects on the screen at the front of the classroom.

Most of the knowledge Casey transmits to students comes from textbooks and worksheets, and involves the understanding of broad concepts. Students have little opportunity to write about themselves or bring their personal experiences into class. Nonetheless, students display a diligent acceptance of the work Casey assigns. For example, when I observe a "circle discussion" (which appears somewhat like a Socratic seminar in structure) debating the U.S. role in the Vietnam War, some students simply restate what they have been taught, contributing to the discussion with phrases like "In classwork 4.16, it says that . . ." or using terms that Casey has reviewed right before the seminar (like "the domino effect"). Although there is a lot going on in the world during the 2015–2016 school year (e.g., presidential primaries, publicized police brutality, terrorist attacks), I rarely observe the use of current media in Casey's class, which reflects NETR's and Triumph's emphasis on canonical knowledge.

Casey's instructional strategies—which echo how the school's curricula are presented—are also indicative of the efficient methods he acquired at NETR. Most lessons follow a similar format: a Do Now, followed by an introduction of the day's topic, some "turn-and-talk" or brief group work related to this, a short class discussion to share their findings, then independent work. Students tell me that this "technique . . . gets a bit boring at times" and suggest "we are doing the same exact thing over and over." However, Casey's instructional strategies might be more varied than the other teachers at the school. One student tells me, "He lets us work in groups. . . . We learn while we are having fun, and a lot of teachers in the building don't do that as much." Moreover, another student justifies what she feels are repetitive techniques because "he made us learn."

Although he acknowledges that he was a bit of a troublemaker when he was in middle and high school, Casey enforces the school's strict discipline policies without compunction. He manages the class proactively through clear directions, merits, positive narration, and circulating around the room; and he displays reactive management by issuing demerits and other punishments (e.g., detention, suspension) when students talk out of turn, violate dress code, fail to complete assignments, and so forth. I see students serving in-class suspension[3] in his room during 2 of the 5 days I observe. However, Casey seems to soften disciplinary blows with witty comments or sarcasm. For example, when one student tells him that he teased a peer because it was "fun," Casey responds sarcastically, "You know what else is fun? The demerit I am about to give you. No, that's not fun." When he is teaching students about sovereignty, he fittingly jokes, "In my personal classroom, I am the sovereign and no one can tell me differently." At Triumph, he feels it is easy to enforce rules because "You do what I say because I am saying it" is an explicit expectation and students rarely resist consequences. A student tells me, "When he is strict, he is just doing his job."

In line with his NETR training, Casey intentionally seeks to balance this discipline with humor. And in general, students seem to appreciate this. When I ask them about his teaching, they tell me that he enforces "the same rules" as other teachers and employs similar instructional strategies, but is different because "he jokes around a lot." For example, when he writes instructions on the board in somewhat messy handwriting, he playfully observes, "I wrote this on the board in my beautiful handwriting." A couple of students giggle at this, to which he responds lightly, "Don't laugh; I worked hard on that." For Teacher Appreciation Week, TAMS requires all of the students to write notes for all their teachers, and Casey tells me that "80% of mine mentioned class being funny or me being funny." When he told his girlfriend this fact, she asked, "Do you really teach or is this just a stand-up routine for you?" This causes Casey to wonder if he infuses too much humor into class, which would be "danger[ous]" because it could quickly spiral into distraction. He tells me, "I think [NETR] . . . would say you have to be careful with sarcasm and self-deprecation and not cross the line." Thus, NETR has also made Casey keenly aware of a boundary in his connections with students, a tightrope that he must traverse between warm relationships and strict discipline, between authenticity and authority.

Casey seems to make use of his training on calling home to parents. Although initially hesitant about calling the parents of students outside his school assigned advisory group, he reaches out to an increasing number of parents over the course of the year for both "praise calls" and disciplinary reasons. And he finds he especially enjoys calling home with positive reports about students because parents seem to respond gratefully. Casey thus develops a growing appreciation for calling home. He explains, "There is certainly a huge power to the family that I saw in action. . . . I'm having to capitalize on more now." But he acknowledges that he did not end up calling nearly all the parents he should have, and recognizes this as the "biggest area of growth for me next year."

Casey also readily draws on NETR moves in his interactions with students. Casey attempts to connect with individual students through brief interactions in which he casually teases them or practices "the sneeze" from NETR coursework to integrate what he says are "small, insignificant details" about a person into their conversations. One student recalls how Casey "really took an interest in" his fascination with "Batman" and often integrated this into their interactions.

Although some of the students seem to have a desire to be better known and understood by their teachers, most do not expect this at Triumph. One student admits that she wanted to connect more with Casey, explaining that when he told the class that he had experienced depression in his life, "I really wanted to tell him my story . . . so he could give me advice." However, she does not share this because there is little space for students to connect with Casey on a personal level. Students do not fault Casey for not knowing more about who they are outside of class, though, suggesting that they are "private" with teachers. One student admits, "I don't think any of the teachers [know us]." In our interviews, I find that Casey actually knows more about his students than they realize because the school counselors, social workers, and other teachers meet to discuss individual students regularly. Nonetheless, the students tell me they feel Casey "understands the basics of being a teenager," knows about their academic behavior, and "pushes" them to succeed, indicating he cares for them. This is consistent with NETR's emphasis on showing academic care for students, pushing them toward possibility.

Students descriptions of the school correspond with ideas of possibility. One student tells me, "I would say that this school in particular is going to definitely help us not only in high school but in college." As such, they value the academic care Casey shows by holding them to particular academic and behavioral standards. One student recalls Casey reinforcing ideas of possibility when he tells students: "You always have to keep your head up high and be strong, even when you are facing adversity . . . you always have to push yourself." Another student remembers him telling the class, "Triumph exists to give people who aren't at the very top a good chance for education even if they do not have enough money . . . so that we can rise . . . in the social groups and everything." Casey thus fortifies students' belief that Triumph will help them navigate society to achieve their own version of the American dream.

However, Casey tells to me that he knows his students face additional challenges because they are people of color, but that they do not seem to realize the institutional barriers that exist for them. He describes how his students watched a video in homeroom that used Lego blocks to illustrate the stark difference in the statistical social mobility of Black and white students. Casey remembers that when students saw how much harder it was for a Black student to rise up in social classes than a white student, "you could see faces drop around the room. People would stop taking notes and just stare at the screen."

Casey feels this video was an "important" lesson for students because "at some point you've got to be real with kids," but he acknowledges that he doesn't often have explicit conversations with them about the challenges they will face. He tells me, "I want to empower students to take ownership of their own life, and understand that life's not fair sometimes, and that they are fighting an uphill battle." But he adds, "I do not want to impart this identity in them. . . . If a kid doesn't feel different, if a kid doesn't feel other, I don't want to tell them that they are." Although the school provided the aforementioned video, Casey tells me administrators explicitly caution teachers against "imparting" an awareness of oppression onto students. Moreover, Casey feels his NETR training did not provide him with the tools to have critical conversations with students about social realities without simply reaffirming the importance of social navigation.

At Triumph Academy with its interactional culture of possibility, Casey readily draws upon his NETR training to connect with students, carefully tempering his strict authority with his authentic humor. He readily modifies the school curriculum to fit his teaching style and draws upon instructional strategies like those employed throughout NETR. His students come away with an appreciation for his jokes, his academic care for them, and the stories he tells them about his life. However, students also admit that they do not share much of themselves with Casey, even if they wish to, perhaps in part because there are few opportunities in class for them to do and this is not a norm at the school. Still, students generally express being satisfied with Casey as a teacher because he seems to understand them as students, and that is what matters when they believe school achievement leads to life success. Casey, who is satisfied with his position here, remains at the school.

ELISABETH AND NARCISSISM AT LAKESHORE MIDDLE SCHOOL

A self-identified introvert, Elisabeth is soft spoken, earnest, and generous with her attention. She is also one of the only PTR residents who expresses a desire to work in a low-income urban neighborhood, having enjoyed her time with City Year after college. However, after PTR, she changes course. Although she applies to some urban districts, she does not find a job likely because of PTR's lack of connections with urban schools. Still, Elisabeth seeks out work in public schools and gets a job at Lakeshore Middle School (LMS).

Lakeshore is an affluent suburb of the central city with median home prices nearing $800,000. Most citizens of the town are highly educated, upper-income earners. Situated among the town's undulating hills, waterways, and tall trees, LMS looks like a grand library. It features brick walls, three floors of windows, palatial stone columns with a steeple at the center, and an American flag swaying in the breeze. However, the building's internal infrastructure feels dated with buttercup-yellow tiles, calico floors, classroom windows that creak open and shut, and no air-conditioning.

LMS's student population comes from the immediate area and resembles that at Xanadu. Only 6% of LMS students qualify for free or reduced lunch (FRL). Moreover, there is limited racial diversity: the vast majority of students are white, while close to 15% identify as Asian American, and 7% are Latinx or African American. Unlike Xanadu, though, Lakeshore is public and quite large, serving just over 1,000 students in sixth to eighth grade. However, the school has managed to create a more intimate feeling with the use of student teams. Each team consists of approximately 80–100 students in one grade level who mature under the tutelage of the same teachers. The eighth-grade teams are each named after a precious metal or stone, and Elisabeth acknowledges that students derive a strong sense of belonging from this structure.

Because Lakeshore has grown significantly in recent years, the school had to add another "half team" of students. Elisabeth teaches within this small half team—called "Opal Team"—and is the only teacher at the school teaching both English and social studies. Although classes and passing periods are short, Elisabeth's dual role means she sees the same 50 eighth-grade students twice every day, and can more readily get to know them and serve them as individuals. Moreover, the school sponsors enrichment activities for students that teachers participate in, like grade-level field trips. Lakeshore is large, but the students in Elisabeth's classes already know each other well and express a lot of pride in being part of Opal Team. They also all tell me that they "like" school.

Similar to Xanadu, there are undercurrents of excellence at Lakeshore. Parents served by the school closely follow their children's academic achievement and extracurricular activities. Elisabeth finds that many of her students suffer from anxiety because they are "overscheduled," but still feel the need to "get all As." However, the school culture is not one that overly stresses excellence. For example, Elisabeth tells me that Lakeshore is in its pilot year for PARCC tests, and the school leadership's attitude about it is,

"Oh well, just try your best!" Students at the school, including students of color and those who qualify for FRL, already score "far above" the state average on standardized tests, so teachers are not expected to spend much class time preparing students for state exams. And Elisabeth does not feel any pressure from the administration to inflate grades. Although all of this sounds like Xanadu, Elisabeth identifies one primary difference between the schools: Xanadu serves children of the "intellectual elite" who are very intentionally choosing progressive education for their children, whereas parents of children at LMS likely have "very different political beliefs and attitudes about education."

Unlike the teachers at the no excuses schools, Elisabeth has complete authority over how she establishes her classroom space. When I first walk in, I notice a cozy reading area toward the back of the spacious room, complete with a colorful rug and small bookshelves filled with books. When I first observe (day 4 of the school year), colorful student work already lines the walls, reflective of the two creative projects Elisabeth has assigned so far. In her social studies class, Elisabeth works with her students to add yet another cooperative document to the wall: their class constitution. This carryover from student teaching at Xanadu requires students to generate their own class rules, debate about the merits of each, and then ratify their final agreement and put it on the wall. This allows students to shape the culture of the class, communicating to them that this learning experience is about them.

Elisabeth further attempts to establish a safe space through her classroom management. Her demeanor is soft and warm, her presence understated but her words clear and direct. She gives the impression that she takes her work quite seriously but often laughs along with the students. Moreover, Elisabeth imposes a couple of obvious structures to gently guide student behavior—for example, counting down from 5 when she wants their attention and asking them to raise their hands before contributing to group discussions. But beyond that, she gives students a great deal of freedom. I notice moments when students seem to test the limits of Elisabeth's loose control: talking over her soft directions, joking with peers during group assignments, wandering aimlessly around the room. But for the most part, Elisabeth ignores these behaviors and students rarely exhibit disruptive forms of resistance. One student tells me that although students sometimes misbehave, "it's not getting to the point where people are taking advantage of her." And in general, students voice appreciation for Elisabeth's emotional constancy, as she is "really friendly and nice all the time," as opposed to "harsh" or overly strict.

Throughout the year, Elisabeth finds many ways to gain knowledge about individual students. She does this in part through her curricula. For example, one of students' early homework assignments is to write a "chunky paragraph" about their name (or nickname, or the heritage of their name, an assignment she saw modeled in PTR). Several of Elisabeth's students say they value when assignments provide opportunities to share aspects of their "personal life" with her. Elisabeth further connects with students through short, casual conversations before school, during passing periods, on field trips, or after school. Moreover, she often exchanges emails with students and attends some of their extracurricular events.

When I ask her about particular students, I find that Elisabeth knows a great deal about all of them, most of which she has derived from conversations with the students themselves. Her reflections on these conversations demonstrate empathy and understanding, as she describes the challenges that students face beyond the classroom. Finally, Elisabeth communicates that she cares about individuals in her class by writing them each a personalized card when it is their birthday, the idea for which seems to have emerged from an early PTR session that discussed the power of affirming notes from teachers. One student tells me: "Mine was so sweet and it was so nice, probably the best birthday card I've ever seen." In these ways, Elisabeth communicates to students that she values them as people, not just students.

She also makes a point to reach out to parents. Early on, Elisabeth realizes that parents at Lakeshore are "involved," "interested," and value communication, which was much the case at Xanadu. She thus actively tries to engage them, sending group emails to all the parents about her class. She also often reaches out to individual parents if she has a concern about their child, and parents regularly take initiative to email her, too. Then in the winter, the school hosts a large "speed-dating"-like parent conference day in the cafeteria where parents move from teacher to teacher. These brief one-on-one conferences give Elisabeth a chance to learn from parents and share observations she has made about individual students. She characterizes all of her parent interactions as positive but admits that it is sometimes "stressful" to negotiate between parents' insistence on excellence (in grades and requests to recommend their children for honors high school classes) and what Elisabeth perceives are students' social and emotional needs.

Although Elisabeth is supposed to "get through" specified material in both her courses—a series of novels in English and an American history textbook in social studies—she has "total freedom" in how she approaches this material and can supplement it with whatever she wishes. Thus, Elisabeth creates most of her daily lessons from scratch, complete with guiding questions for each unit, as she learned in student teaching at Xanadu. She also finds ways to relate the curricula to the students in her classes and invites them to make their own meaning of the texts she assigns. Students generally seem to appreciate her "more relatable" approach to the curricula. One student explains, "The curriculum this year is just a lot better and the way she handles it is a lot better [than in previous years]." Another adds, "The books that we read, sometimes they relate to my personal life and what

I like to do." Students appreciate that they are invited into the curriculum instead of having it imposed upon them.

Progressive pedagogy echoes throughout Elisabeth's classroom. Before the year begins, she tells me that she does not want to be "that sage on a stage," but "the kind of teacher that lets kids guide" the learning, where they feel "empowered to investigate and be creative." Not all of Elisabeth's lessons reflect this, as she sometimes assigns worksheets or quizzes used by other teachers at Lakeshore, and a couple of the students tell me that they do not like that they are required to read so much out of the history textbook or annotate their novels for homework. But overall, Elisabeth does seem to practice what she preaches. And students tell me Elisabeth is "different" from other teachers, because she "often does a bunch of fun activities," and her teaching style seems like "a nice break from the traditional teaching we've been used to these past 8 years."

In a class-wide debate activity on the Indian Removal Act of 1830—an activity Elisabeth derived from Leah's lessons—Elisabeth assigns all students to one of five historical perspectives. When it is time for the debate, students walk into the room with costumes and props; some young men wear suits or don American flags to represent Jackson, while one student with Huron roots brings in ancestral headdresses and other ceremonial objects to share with her Cherokee group. Elisabeth, too, dresses for the occasion, wearing a long black judge's robe. Most students actively engage in the debate, with very little intervention from Elisabeth, offering eloquent opening statements, vociferously defending their respective causes during debate, and ending with passionate closing statements (some in the form of spoken word poetry). Like at Xanadu, and consistent with a culture of narcissism, many students "ham it up."[4] And after I observe and film this class, students repeatedly ask Elisabeth if they can watch the film.

Instead of taking curriculum at face value, Elisabeth encourages students to take a critical stance in their reading of novels and discussion of history. For social studies, she asks students to respond to Chimamanda Adichie's "Danger of a Single Story" to help them bring a "critical lens" to what the required textbook says about history. Moreover, Elisabeth and her students also regularly make connections between historical and literary content and current events. When they read *Witness*, which confronts the arrival of the KKK in a small Vermont town in 1924, students discuss a present-day incident in which the activist group "Anonymous" hacked into the KKK splinter groups and released the names of those involved. In reference to this, Elisabeth asks students to consider, "Is it okay to do something bad for the greater good?" In both classes, she relies upon a lens that she discovered through Facing History and Ourselves, probing students to consider who the "upstanders, bystanders, perpetrators, and victims" are in historical events and novels. She asks students to contemplate, "If you don't stand up for something, are you taking the side of the oppressor?" This instructional approach—which she tells me she learned in PTR coursework and student teaching—challenges students to think critically about the content she presents and their own actions in the present day.

But while Elisabeth believes in promoting a critical and antiracist perspective, she allows students space to come to their own conclusions about course topics. She tells me that this "very privileged room of kids . . . will go on to positions of great authority" and should learn to consider the needs of other people through the development of "empathy." However, Elisabeth admits she is hesitant to get "up on my soapbox" or "push issues that I think are really important." As she experienced at PTR, she wants students to "come to those realizations themselves" by being asked prodding questions that inform group discussions and self-reflection. The resulting discussions are somewhat dependent on the students in her room, most of whom are white and affluent, and there is not always "consensus" around how society should be. Moreover, the few students of color in the room are usually quiet during these conversations. Elisabeth's approach is consistent with progressive pedagogy and a culture of narcissism: students are empowered to think for themselves. But this does not necessarily advance collective action.

In the end, *all* the students I interview tell me they enjoy Elisabeth's class. One student tells me, "It's really fun actually, I definitely enjoy being in it." Students also express feeling valued and cared for by Elisabeth, both academically and personally. One says, "I feel like she cares about how her students are doing not just in school, but like emotionally too and . . . everything that's outside of school." And when I ask if they feel safe in class, all the students I interview tell me they do. Another student elaborates, "I feel very safe . . . since you are able to sort of speak your mind and have your ideas be respected." And at the end of the year, the students in Opal Team decide to put their class constitution into their team time capsule, reflecting how much they valued Elisabeth's class and the norms they set for each other within it.

Students' appreciation for her class seems largely a result of Elisabeth's attempts to understand and value individual students and personalize instruction for them. While some of this can be attributed to her thoughtful personality, much of it stems from PTR. The conditions Elisabeth encounters at Lakeshore—which include a racially and socioeconomically homogenous student population, little administrative oversight,[5] a manageable number of students whom she sees twice each day, and a supportive interactional culture—allow Elisabeth to remain faithful to PTR's teaching around both teacher–student relationships and pedagogy. Thus, Elisabeth ends her year at Lakeshore feeling successful and remains at the school.

LEAH AND EXCELLENCE AT ZENITH HILLS MIDDLE SCHOOL

Leah is a self-possessed and incisive resident who holds herself to a high standard throughout PTR. After graduating, Leah becomes one of the three PTR residents who gets a job at a public school. She focuses her search on the suburbs and finds employment at Zenith Hills Middle School (ZHMS).

Zenith Hills is among the top three most affluent communities in the state, with a median home price of nearly $1 million. The neighborhood immediately surrounding ZHMS features heavy shade from old-growth trees and stately homes with perfectly manicured lawns and cheerful planted flowers out front.

ZHMS resembles a small college, featuring two to three stories of red brick with windows trimmed in white and a prominent American flag. Despite its stately façade, the yellowed brick walls and patterned tile floors inside feel outdated and it has no air-conditioning and insufficient heating. Like at LMS, only 6% of students qualify for free or reduced lunch. However, wealth is more noticeable at ZHMS, as some of the students characterize being "normal" here as having "money" and wearing brand-name clothing like "Lululemon." However, ZHMS is slightly more racially diverse, with 10% Asian American, 5% Latinx, 5% African American, 5% two or more races. Leah tells me that most of the non-Asian people of color at the school come from the City Bussing Program (CBP), a 50-year-old institution that was established to allow students from the central city (many of whom are middle class) to attend more affluent public schools in nearby suburbs.

ZHMS is also the largest school in my study, serving nearly 1,200 students grouped by teams that share common teachers. However, the ZHMS teams are larger than those at LMS, and Leah observes that most students do not know each other's names by eighth grade. In this context, Leah teaches five different sections of eighth-grade history. This means she is responsible for serving over 100 students in 50-minute classes. Unlike the three other focus teachers, who have far fewer students on their rosters, Leah only sees her students once a day.

The culture of ZHMS seems largely consistent with Anyon's description of excellence. Unlike at LMS, parents at ZHMS seem to have effectively pushed the school away from enrichment activities that appear "fluffy"—like school field trips and socioemotional learning opportunities—and toward "harder" skills. Parents expect their children to get good grades, and there is concern among faculty about the prevalence of "grade inflation" here. Although there are no parent–teacher conferences after sixth grade, parents can email teachers and administrators at any time. But a more veteran teacher advises Leah that she should never meet with a parent alone, because "literally, they will twist your words." Thus, it seems that parents wield a great deal of power at the school; and like those in Anyon's study, parents at ZHMS "know what they want for their kids."[6]

Leah and the students acknowledge and respond to this culture of excellence. One student tells me, "None of the teachers really care about how okay you are" because "at the end of the day, they think school is more important" because "they're trying to prepare us for the future." Thus, students do not feel coddled but do feel the need to compete. Leah tells me that at ZHMS, "the atmosphere is very competitive." She adds that students seem to have a distinct "sense of entitlement" related to this in that "there's a desperateness to wanting to be the best without quite understanding what it takes to do hard work."

Leah, too, occasionally capitulates to excellence. For example, early in the year she assigns a name quiz for which students will receive a quantifiable grade based on how well they are able to identify their fellow classmates. By assigning this quiz, Leah acknowledges students may only put in the effort to learn each other's names if it will affect their performance. When completing this quiz, however, some students "cheat" by surreptitiously conferring with those around them or walking up to view student pictures in the back of the room. While this behavior reveals how little students know about their peers, it also suggests that they are so concerned with achievement that they are willing to cheat on a name quiz. This action surprises Leah, and she increasingly attempts to work against the culture of excellence.

One of the ways Leah attempts to counter the large and competitive culture is by establishing a warm community in her classroom. She puts up inspirational posters and creates a giant empty timeline that she posts in the back of the room for students to fill. She also attempts to build community through class structures and activities. Early in the year, Leah decides to organize the desks into cooperative groups of three or four to "facilitate more cooperation and discussion." Additionally, she requires students to bring in a photo of themselves and write their name and why they selected this photo underneath it; Leah puts these photos on the wall and then asks students to circulate around the room in a gallery walk, making note of their classmates' names and stories and placing sticky notes next to the photos of two people with whom they have something in common. Like Elisabeth, Leah asks students to collectively assemble their class constitution, too. All of this is consistent with her preparation at PTR, as she works to establish a more intimate culture within a large competitive institution.

As she stands in front of the class, Leah's demeanor is charismatic and engaging, her voice clear and firm. She punctuates her lessons with self-effacing humor and witty social commentary. For example, during a lesson on the Mexican-American War, she jokes, "President Polk, Mr. Manifest Destiny, that's not what people called him at parties, but that's what we call him." At other moments, she playfully slips into a British accent. She also anticipates and responds to students' thoughts and behavior in ways that are understated, yet effective: she reveals how she planned for assignments, notes when class discussions might feel "uncomfortable," and acknowledges when extreme cold or heat in the classroom might impact students' ability to learn.

Despite wishing for more preparation in classroom management at PTR, Leah has little trouble managing her classes at ZHMS. She tells me her aim is to embody Delpit's idea of a "warm demander," where she holds students to high expectations and supports them to achieve with personalized attention.[7] One student tells me that Leah "expects a lot from me" but is "really understanding," indicating that perhaps Leah achieves this aim. Leah also uses subtle cues to support her students to complete their work effectively. When students talk during independent assignments or seem to be off topic on group assignments, she softly calls out their name(s), utters, "Shhh," or uses her physical proximity to remind them to return to the task at hand. Leah never raises her voice or issues punishments to any student. In January, she tells me, "I really have had like almost no classroom management issues." Students confirm this, one suggesting, "She knows how to run the class pretty well."

However, Leah quickly realizes that school structures are not very conducive to connecting with students, so she "create[s] structure for myself to have more individual moments" with them. Leah establishes opportunities for individual connections by staying after school to help students with assignments, standing at the door in between classes to greet students, and attending a few of the students' extracurricular events. Within the scope of her classes, Leah seeks out knowledge of students through Google surveys, personal writing assignments, individual projects, and by simply asking questions of them if there is extra time in class (like "What is your favorite thing to do on a rainy day?"). She also seeks out information about them from the counselor and other teachers, but this information feels "hard won" to her, and she ends up learning the most through students themselves. Leah then draws upon her knowledge of students to demonstrate care for them when she writes personalized cards for their birthdays (like Elisabeth does), which students tell me they appreciate. The actions reflect her attempts to recognize students as individuals, not just students, and many of these strategies reflect what she learned at PTR.

Leah also attempts to reach out to families. She describes ZHMS's structures for connecting with parents as "lacking," especially when compared to Xanadu where "they have super intensive parent conferences." She sends emails to all the parents to introduce herself and curricular units, and sends individual emails to a parent if she is concerned about their child. But Leah seems more tentative in initiating connections with parents than Elisabeth, perhaps because of the warnings she received from her colleagues. She also fields emails from many parents, most of which focus exclusively on students' grades. Overall, these interactions feel largely impersonal to Leah, who explains, "It's really weird to me that I've never seen their faces before; if I have to call them or if I get an email, I have no idea who they are." Although she ends up meeting a group of parents at a "Back-to-School" night in the fall, the event does not allow time or space to have individual conversations with parents, and she continues to feel "very divorced from their families" throughout the year.

Nonetheless, Leah hopes that the department's curriculum can help foster connections with and among students. The Social Studies Department created the "Fighting for Racial Justice" curriculum 2 years before when they began to feel that the extremely privileged students at the school needed to understand the history of oppression in the United States. Instead of glorifying the country and those in power, this curriculum focuses on the injustices committed against African Americans, Native Americans, and Latinx people, and how these groups attempted to resist oppressive actions.[8] The units confront issues of slavery and reconstruction, the Mexican-American War, the Trail of Tears and the reservation system, and the role of structural and institutional racism. The year concludes with a Facing History and Ourselves unit that requires students to reflect on their own lives. Leah suggests that this curriculum is one of the reasons she wanted to teach at ZHMS, as she feels it corresponds with her own "aspirations" for students, regarding "questioning and being engaged with issues in the world." In the words of Jean Anyon, this curriculum is also the most "sophisticated, complex, and analytical," as well as the "most honest" and overtly "socially critical" of all the curricula I observe in this study.[9]

Like Elisabeth, Leah has a great deal of flexibility regarding her pedagogical approach to the curriculum. She often uses some of what her department has "brainstorm[ed]" for each day, but also designs her own unique activities and projects. Most of her lessons begin with a Do Now, involve cooperative learning, incorporate technology (like online surveys, short videos, PowerPoints), and avoid lecture. She employs several active learning strategies like gallery walks, Socratic seminars, four corners activities, art projects, and class debates. For example, when they study the Chicano movement in Los Angeles, she asks students to make large murals out of pastels to reflect their understanding of the movement; no other teacher does this, and the beautiful murals are prominently displayed in the hallway surrounding Leah's class.

Students express appreciation for her pedagogy, calling it "fun" because "every day we do a different fun activity," it is "hands on," focuses on "current events," and they get to "socialize" and "move around the classroom." Another student adds that in Leah's class, "you are always entertained; you are never bored." Although her class appears more structured than Elisabeth's, Leah has the freedom to use the progressive pedagogy she absorbed through PTR.

Nonetheless, the interactional culture at ZHMS seems to negatively impact the students in ways that challenge Leah. She feels the competitive academic culture causes students to avoid "tak[ing] risks" in class discussions because they feel "pressure" to "have the right answer." In interviews, students also identify a competitive social culture, a hierarchy of "popular groups and less popular groups," where "gossip," bullying, "drama," and insensitive comments are common.

Moreover, ZHMS has the most racially hostile climate of the schools in my study. For example, Leah tells me that many of the African American and Latinx students have written about "feeling not included" on campus. One of her Asian American students also tells Leah the students "are generally racist" and do not stand up for each other in the ways he wished they would. Furthermore, Leah tells me that she hears "racist comments all the time between classes," but that her white students do not seem to understand that these are "racist things until I point it out." This hostile culture might be one of the reasons why the test scores of African American and Latinx students at the school fall well below their peers.

Leah attempts to address racism and bullying through her curriculum and interactions with students. Students seem to recognize this; one white student suggests Leah would have "no problem stepping in or trying to help kids" if she saw bullying or heard racist remarks. Leah also tells me she intentionally focuses "more of my own emotional energy and time on students of color who [are] not performing well academically and struggle with how they fit into the Zenith Hills community." On 2 of the 5 days I observe, the same group of four to five African American and Latina girls stay after school to work with Leah on class assignments. One of these young women later enthusiastically tells me, Leah is "my favorite teacher!" She adds that she feels she can "come and talk to her about my social problems and we don't sit here and talk about like only academics." In these ways, Leah attempts to create a safe space for her students of color. However, she acknowledges that many of the students who seek her out for extra help still do not "talk that much in my class," suggesting that they still do not feel safe with their peers at ZHMS.

While most students voice appreciation for Leah and her teaching, telling me they like her class "a lot," she ends the year feeling like "the institution itself is not set up" to support connections with students. Although Leah feels like she fostered meaningful connections with the students who came for help after school, she admits, "That wasn't many students. That's sad for me." She tells me that she is envious of Elisabeth's teaching assignment at Lakeshore because Elisabeth serves a smaller number of students whom she sees twice a day, does not have to deal with students who "react poorly to low grades," and works at a school that "feel[s] like a community."

Although she has some pedagogical freedom, her teaching load and the competitive culture of the school make it harder for her to connect with students in ways that are consistent with PTR. Leah concludes, "The [progressive] philosophy is still important to me. Everyone wants to be seen as an individual," but she says she "can't figure out how to do that for so many students. Keep their individual needs in my head." And she ends the year feeling "conflicted" about her job because "I don't feel a great call to teach the children of Zenith Hills."

TRAVERSING INTERACTIONAL CULTURES

Both NETR and PTR left visible imprints on the beginning practice of all four of these teachers, as they faithfully attempted to apply what they had learned in their first year of practice. And in many ways, these two dissimilar approaches to teacher preparation—one based on the use of discrete "moves" and the other based on immersion in a particular environment—both shape the identity of these teachers. Moreover, the intensive residency structure and focus on teacher–student relationships in each program seem to have benefited these four teachers, as their students voiced appreciation for them and presented few classroom management issues. However, the teachers did not all feel equally prepared or able to implement their program learning in the field, and this seems to be related to the interactional culture and institutional structures at the school sites where they secured jobs. Casey and Elisabeth ended up at schools with interactional cultures that mirrored their residency programs, where they eagerly implemented what they had learned to connect with students; meanwhile, Leah and Julie taught at schools with cultures that were inconsistent with their program and thus felt less able or willing to rely on the tools they acquired in teacher preparation. Their successes and challenges illuminate the power and limitations of mission-driven teacher residency programs.

Much of what the four residents in this study learned in their different programs carried over to their first year of practice in obvious ways. Both Julie and Casey from NETR attempted to modify existing curricula to suit their personalities and employed formulaic and efficient pedagogical techniques. At different points, they also employed both proactive and reactive classroom management strategies (like relying upon the use of merits and demerits, affirming desired behaviors, and issuing punishments for infractions). Moreover, they consistently displayed high academic standards for their students, which caused students to feel like these teachers cared about them, at least academically. Julie and Casey also both very much identified as no excuses teachers, believing in the potential of the model and priding themselves on being strict. However, Casey was more able and willing to implement NETR's proposed relational strategies than Julie, seemingly because of school factors.

At first glance, PAMS where Julie worked and Triumph where Casey worked did not appear terribly different from one another: both were no excuses schools in urban areas that predominantly served a population of Latinx students from low-income backgrounds. Both even featured similar bell schedules, disciplinary policies, and signage because the Pinnacle network was modeled after the Triumph network. But while Triumph was characterized by a culture possibility, where students bought into the school as a means of advancing their life outcomes, PAMS was dominated by resistance.

At Triumph, a school of choice, Casey readily implemented tools and strategies he learned in NETR. He intentionally practiced "the sneeze," reinforced messages of possibility and navigation, and "sweat[ed] the small stuff" without compunction. He also found a way to balance his authentic humor with strict authority and efficient lessons. But Julie did not find the culture of PAMS to be as conducive to these strategies. While she initially attempted to follow her NETR training around relationships and classroom management, she grew increasingly resistant to the use of reactive management because it seemed oppressive when imposed on involuntary students. Moreover, she flouted order and efficiency when she created space for students to relax and relied on her own warm personality to connect with students through informal interactions. While contrary to NETR lessons, most of these behaviors actually seemed to benefit Julie's relationships with students because she was not fully complicit in a system that many of them resented; this caused her to conclude, "We have to start treating them like human beings."

But it is worth noting that Julie's training was so powerful that she seemed to abandon this hard-won lesson when she later joined a charter school that was more congruent with a culture of possibility. Because "families and students voluntarily chose" this school, Julie felt more "comfortable" being a "disciplinarian." Imposed on students who opted into the no excuses model, the discipline system seemed less oppressive to her. Thus, in accordance with NETR, Julie found a school "where I can truly 'row in the same direction' as my coworkers and superiors." Even though she seemed to identify the limits of NETR's approach to both relationships and instruction at PAMS, Julie faulted PAMS, not NETR, for these shortcomings. At an influential postcollegiate juncture in her life, NETR cultivated a powerful collective identity—the NETR brand—that Julie held on to, even when her teaching experience contradicted it.

The cases of the two residents from PTR offered analogous findings. Leah and Elisabeth drew heavily on their progressive preparation. They sought out knowledge of students through personal assignments, led community-building activities, facilitated active and varied lessons, relied upon student-centered and cooperative learning structures, discussed current events, and used their curricula to interrogate social structures. They both demonstrated empathy for students in conversations and care in personalized birthday cards. And though PTR empowered teachers to find their own unique approach to teaching, Leah and Elisabeth shared lessons and strategies because they remained close friends and often collaborated. Much like the two residents from NETR, Leah and Elisabeth shared a collective identity as progressive teachers.

But again, Elisabeth was able to form more meaningful connections with individual students and their families than Leah because the culture of the school and the conditions of her particular assignment were more congruent with PTR. Both Leah and Elisabeth taught at affluent suburban public schools that served a predominantly white student body. Both schools were also large, included similar bell schedules, had limited administrative oversight, and organized students into teams. However, LMS and ZHMS had dissimilar interactional cultures. ZHMS was dominated by the theme of excellence, while LMS was characterized by narcissism.

At Lakeshore, Elisabeth readily employed behavior she had learned at PTR, forging close connections with her 50 students, many of whom she engaged with before school, during lunch, after school, and on field trips. She also met with most of their parents and emailed regularly with others in interactions that focused at least in part on students' social and emotional well-being. Moreover, it was easy for her to build a safe and inclusive community in her classroom because students already knew and liked each other. While Leah attempted to implement many of the same strategies to connect with students and families throughout the year, the school culture and institutional structures seemed to impede her ability to foster as many meaningful relationships with students.

Leah had twice as many students to serve, most of whom did not even know each other's names at the beginning of the year. Despite her attempts to create a safe and inclusive culture in her class, she felt the competitive social and academic climate prevented students from taking risks in class; and she used a lot of "emotional energy" trying to counter the racial hostility she perceived. Furthermore, she had limited interactions with parents, largely restricted to email and focused on student achievement. She did not have a chance to bond with students during "fluffy" activities like field trips, and she felt like she really only formed meaningful relationships with those who came after school for extra help. At the end of the year, Elisabeth reported a sense of satisfaction with her job, while Leah felt conflicted. Leah primarily blamed structures at ZHMS for inhibiting the formation of meaningful teacher–student relationships, as the progressive philosophy remained an "important" part of her identity.

Research suggests that teachers should learn to teach in a school context similar to the one where they will ultimately work.[10] The most obvious contextual similarities are educational model, student demographics, neighborhood urbanicity, class sizes, and bell schedules. And many preparation programs take these factors into consideration when they prepare their teachers for particular school environments. However, the cases of residents from NETR and PTR suggest that a school's interactional culture, which is not obvious on the surface, could influence teachers' ability to connect with their students. In fact, the relational aspects of a teacher's practice might be even more context dependent than the so-called cognitive aspects of practice (like lesson planning and pedagogy). All of the teachers represented here (including Leah and Julie) used a pedagogical approach that was consistent with their programs; but the culture of the school seemed to notably influence these teachers' relational practice, more so even than school structures (like size and bell schedule, which were similar across sites).

Incongruence between program and school sites challenged residents to connect with students in ways that were less consistent with their program, and at least in Julie's case, more consistent with her naturally warm personality. However, the identity residents cultivated in the programs—one that was tied to the ability to exercise particular relational competencies—was so powerful that residents at schools with less congruent cultures ended up criticizing or rejecting their school sites in favor of their programs. While some research suggests that preservice teachers might "resist coherent messages" from their programs "when they find it difficult to engage in recommended practices" at their school sites,[11] this is not the case for these residents.

Both NETR and PTR provided powerful formative experiences for these teachers, but what residents learned in these self-insulated worlds was not quite applicable to all settings. This is an important finding for mission-driven teacher educators looking to adequately prepare teachers to work in specific contexts. Teachers should either be trained in a culture like the one to which they will matriculate, or they should be trained in multiple different contexts and learn to recognize, respond, and adapt to a variety of school cultures as part of their teacher identity.

NOTES

1. Anyon, Jean. (1981). Social class and school knowledge. *Curriculum Inquiry, 11*(1), p. 32.

2. I did not go into this study looking for school's that reflected Anyon's four themes for teacher–student interaction. I simply selected these four teachers and followed them into their

schools. But by happenstance, the four schools at which I observed them each largely reflected one of Anyon's themes.

3. At Triumph, students serving in-class suspension sit at the front of the room, back to their peers, wearing an inside-out sky-blue T-shirt over their clothes, while completing work without interacting with others.

4. Anyon, Jean. (1981). Social class and school knowledge. *Curriculum Inquiry, 11*(1), 21.

5. By this I mean, "loose coupling," a term that suggests that there is very little oversight or control from school or district administrators. It comes from Meyer, John W., & Rowan, Brian. (1978). The structure of educational organizations. In M. W. Meyer (Ed.), *Environments and organizations.* San Francisco, CA: Jossey-Bass.

6. Anyon, Social class and school knowledge, p. 24.

7. Delpit, Lisa. (2012). *Multiplication is for white people.* New York, NY: New Press.

8. Notably, this curriculum omits a focus on the school's largest nonwhite group: Asian Americans, who have a similar history of oppression in the United States. One of Leah's Asian American students identifies and criticizes this omission.

9. This corresponds with the executive elite school Anyon documented in "Social Class and School Knowledge," pp. 26 and 37.

10. Feiman-Nemser, Sharon, Tamir, Eran, & Hammerness, Karen. (2015). *Inspiring teaching: Preparing teachers to succeed in mission-driven schools.* Cambridge, MA: Harvard Education Press; Clift, R. T., & Brady, P. (2005). Research on methods courses and field experiences. In M. Cochran-Smith & K. M. Zeichner (Eds.), *Studying teacher education: The report of the AERA panel on research and teacher education* (pp. 309–424). Mahwah, NJ: Erlbaum.

11. Clift & Brady, Research on methods courses, p. 331.

Chapter Nine

Relationship Lessons

Fundamentally, care was more motivating than authority, reciprocal relationships more effective than power over, listening more useful than lecturing, healing more beneficial than punishment.—Carla Shalaby, *Troublemakers*[1]

We know that the individual teacher in the classroom makes more of a difference in a student's progress than any other factor the school can control.[2] Research also shows that teacher–student relationships play an important role in this process, with meaningful relationships facilitating better academic and social and emotional outcomes for students.[3] But neither teachers nor teacher–student relationships receive the respect they deserve.

Just as teaching is considered a low-status profession in the United States, due in part to its historical association with "women's work,"[4] so too are the relational aspects of teaching—which may be considered "feminine"[5] or "soft"—relegated to the subtext of educational discourse and scholarship. But the relational side of teaching is incredibly complex, especially when teachers are working across lines of perceived difference (not just in terms of race, which has been my focus in this book, but also in terms of ethnicity, language, socioeconomic status, gender, sexual orientation, religion, etc.). Because every student deserves a teacher who sees and cares for them, the development of teacher–student relationships warrants more consideration in schools, in policy, and in teacher education.

In the field of teacher education—which informs teachers' thinking and practice at a fundamental level—the relational aspects of teaching are undertheorized, undersupported, and underexamined.[6] Therefore, many teacher education programs likely neglect a focus on teacher–student relationships, thereby perpetuating tacit assumptions about these relationships. This is irresponsible, because not only would teachers benefit from support to develop meaningful relationships with students, but as this book demonstrates, teacher education can have a powerful impact on teachers' relational practice. This may be especially true in teacher residency programs.

The two programs represented here, No Excuses Teacher Residency (NETR) and Progressive Teacher Residency (PTR), shared some common residency components: they operated around a distinct mission, interwove coursework and practice, relied upon extensive fieldwork with students, and ensured that residents received thoughtful and coherent feedback about their practice through trained coaches (NETR) or skilled guiding teachers (PTR). Both programs also *intentionally* approached the development of teacher–student relationships. Residents from both programs cited their extended fieldwork—particularly the fieldwork that allowed them to foster more natural relationships with students during less structured time—as particularly salient in their learning to connect with students.

In their first professional teaching positions, graduates of these programs clearly demonstrated pedagogical and relational practices they had learned in their residency programs. This was easier for teachers when school structures—especially a school's *interactional culture*, the dominant trends that characterize teacher–student interaction in educational spaces—were conducive to these practices. However, even when their school culture did not support the kinds of relationships they had learned in their programs, residency graduates criticized their school sites, maintaining their faith in what they learned in teacher preparation. This suggests that residency programs may be quite influential for teacher–student relationship development, at least early in novice teachers' careers.

However, residency programs are by no means a panacea for meaningful student connection, because the relationships teachers form with their students will largely depend on their preparation program's vision of and support for such relationships. In fact, the differences between NETR and PTR shed the most light on the process of teacher–student relationship development, with powerful implications for the students served by graduates of these programs.

A TALE OF TWO RESIDENCIES

The two programs represented throughout this book reveal a great deal about how relationships can be conceived of and developed quite differently in teacher education spaces and beyond. NETR conceived of relationships as *instrumental*: a teacher-directed process that must be undertaken to ensure maximum effort and compliant behavior from students; the program taught residents to acquire "professional relationship capital" with students toward this end by using discrete moves like calling home to parents or having one-on-one conversations with students to address "problem[s]" in class. But the program focused so heavily on going through the motions of relationships that it largely ignored the affective components of these connections.

In contrast, PTR established relationships as *reciprocal*, where teachers gathered complex information about students as "whole people," primarily through conversations with, and reflective assignments from, the students themselves. Residents were also taught to self-reflect and cultivate empathy and care for students by observing and supporting them within the classroom and at extracurricular events. While residents learned to draw on these sources of knowledge and experiences to design curricula and instruction for students, the program did not provide residents enough guidance around other relational actions, such as classroom management or connecting with parents.

However, even without their explicit relational visions, each program's pedagogical approach alone would have communicated a great deal about the role and character of teacher–student relationships in these programs, as such relationships cannot be disentangled from the medium through which they are forged. In NETR, teachers were treated as interchangeable technicians who could enter any classroom, pick up predetermined unit plans, "modify" lessons if needed, and implement a range of discrete moves to manage student behavior as they disseminated standardized knowledge. The urgency to achieve their end goal—advancing the achievement of students who faculty identified as "behind" their peers—resulted in pedagogy that was directive and teacher centered and curricula that generally reflected the Western canon (not the student population). In the context of this urgent mission, relationships with students became transactional, a controlled means to advancing student achievement; there was no time for "thinking and feeling," for messy human connections, when it came to efficiently increasing test scores.

Alternatively, PTR upheld the notion that knowledge was something to be co-constructed between teachers and students. Teachers had to be highly skilled professionals who could design and implement curricula that responded to the students, and instruction that invited students to make sense of content through discussions and assignments. But to enact this vision, teachers first had to gain holistic knowledge about students, to foster the kinds of connections between themselves and students and among students that would support classroom dialogue. Such relationships were time consuming and variable, but nonetheless fundamental to the entire learning experience proposed by PTR. Plus, the affluent and mostly white students at Xanadu often seemed to feel entitled to this kind of relational attention from teachers, for they viewed themselves as partners in their learning.

While they might appear extreme or idiosyncratic, NETR and PTR represent pervasive values, instructional methods, and relational tools that are visible across the landscape of education in the United States. Whenever the focus of schooling turns to quantifiable educational outcomes or results (e.g., standardized test scores, budgetary efficiencies), students are treated as products (or broken windows), leading teachers toward more standardized and superficial relationships with them. Conversely, when the tide shifts toward "whole-child" models of education, teachers must form highly individualized and reciprocal relationships with them to support their holistic development. Because teacher–student relationships are intertwined with context, content, and pedagogy, different schooling models invariably lead to the different kinds of relationships.

However, it is important to consider which students have access to each educational and relational approach. Both programs in this book aspired to serve students of color in some capacity and thus sought to equip their residents with some form of racial competence. However, neither program quite fulfilled this aspiration because PTR centralized "thinking and feeling" about race without fieldwork that enabled them to act on this learning, and NETR focused almost exclusively on actions like teaching historically marginalized students to "navigate" the culture of power.

PTR teachers learned to identify and interrogate social forces like racism and their own privilege. They also learned to speak critically about racism in mostly white contexts, which is undoubtedly an important step in supporting white students to understand how forces like racism shape society. However, many of these conversations, at least in the context of PTR coursework, remained unmoored, without an explicit overarching mission or framework to support antiracist work. Because residents directed much of the learning in PTR coursework, and learned most relational actions in fieldwork, the program's white homogeneity—both in its resident population and the students they served in fieldwork—became a great limitation. Residents did not have many opportunities to cultivate cross-racial relationships, and when they sought out teaching jobs, they did not feel comfortable going into schools that primarily served students of color. This suggests that critical knowledge about racism can only go so far without experience with, and explicit support for, working with students of color.

Conversely, NETR teachers secured employment at schools serving almost entirely students of color, due to the program requirement that they teach at urban public and charter schools. Equipped with the tools of navigation—teaching those from historically marginalized backgrounds how to adopt behaviors common to the dominant culture to succeed in spaces of power—residents felt prepared and entitled to serve a population that mirrored that of the no excuses schools where they completed their fieldwork. But this strictly navigational approach to schooling precluded critical discussions of race. Residents did not have the opportunity to address racism within the no excuses context, or within themselves; there was no space to do the "internal work" of antiracism. Instead of preparing teachers to support students to understand and confront the structural barriers they may face because of their race, NETR's approach tacitly endorsed the existing culture of power, essentially representing those who cannot or do not effectively navigate it as deficient in some way. This approach denies meaningful recognition to those who do not ascribe to the dominant culture.

The philosopher Charles Taylor writes of the importance of recognition (individually and in society), of people understanding another's "defining characteristics as a human being." While recognition can help people better understand themselves and support them to live full and happy lives, "nonrecognition or misrecognition can inflict harm, can be a form of oppression."[7] Teachers might unintentionally misrecognize students through deeply ingrained deficit thinking or stereotyping, or they might not recognize students at all if they are focused on teaching the class as a whole without taking the time to connect with the individuals in their care. Thus, recognition is not a given in schools; instead, teachers must *learn* how to recognize and connect with all their students, especially across lines of perceived difference such as race. And how they are taught to do has great implications.

REPRODUCTION THROUGH RELATIONSHIPS

Upon the establishment of universal public education, Horace Mann declared schools "the great equalizer," the place where all children can go to gain access to an educational experience that uplifts them all equally.[8] This pervasive idea has led to varying educational movements like those represented above, as reformers attempted to best serve all students. However, the reality of schooling has never lived up to its ideals. Instead, socioeconomic status has largely predicted a student's educational attainment, and the "achievement gap" between students from low-income backgrounds and those from upper-income backgrounds has only increased over time.[9] The long-standing disparity between the educational and life outcomes of non-Asian students of color and white students also persists.[10] And the way teachers form relationships with students in different settings likely contributes to these social inequalities.[11]

Teachers represent significant adult figures in students' lives.[12] From an early age, children often spend more waking hours with their teachers than they do with their parents. Through their expressly granted authority and this extended proximity to students, teachers can wield a strong influence over the way children think about themselves, others, and the world. The way teachers interact with their students, and the way they position students in relation to themselves, their peers, and the act of learning, can thus have great implications.

The two programs represented in this book both aimed to achieve a "social justice" vision of their own, attempting to counteract the tide of social reproduction that has pulled at schools for centuries. In NETR, the goal was "social justice through good teaching technique." The theory of action behind this idea was that if students from historically marginalized backgrounds had access to teachers who could effectively and efficiently equip them with dominant forms of knowledge and ways of behaving, these students could perform well on standardized tests and get into college so they could advance socially and economically. But the program reinforced the traditional hierarchy of teacher–student relationships, which positions students as receptacles to be filled with a predetermined set of knowledge and skills. [13] And forming connections with student was only envisioned as a means of advancing this end. With this in mind, all NETR graduates went on to teach students of color in urban charter and public schools.

In PTR, the social justice goal was very different: to prepare "change agents" who could carry the tools of progressive education to both privileged students and to those who rarely have access to this kind of education. These tools included knowledge of society, critical thinking, and the ability to form reciprocal relationships. In PTR, reciprocal relationships that very much resembled what Martin Buber calls an "I–Thou" relation—characterized by dialogue, reflection, empathy, care, and agency—became the foundation of the entire progressive learning experience, with the idea that teachers could not teach effectively without first knowing their students and establishing community among them. By dismantling the hierarchical teacher–student dynamic, teachers and students were allowed a process of joint personal development in the classroom, a process that could be liberatory for students, especially those from historically marginalized groups. [14] However, the intensive focus on PTR residents' personal development in a progressive space, coupled with the lack of support for meaningful work with students of color and low-income students, led residents to seek out teaching jobs at schools that more closely resembled Xanadu Community School. All the graduates of PTR ultimately chose to teach at independent and affluent, suburban public schools serving mostly white students. [15]

This distribution of NETR and PTR teachers led to separate and unequal relationships in schools. Already privileged students received PTR teachers who formed meaningful reciprocal relationships with them, which emphasized their inherent value as human beings and their agency over their educational (and life) experiences. Such interactions prepared them to critically analyze social situations, to engage with authority figures, and to someday hold positions of authority themselves. Meanwhile, historically marginalized students received NETR graduates who formed instrumental relationships with them as a controlled means to a particular end: student compliance. Students learned that their value was tied to the degree to which they navigated the system by working hard and behaving in line with what mostly white authority figures demanded, not in their own right. Such relationships essentially conditioned students for positions of subservience. This phenomenon may be indicative of a larger trend in our schools: privileged students have more access to reciprocal relationships with their teachers than historically marginalized students.[16]

I saw this pattern reflected in teacher–student interactions throughout the schools where I observed residency graduates. At the two Title-1 schools that predominantly served students of color where I followed NETR graduates, teacher–student interactions centered around control. Teacher control took the form of both disciplinary enforcement and mystifying logics like possibility—the idea that if students worked hard and behaved for teachers, they could achieve whatever they wanted in life.[17] At the two affluent schools where I followed PTR graduates, students had a great deal more agency and power over their learning, placing them on more equal footing with their teachers. In one school, this translated into self-directed learning experiences and self-advocacy; in the other, it manifested in individualistic competition for good grades and social status. In the former two schools, teachers saw their students as academic beings who needed to complete their work and behave without excuses; at the latter schools, teachers viewed their students as "whole people," with meaningful lives beyond the classroom that influenced their work within it. This reinforces the idea that privileged students in general likely have more access to this full human recognition in schools and society.

In some ways, partial and instrumental relationships like those advanced by NETR seem better than no teacher–student relationship. Many no excuses schools do not emphasize forming relationships with students in any capacity, and thus the students of the NETR graduates whom I observed felt these teachers' attempts to connect with them were better than most of the teachers at their schools. Although they did not see themselves reflected in the curriculum, or often feel understood as people outside the classroom, students did report feeling cared for by the NETR graduates in an academic sense. In the absence of full and holistic recognition, it seems the teacher who even partially recognizes students is a step above the rest.[18]

But ultimately, instrumental teacher–student relationships are not enough for any student. As Paulo Freire explains, "The world of culture, which is also the world of history, is the world where freedom, choice, decision, and possibility are only possible because they can also be denied, despised, or refused. For this reason, the education of women and men can never be purely *instrumental*. It must also necessarily be ethical."[19] Being ethical, according to Freire, requires a dialogical and reciprocal relationship between teacher and student, an I–Thou relation that allows for the critical interrogation of structures in school and society. For without this give-and-take, this process of joint personal development, classrooms may reproduce established power structures in society, where mostly white teachers socialize what is now a majority of students of color into relationships of obedience.[20] In a country where the Constitution once sanctioned the partial recognition of African Americans—as only three-fifths that of a white person—American society still has much to do to overcome the residual devaluation of children of color. And partially recognizing students, connecting with them only as a means of advancing their academic output, is not going to correct past oppression; it will only reinforce it.

In the end, NETR's social justice aspirations were likely limited by its instrumental vision of relationships, which many no excuses schools seem to share (if they confront teacher–student relationships at all).[21] This might be one of the reasons why some research has found that no excuses schools improve students' standardized test scores but ultimately fail to improve their life outcomes.[22] To truly move forward, students must be able to embrace their own agency and learn to understand and confront the structural barriers they may face because of their skin color and/or socioeconomic status. If NETR embraced a new vision of relationships, though, it might have to reevaluate other aspects of its approach to education, too, because teacher–student relationships cannot be fully disentangled from pedagogy or school discipline.[23]

PTR, on the other hand, upheld a meaningful vision for teacher–student relationships but failed to support residents to carry this vision to historically marginalized students. To change this, the program would have to embrace a more explicit focus on racial and socioeconomic equity, recruit more residents of color, incorporate clear frameworks (e.g., culturally responsive pedagogy) to support cross-racial practice, and require fieldwork at schools serving a much more racially diverse population of students. But in attempting to support more fieldwork in racially diverse schools, it is possible that PTR might also come to realize the limits of its own approach.

While these changes seem profound, neither NETR nor PTR is satisfied with resting on its laurels. PTR's subsequent resident cohorts have been more racially diverse than when I observed, and NETR has redesigned much of its coursework around relationships and race. The leaders of both programs continue to aspire to improvement, and that in and of itself is hopeful.

A "THIRD WAY" FORWARD FOR TEACHER EDUCATION

Teacher residency programs are often hailed as a "third way" to prepare teachers, one that borrows the best aspects of traditional and alternative programs, but remedies their weaknesses.[24] As noted above, the two residency programs represented in the book proved highly influential over the relational practice of beginning teachers. And while promising in different ways, each program had shortcomings that inhibited its ability to promote meaningful teacher–student relationships across racial and cultural differences. However, there are other unique teacher education programs that seem to be approaching meaningful relationships in encouraging ways that may warrant further research.

One such program is High Tech High's Teaching Apprenticeship Program (TAP). Like NETR and PTR, TAP is a teacher residency program with close connections to one school. It emerged out of High Tech High, a network of schools in San Diego, California, with a clear mission and vision for both teaching and teacher–student relationships. Similarly, TAP requires extensive fieldwork in High Tech High schools that aims to prepare teachers for a specific set of affiliated charter and public schools, much like NETR does; this reduces the alignment issue that PTR faced when it attempted to prepare teachers for a broader range of schools. Like PTR, TAP's philosophy is based in ideas of "student-centered" progressive education; but according to Sarah Fine, the program director of TAP, the High Tech High network has been engaged in extended critical discussions about "anti-racist pedagogy and culturally responsive or sustaining pedagogy and how that fits in with and/or pushes the boundaries of what historically our schools have been trying to do." TAP centralizes antiracist education and attempts to equip residents with "a set of perspectives and then practices that help them operationalize those commitments." For example, residents in the program complete a yearlong seminar focused on equity that helps residents cultivate racial competence through "self-work," analysis of "structural inequalities [that] have shaped our society and our schools," and culturally responsive and critical pedagogical practices. One of the practices emphasized by the program is "empathy interviewing," where teachers ask thoughtful questions of individual students to "jump-start relationships." TAP is also committed to serving a cohort that is at least 50% people of color and places residents in classrooms with racially diverse students and cooperating teachers, whom the program also supports with 5 days of training. Although only in its second year, TAP is a formalized extension of the High Tech High Intern Program, which has received accolades for its ability to prepare teachers to support deeper learning. [25]

UCLA's Teacher Education Program (TEP), where I completed my own teacher education, is another example of a program that thoughtfully prepares teachers for meaningful relationships with all students. [26] Since its inception in 1992, the TEP at UCLA has operated with a clear social justice vision, one focused on preparing teachers and students in low-income schools with the tools to transform society, not just navigate it. [27] Like NETR, all TEP graduates are expected to teach in an urban Title-1 school after graduating. But unlike NETR, teacher–student relationships are not treated as a separate element of teaching; instead, the relational aspects of teaching are woven throughout the program. Though not called a residency program, TEP integrates many of the components of successful residencies. A cohort of racially diverse preservice teachers in TEP complete extended clinical placements in public schools across LA with mentor teachers that they select themselves after observing in their classrooms. Coursework incorporates theory but responds to practice, equipping teachers with the tools of sociocultural theory and culturally responsive pedagogy, discussing the history of education in the United States and Los Angeles more specifically, and grappling with the "moral, cultural, and political dimensions" of teaching students with a range of academic and personal needs. Like PTR, TEP features extensive self-reflection and social analysis, coupled with a focus on getting to know and care for students as complex human beings. But unlike PTR, TEP supports preservice teachers to develop racial competence through its explicit social justice structures and fieldwork with racially diverse students before they become full-time classroom teachers. TEP also continues to support its teachers into their first year of practice with a field supervisor who observes and provides feedback on their teaching and additional coursework focused on instructional methods or local neighborhood issues as the teachers complete a thesis for their master's in education. It is thus not surprising that many of the Los Angeles Unified School District or even the Los Angeles County Teachers of the Year are graduates of this program.

NETR and PTR, plus the two programs described above, offer guidance for teacher educators looking to better prepare teachers for meaningful relationships with all students. In addition to recruiting more racially diverse candidates, teacher education programs should attempt to do the following:

- *Articulate a clear vision around teacher–student relationships,* one that aligns with theory and research around the importance of reciprocal and responsive relationships. In the process, programs should consider how their context, pedagogy, and disciplinary approach influences the enactment of such relationships.
- *Employ coherent coursework aimed at the development of multifaceted relational competencies that support this vision,* from knowledge of self and students, to dispositions like empathy and care, to actions like connecting with parents and designing responsive curricula and instruction (described further in Chapter 7).
- *Explicitly address equity or social justice and integrate "internal work" throughout program structures.* A critical component of this is racial competence. To help preservice teachers develop racial competence, programs must support them to confront their own deep-seated biases as they gain understanding of the social and institutional forces that impact their students. Although not the focus of this study, the same is likely true for supporting teachers to work across lines of gender and gender identity, class, dis/ability, and sexual orientation.

- *Require meaningful fieldwork with students from diverse ethnic, cultural, class, and linguistic backgrounds to support the development of relationships with all students.* Because as this study indicates, "thinking and feeling" is insufficient without action.
- *Establish clinical experiences that also allow preservice teachers time to connect with students in informal ways.* Residents in both NETR and PTR cited the fieldwork experience that allowed for more natural interactions with students (Tutorial in NETR and the Xanadu placement in PTR) as most salient in relational development. Residents reported that the individual personal conversations they had with students gave them insight into the human beings they served and helped them consider how to best connect with future students.
- *Support teachers to connect with students in schools that are not fully aligned with the culture and structure of their programs.* UCLA's TEP may offer some guidance on this point, as it exposes preservice teachers to a range of schools with different cultures early in the program and then explicitly addresses the challenges of teaching in different school cultures throughout coursework. Graduates learn strategies for working within (and sometimes against) different cultures as they form relationships with their students. Moreover, they continue to receive support from the program in their first year of practice.

There is much that teacher education programs can and should do to centralize and support the development of meaningful relationships between teachers and students. Such programs have a responsibility to initiate this process, as they prepare teachers at a fundamental level.

LESSONS FOR SCHOOLS

Relational behavior begins at home *and* at school. The way that teachers connect with students in their classroom has implications for the way we interact in society. Therefore, all educators must foreground teacher–student relationships, uplifting the human side of education so that it becomes at least as prominent as the more procedural and so-called cognitive aspects of the endeavor. Although teachers may (or may not) build the capacity to form meaningful relationships with students in preservice teacher education, the work does not end there. Instead, the real and sustained work of humanizing relationship-building must be supported by schools. As I learned from and with the four residents I followed into their first classrooms, certain school structures may better facilitate the formation of teacher–student relationships than others.

First, size (and teaching load) matters, and bigger is not better. The no excuses schools in this study seemed to have figured this out, with smaller schools, smaller classes, and fewer students for each teacher to serve. It is clearly easier to form relationships with individual students when a teacher only has 30–60 students in total to connect with, not over 100.[28] This was the case in both affluent and low-income contexts.

Second, proximity matters. It helps when teachers can see their students more often or for longer sessions. Teachers who worked with students for longer periods of time, or more than once a day, felt better able to "see" their students. The one teacher in my study who taught five different classes of students each day, and saw them each only once a day, found it hard to really get to know them.

Third, informal connection matters. Teachers should have informal time with students—through advisories, field trips, passing periods, lunches, and so forth—to connect around nonschool issues. The teachers in this study often learned more about students in their informal meetings during short passing periods, between classes, or at lunch than they did in class.[29] But teachers also need support to connect with students in these less formal settings; if they are simply placed with students without planning or preparation to support relationship development, teachers will likely have to exert more energy on behavior management than connecting.

Fourth, parent–teacher connections matter. Schools should work with parents or other primary caregivers to create opportunities for these interactions. When schools put structures in place for teachers to connect with individual parents, the teachers in this study made these connections and learned a lot about their students in the process. Systems to call home to parents regularly, with support for language translation if needed, can be helpful, as can formal parent meetings with child care provided and in locations that may be outside the school (e.g., libraries).

Finally, academic norms matter, as they contribute to school culture. In the no excuses schools in this study, urgency was the enemy of human connections. Urgency bled the joy out of classes, supported the strict enforcement of discipline, informed an efficient pedagogical approach, and precluded informal connections with students. In the affluent schools, excellence[30] had a similarly detrimental effect on teacher–student relationships and relationships between students. Excellence reinforced the need to compete with one's peers, the intensive focus on grades, the reduction of "fluffy" activities that might have facilitated less formal connections between teachers and students and among students. To change these trends, educators must accept that academic rigor and relationships are not in fact antagonistic. Instead, meaningful holistic relationships with students can support deeper learning.[31]

As this study suggests, school factors influence the development of teacher–student relationships. While teacher education programs can do a lot to prepare teachers to form meaningful connections with students, schools need to do their part, too.

RECOMMENDATIONS FOR TEACHERS

Within schools, the teachers are undeniably the ones implementing this work; they are the lynchpins of the entire educational and relational experience in schools. As I know from personal experience, this work is incredibly challenging, with new demands placed on teachers every day. However, even amidst these demands, teachers must prioritize relationships with students, because such relationships truly are the core of this profession. To support relationships, teachers can do the following:

1. *Learn about students.* Their families, their interests, their cultural or religious practices, their hobbies, their challenges, their fears, their hopes and dreams. This can be done through surveys, personal letters, class assignments, and conversations with students and parents or guardians.
2. *Explore the community surrounding the school with an asset-based lens.* Walk or drive around the neighborhoods where the students live, and find the beauty and unique resources there, as opposed to simply looking at this through a deficit lens.
3. *Reflect on yourself and your practice often.* Consider why you came into this work and why you chose to serve the population you did. Take some time to think about the social forces that have shaped your life, and think about those that impact your students. Acknowledge the differences, and respond with humility. Reflect on whether you feel more able to connect with some students than others, and if so, why that might be.
4. *Commit to equity and antiracism.* Read books, articles, and websites about social issues that you know affect the students you serve (e.g., racism, xenophobia, sexism, homophobia, transphobia, classism). Talk to others who have experience with these issues, gain understanding, and commit to enacting best practices for supporting your particular students.
5. *Be authentic.* Show them pieces of who you are. Admit expertise in the areas where you are expert and ignorance in the areas where you are not. Share your authentic passions with students as a means of driving your curriculum forward, and make space for theirs.

6. *Cultivate empathy for students.* Try to understand where they are coming from, why they might have made certain decisions, how their life shapes their behavior. Sometimes, there are genuine excuses for behavior that digresses from school norms. Allow yourself to feel some of what they feel, if even for a moment.

7. *Care for students, both academically and personally.* Help students with assignments, hold them all to high expectations, tell them you believe in them; but also, check in with them if they seem upset, ask how you can help, attend one of their extracurricular events. Small gestures like greeting students at the door with a smile as they enter your classroom and telling them that you look forward to seeing them the next day can also be meaningful.

8. *Connect with families.* Send letters home with students, call parents or guardians with concerns *and* affirmations, email them, text them, encourage families to come to school events, even schedule home visits. Find ways around language barriers with faculty or staff members helping you translate. Do not let this crucial part of practice slip through the cracks.

9. *Design responsive curricula and instruction.* Feature authors or historical figures that reflect students' ethnicities and cultural heritage. Employ varied instruction that responds to students' particular needs and preferred modes of learning. Create assignments that allow students to demonstrate their individual knowledge and expertise. Do not be afraid to ask students to interrogate existing structures around the content you teach and society at large. Read about culturally responsive teaching, culturally relevant pedagogy, and critical pedagogy for more on this.

10. *Finally, create a safe and inclusive space in your classroom.* Have students help create a class compact. Have them participate in determining what kind of environment they want to learn in. Do not let racist or unsafe comments go unaddressed. Put systems in place to help students work together. Do your best to maintain a calm, considerate, even-keeled tone, even when challenged. Try to keep students in the classroom—as opposed to immediately sending them out for disciplinary infractions—to avoid severing those ties that connect students to the class community.

Teachers are really the ones with the power to make a difference by connecting with students, and following these recommendations may help ensure more meaningful relationships.

RELATIONSHIPS IN, AND FOR, THE FUTURE

We expect schools to equip students for the future. To many, this means providing students with the content knowledge and accompanying cognitive skills to fulfill basic functions in society (e.g., deciphering a bus schedule, completing governmental forms, applying for and performing in jobs). But others believe that schools should be focusing just as much on students' social and emotional learning, including the ability to self-reflect, to cooperate, to behave with respect and care for others.[32] Meaningful relationships with teachers support both outcomes.

Through such relationships, teachers can invite students into the academic content, prompting new passions; teachers can start a dialogue that enables students to articulate their own thoughts and feelings, to discover who they are; teachers can make their students feel "seen" and model how to see and connect with others. But the inverse of this also seems true: if teachers fail to foster such connections, their students might have less access to both the academic and social and emotional competencies they need to not only function in society, but to build a better one.

As noted above, there is much that teacher education programs, schools, and teachers can do to support more meaningful relationships with students. Future research also needs to centralize teacher–student relationships, as much as topics like curriculum, pedagogical strategies, and standardized testing (which currently dominate much of the educational literature). More research is needed into how traditional and alternative programs approach teacher–student relationship development, and how graduates of these programs enact program learning in beginning practice. Researchers should also explore how teachers across different types of schools enact relationships in the classroom. But as the study documented in this book suggests, teacher–student relationships are complex and intertwined with content, context, pedagogy, and discipline; they cannot be studied in a vacuum. Therefore, future research should attempt to consider institutions holistically in order to better understand their approach to relationships.

The potential of the United States, or of any nation, relies on the preparation of its citizens to build community, think critically, and improve social structures. Establishing meaningful teacher–student relationships in schools can help mend the tattered fibers of this country's rich and diverse tapestry by teaching students that our differences do not have to become divides. Relationships with students may thus be the most important aspect of teaching, for through these connections, teachers model our future.

NOTES

1. Shalaby, Carla. (2017). *Troublemakers: Lessons in freedom from young children at school.* New York: The New Press, p. 145–6.

2. Sanders, W. L., & Rivers, J. C. (1996). *Cumulative and residual effects of teachers on future student academic achievement.* Knoxville: University of Tennessee Value-Added Research and Assessment Center.

3. Cooper, Kristy. (2013). Eliciting engagement in the high school classroom: A mixed-methods examination of teaching practices. *American Educational Research Journal, 51*(2), 363–402; Furrer, C., & Skinner, E. (2003). Sense of relatedness as a factor in children's academic engagement and performance. *Journal of Educational Psychology, 95*(1), 148–162; Hallinan, M. T. (2008). Teacher influences on students' attachment to school. *Sociology of Education, 81,* 271–283; Martin, Andrew J., & Dowson, Martin. (2009). Interpersonal relationships, motivation, engagement, and achievement: Yields for theory, current issues, and educational practice. *Review of Educational Research, 79*(1), 327–365; Roorda, D., Koomen, H., Spilt, J., & Oort, F. (2011). The influence of affective teacher–student relationships on students' school engagement and achievement: A meta-analytic approach. *Review of Educational Research, 81*(4), 493–529; Sosa, Teresa, & Gomez, Kimberley. (2012). Connecting teacher efficacy beliefs in promoting resilience to support of Latino students. *Urban Education, 47*(5), 876–909; Schonert-Reichl, Kimberly. (2017). Social and emotional learning and teachers. *The Future of Children, 27*(1). Retrieved from https://files.eric.ed.gov/fulltext/EJ1145076.pdf

4. Griffin, Glenda. (1997). Teaching as a gendered experience. *Journal of Teacher Education, 48*(1).

5. Nel Noddings embraced this fact, titling her first book *Caring: A Feminine Approach to Ethics and Moral Education.* The feminine is not, of course, inferior in any way, but because of the historical subjugation of women in the United States and many other countries, the association of teaching with women and the association of caring and relationships with the feminine has resulted in a reduced-status position.

6. Grossman, Pam, & McDonald, Morva. (2008). Back to the future: Directions for research in teaching and teacher education. *American Educational Research Journal, 45*(1), 184–205; McDonald, Morva A., Bowman, Michael, & Brayko, Kate. (2013, April). Learning to see students: Opportunities to develop relational practices of teaching through community based placements in teacher education. *Teachers College Record, 115,* 1–35.

7. Taylor, Charles. (1994). The politics of recognition. In A. Heble, D. Palmateer Pennee, & J. R. (Tim) Struthers (Eds.), *New contexts of Canadian criticism.* Peterborough, ON, Canada: Broadview Press, p. 25.

8. Graham, Patricia A. (2005). *Schooling America.* New York, NY: Oxford University Press.

9. Reardon, Sean. (2013). The widening income achievement gap. *Educational Leadership, 70*(8).

10. In numerous reports on the "achievement gap," most groups of Asian American students have performed as well as, and often better than, white students on average. Hsin and Xie (2014) find that this is because Asian American students often work harder than white students, believing that achievement is a product of effort, not innate ability. But these authors also caution that this cultural belief in hard work can come at a social and relational cost, suggesting that teachers need to work hard to support Asian American students through relationships, too. See also Morin, Monte (2014, May 5). Study examines achievement gap between Asian American, white students. *Los Angeles Times.*

11. Golann, Joanne W. (2014). The paradox of success at a no-excuses school. *Sociology of Education, 88*(2), 102–119; Bowles, Samuel, & Gintis, Herbert. (1976). *Schooling in capitalist America: Education reform and the contradictions of economic life.* New York, NY: Basic Books.

12. Tatar, Moshe. (1998). Teachers as significant others: Gender differences in secondary school pupils' perceptions. *British Journal of Educational Psychology, 68*(2), 217–227.

13. Freire, Paulo. (1970). *Pedagogy of the oppressed.* New York, NY: Continuum; Noddings, Nel. (2013). Freire, Buber, and care ethics on dialogue in teaching. In R. Lake & T.

Kress (Eds.), *Paulo Freire's intellectual roots: Toward historicity in praxis*. New York, NY: Bloomsbury.

14. Freire, *Pedagogy of the oppressed*.

15. With the exception of Ashley, the one African American resident, who chose to enter an urban charter school in New York City; but she only remained for one semester before she quit and went on to an independent school that was more consistent with Xanadu.

16. As noted in Chapter 7, this is a phenomenon that Anyon observed; see Anyon, Jean. (1981). Social class and school knowledge. *Curriculum Inquiry, 11*(1), 3–42. It is also one that Bowles & Gintis commented upon in *Schooling in Capitalist America*. More recently, this phenomenon has been represented in the following: Valenzuela, Angela. (1999). *Subtractive schooling: U.S.–Mexican youth and the politics of caring*. New York, NY: SUNY Press; Golann, Paradox of success.

17. Anyon, Social class and school knowledge.

18. Green, Elizabeth. (2014). *Building a better teacher: How teaching works (and how to teach it to everyone)*. New York, NY: Norton; Golann, Paradox of success.

19. Freire, Paulo. (1998). *Pedagogy of freedom: Ethics, democracy, and civic courage*. Lanham, MD: Rowman & Littlefield, p. 57, emphasis mine.

20. Golann, Paradox of success. For further analysis of how these programs may have contributed to social reproduction, see Theisen-Homer, 2020.

21. Mehta & Fine also find a lack of meaningful teacher–student relationships in the no excuses schools they study. See Mehta, Jal, & Fine, Sarah. (2019). *In search of deeper learning: Inside the effort to remake the American high school*. Cambridge, MA: Harvard University Press.

22. See Dobbie, Will S., & Fryer, Roland G. (2016). Charter schools and labor market outcomes. *NBER Working Paper Series*.

23. Fine, Sarah. (2017). *Struggling toward humanization: Restorative justice, deeper learning, and the pursuit of transformed relationships at an urban charter school*. (Doctoral dissertation). Harvard University, Cambridge, MA., p. 39.

24. Berry, Barnett, Montgomery, Diana, Curtis, Rachel, Hernandez, Mindy, Wurtzel, Judy, & Snyder, Jon D. (2008). Urban teacher residencies: A new way to recruit, prepare, develop, and retain effective teachers in high-needs districts. *Voices in Urban Education, 20*(13); Berry, Barnett, Montgomery, Diana, & Snyder, Jon. (2008). *Urban teacher residency models and institutes of higher education: Implications for teacher preparation*. Chapel Hill, NC: Center for Teaching Quality.

25. High Tech High's Teacher Intern program started in 2004. The Intern Program is recognized in Darling-Hammond, Linda, & Oakes, Jeannie. (2019). *Preparing teachers for deeper learning*. Cambridge, MA: Harvard Educational Press.

26. See the program's website at https://centerx.gseis.ucla.edu/teacher-education/about-us/ for more information.

27. For a discussion of the difference between navigation and transformation, see El-Amin, A. (2015). *"Until justice rolls down like water": Revisiting emancipatory schooling for African Americans—A theoretical exploration of concepts for liberation* (Unpublished doctoral dissertation). Harvard University, Cambridge, MA.

28. Sizer, Theodore. (1984). *Horace's compromise: The dilemma of the American high school*. New York, NY: Houghton Mifflin.

29. McDonald, Bowman, & Brayko similarly found informal time supported the development of teacher–student relationships in community organizations in their article "Learning to See Students."

30. I use Anyon's definition of excellence from "Social Class and School Knowledge."

31. Mehta & Fine, *In search of deeper learning*.

32. See the Aspen Institute's National Commission on Social, Emotional, and Academic Development and their 2019 accompanying report *From a Nation at Risk to a Nation at Hope* at https://www.aspeninstitute.org/programs/national-commission-on-social-emotional-and-academic-development/.

Epilogue

The genuine educator does not merely consider individual functions of his pupil, as one intending to teach him only to know and be capable of certain definite things; but his concern is always the person as a whole, both in the actuality in which he lives before you now and in his possibilities, what he can become.—Martin Buber, *Between Man and Man*[1]

As I raise my two little girls, I cannot help but consider where we have landed as a society, and where I wish we were. In some ways, it appears we have become increasingly divided from one another, and alienated from our collective humanity. We are not doing a really good job "seeing" past our perceived divides, seeing the person behind the façade. Our differences often blind us to our similarities. This manifests in the painfully divided political climate, one where a person might physically accost another for having different beliefs. This divide is further evidenced in the police brutality against people of color, in the rising neo-Nazi and white supremacist movements, in the increasing number of mass shootings. Somewhere, somehow, people are losing sight of each other. And those who do not feel "seen" might fall into depression, drown themselves in narcotics, or lash out—sometimes violently—to call attention to themselves. While we maintain surface-level connections with many more people than in the past via social media, we seem to come up short on deep and meaningful relationships with the complex and multifaceted human beings around us.

All of this causes me to despair about the world into which I have brought my daughters. But a wave of change seems to be cresting at the horizon. It seems that we are headed for a social "reckoning."[2] People are beginning to stand up and declare their right to be seen and heard; the long oppressed are making their plight known in the form of movements like Me Too and Black Lives Matter. But this, too, can initially cause backlash among those who do not understand it. If an equitable and just future is to be forged from the mayhem, then programs like those in my study have to respond in kind, move along with the tide, grow, change, and evolve. Much of the work for the future of our nation begins in the classroom, these microcosms of society, sites where children learn how to form relationships with others and better understand themselves. Teachers are responsible for modeling and facilitating the development of meaningful relationships here, but they must first learn how to do so thoughtfully. This is where teacher training comes in. And honestly, it gives me hope.

As I experienced at UCLA, and as I have seen in these two programs, teachers can be taught to form relationships with students. They can learn to reevaluate their own history, reasons for teaching where they do, and motivations for teaching particular lessons. They can learn to honor parents and guardians, to reach out to them in multiple meaningful ways. They can learn to listen to students: what they say, what they imply, what they omit. They can learn to care for students, to push them academically, to try to empathize with their needs/interests/worries. They can learn to draw upon their knowledge and understanding of students to design responsive curricula and instruction. They can learn to view students not as pupils who must acquire a predetermined set of skills, but as multifaceted human beings capable of teaching quite a bit to themselves, each other, and the teacher.

And while connecting with students allows teachers to better serve their students, it also makes their own work more intrinsically rewarding; for in the process of seeing others, they too are seen. Forming meaningful connections with our fellow human beings uplifts us all. So let's build a better society. One connection at a time. And let's start in the classroom.

NOTES

1. Buber, Martin. (1965). *Between man and man*. London: Routledge, p. 104.
2. This term has been used in the *New York Times*, *Newsweek*, *The Atlantic*, *Time Magazine*, and other media to refer to this time of cultural change.

Methodological Appendix

When I became a doctoral student at Harvard in the fall of 2011, I found myself adrift, unmoored in a place that was too far removed from the teaching job in Los Angeles that gave me meaning and vitality. I did not see myself in this Ivy League institution, and I took every opportunity to travel back to Los Angeles to reconnect with the people and the place that fed my soul. I took my first meaningful foray into research in LA. Here, I studied teacher agency because the teachers at the school where I used to work were fighting amidst a great recession for their students and their livelihoods. I also studied teacher dismissal because the resulting reduction in force (RIF) layoffs—conducted in reverse seniority order—had caused irreparable damage at this school and many others within Los Angeles Unified School District (I myself received two RIFs during my 4 years in the classroom). But neither of these topics truly ignited my passion, in part because they dealt more with the forces that drove me from the classroom and less with those that continued to anchor my spirit to this incomparable profession. I continued to feel lost.

I did not find my calling within the university until the spring of 2014 when I read Pam Grossman and Morva McDonald's article "Back to the Future: Directions for Research in Teaching and Teacher Education." In this article, the authors identify that teacher–student relationships are "remarkably undertheorized" and add:

> Any framework of teaching practice should encompass these relational aspects of practice and identify the components of building and maintaining productive relationships with students. Such an understanding might be particularly useful in preparing teachers who can work effectively with students who differ from them in terms of race, ethnicity, socioeconomic status, and language. [1]

This article called to me, because I realized that what I missed most from the classroom were my relationships with the students, relationships that had supported both my own success as a teacher and their success as students. Upon reflection, I also realized that UCLA had largely prepared me, a white woman, to form meaningful relationships with the students of color who I served. This was critical, because a range of scholars have documented the negative effects white teachers can have on students of color without the ability to see and serve them adequately. However, my research on teacher education more broadly indicated that the preparation I received at UCLA might be rare. I found several quantitative studies that linked teacher–student relationships with positive student outcomes; but as Grossman and McDonald identified, I found almost no empirical research in the field of teacher education that directly explored how teacher education programs approached the relational aspects of teaching. This felt like a critical oversight to me, one that guided me to conduct the study that informs the pages of this book.

To study this, however, I first had to find teacher education programs that were intentionally approaching the relational aspects of teaching. I drew on my academic and professional connections, setting up meetings with different educational leaders who eventually directed me to No Excuses Teacher Residency (NETR) and Progressive Teacher Residency (PTR). Both were teacher residency programs, and I began to hypothesize that because of their heavy focus on fieldwork, residency programs might be uniquely positioned to support the development of teacher–student relationships. Plus, there was limited research on teacher residency programs, too, which gave me further incentive to study these programs. Though incredibly different from one another, both NETR and PTR featured an explicit and intentional focus on teacher–student relationship development, which was lacking in most of the other programs I had considered studying. Finally, I anticipated that their differences would yield a particularly rich comparison. I had found my two research sites.

RESEARCH QUESTIONS

I began designing my research project around the question: How does each program conceive of preparing new teachers to form relationships with students, especially across racial and cultural differences? Because "how" questions are often better addressed through qualitative than quantitative research, I knew this would lead me to observations of program coursework and fieldwork, document collection, and interviews with faculty. But I was interested in getting a more complex picture of the experience, so I also asked: How do novice teachers within each residency make sense of their relational training? To address this question, I would attend closely to residents' words and behavior in coursework and fieldwork and interview a representative sample of these residents. But I did not want to stop there, for I had also come across scholarship that criticized teacher education research for not following program graduates into the field to document how they drew upon their preparation coursework in practice.

I wanted this research to address the effects of teacher preparation on classroom relationships. Thus, I asked: How (if at all) do white teacher residents in beginning teaching practice draw upon their preparation when forming relationships with students, especially students of color? Although I strongly believe that more research needs to focus on teachers of color, and understand the justifiable criticism of research that centers whiteness, I chose to follow white teacher residents into the field for a few reasons. When I first visited these programs, I saw that there was only one resident of color in PTR (though I later learned that one of the white residents identified as Latina), and she taught preschool. Having taught high school myself, I wanted to focus on secondary teachers who taught humanities (English or social studies) because I could more readily understand their teaching experiences and the relationships they formed with teenagers though these experiences. I was not yet a parent, and did not understand much about young children or what they needed from relationships with adults. In PTR, there were only four secondary humanities residents, all of whom were white. And I wanted the teachers I focused on in NETR (which was more racially diverse) to be demographically similar to those I selected from PTR. Furthermore, I had found several studies that suggested white teachers often failed to establish meaningful relationships with students of color, indicating that learning to form relationships with students across racial and cultural differences might be especially important for white teachers. Because 82% of teachers (and those in the teacher education pipeline) are white, I also believed the implications of the preparation each teacher received could be better extended if I followed white teachers into the field. Nonetheless, I made a point to seek out the voices of residents of color within these programs to help make sense of the work I would observe in both NETR and PTR.

METHODOLOGY

From these research questions, I designed a study using what my colleague Sarah Fine calls a "case study approach through ethnography and portraiture."[2] Both ethnographic case research and portraiture view phenomena holistically, considering both individual actors and the ways in which their behavior is shaped by context, culture, and relationships.[3] Both methods also operate on the belief that "universal themes" can be revealed in "the particular." Moreover, both rely heavily on the qualitative data sources of documents, interviews, and observations. However, these methods differ in the analysis and presentation of data. As Lawrence-Lightfoot and Davis observe, "Ethnographers listen *to* a story while portraitists listen *for* a story."[4]

I relied heavily on portraiture throughout the research process. This methodology was ideal for this study because "relationship building is at the center of portraiture,"[5] and thus the method mirrored the research topic. In portraiture, the relationship between the researcher and participants is thoughtfully constructed and carefully maintained, as participants are not regarded solely as sources of data, but as human beings worthy of respect and generosity. It is also phenomenological, privileging the perspectives of participants and the subjective and relational nature of their experiences. Moreover, portraiture attends to the "voice of the researcher," and necessitates that the researcher reflects upon their own embodied perspectives and the biases these involve; in my case, this means acknowledging that I approach this work from the perspective of a white female teacher who brings my own preconceptions of society and teacher education from my preparation at UCLA.

Portraiture is also aesthetic. It uncovers subtle aspects of personal and institutional culture and behavior, including cultural symbols, verbal refrains, guiding metaphors, and understated gestures. Portraiture's final products are narrative and analytic, full of thick and thin description that captures the context and participants with detail and complexity. As Lawrence-Lightfoot and Davis assert, "The portraitist is not interested in producing a facile, idealized portrayal; rather she is committed to pursuing the complex truths, vigilantly documenting what supports and distorts the expression of strength."[6] I have aimed to create portraits of these programs in Parts I and II of the book that are nuanced and textured, shining a mirror on these programs in the hope of evoking reflection.

In Part III of the book, though, I utilized comparative case study methodology,[7] drawing upon the ethnographic data in the development and presentation of my findings, which build from the initial portraits. Unlike portraiture, case studies do not attend to the "aesthetic" presentation of findings in the same way. Instead, they rely more heavily on theory to make sense of data and are often more succinct and analytic. Furthermore, case studies are not necessarily phenomenological, and thus allow me the opportunity to step further away from my data to represent findings in broader strokes, including the "patterns and themes that cut across these" cases and portraits.[8]

DATA COLLECTION

Data collection for this study extended from September 2014 through July 2016. In the first year, I embedded myself in the two different programs, which were located in the same metropolitan area. I traveled back and forth between programs, collecting program documents and conducting approximately 40 hours of observations of relevant coursework and activities in each program. During observations, I took rich ethnographic field notes,[9] paying special attention to content related to teacher–student relationships, the pedagogy modeled by faculty, and novice teachers' responses to coursework.

I employed "purposeful sampling"[10] to select three to four program faculty and staff and nine to ten residents in each program for 45- to 60-minute semistructured interviews. For the staff and faculty, I sought participants who had expert knowledge about the program and its relational vision, and who could provide guidance around observing relevant coursework and activities. For the residents, I interviewed a representative sample (in terms of race, gender, content area, and grade-level focus) of each resident cohort. These interviews provided me insight into each program's broader goals, intentional practices, and how new teachers responded to coursework.

During this time, I also began to follow white teacher residents into fieldwork. From my resident interview participants, I selected two white focal teachers from each program who planned to teach middle school humanities (English language arts and/or social studies) at either urban charter or public schools; these shared characteristics enabled me to better compare their experiences. I began by observing each of these teachers in their field placements two to four times in the fall and/or spring. In PTR, I initially observed all four humanities residents in fieldwork, but later narrowed these focal participants down to the two who sought out teaching jobs in public schools. I conducted 20- to 40-minute interviews with each focal participants' guiding teacher (PTR) or coach (NETR) to better understand these residents' developing relationships with students. At the end of residency year, I interviewed each focal resident a second time. A focus on these teachers yielded a much richer understanding of each program and how it influenced individuals, and specifically white teachers.

In the study's second year, I followed these four focal teachers into their first year of full-time teaching at four different school sites. I observed them each for 5 full school days over the course of the year (twice in September and then once in November, February, and May), observing each teacher for a total of 30–40 hours (depending on the length of the school days that I observed). I filmed two of these observations and then engaged in "simulated recall"[11] interviews with each participant after they watched clips of their practice. In addition to these two simulated recall interviews, I conducted six more semistructured interviews with each participant over the course of the year, which varied in length from 25 to 70 minutes. Additionally, I collected documents from each teacher, including syllabi and assignments.

To assess student responses to teacher practices throughout this unit, I collected student work and interviewed 8 to 11 students from each teacher's roster. I relied upon the teacher to help identify students whose parents had completed consent forms, thereby allowing their participation in the study and interview. I conducted interviews in both individual and group formats—per the preference of the students—in February and May during noninstructional time. Individual student interviews lasted anywhere from 6 to 12 minutes, while the group interviews, or focus groups, lasted up to 45 minutes. Most of these interviews were audio recorded and later transcribed verbatim. All of this enabled me to develop a strong sense of how teachers applied learning from their residency programs, as well as how their students responded.

DATA ANALYSIS

In sum, the collected data—typewritten observations, transcribed interviews, memos, and documents—consisted of more than a thousand pages. Analyzing this data was an interactive process that brought me back and forth between data, participants, relevant scholarship, reflection, and back to data. Initially, I analyzed the data from each case site separately,[12] employing inductive and deductive coding schemes. I used thematic coding[13] to consider emergent themes and apply codes to passages related to this. For example, the code "efficiency" emerged over 100 times in observation and interview data from NETR, while the code "individualized instruction" emerged over 70 times in PTR data. During this process, I also drew upon the "impressionistic record"[14] and "analytic memos"[15] that I generated in the field to help me refine my codes. Next, I drew upon a conceptual framework I had generated of components of teacher–student relationships to apply deductive codes to data. These codes included: knowledge of self, knowledge of students, knowledge of society, care for students, responsive curricula and instruction, classroom community/management. For example, I applied the code "knowledge of self" (a relational competency from my conceptual framework), to instances where coursework challenged residents to reflect on their previous educational experiences, where faculty discussed the importance of self-knowledge or reflection, or where residents discussed the ways in which the program promoted self-knowledge or reflection. Excerpts often received both inductive and deductive codes.

When data collection was complete, I engaged in a cross-case analysis.[16] During this phase, I applied codes that emerged from individual sites that seemed relevant to both and made note of similarities and differences across cases. I then generated core-focused codes from my inductive and deductive codes to aid in the development of initial theories. During this stage, I began noticing a trend toward codes like reciprocity, dialogue, and reflection in one program and efficiency, instrumentalism, and control in the other; this led me to identify the relevance of Buber's I–Thou relation as a frame to better understand the two residencies' relational approaches. I then returned to the data again, looking for both confirming and disconfirming evidence of these theories.

By triangulating data sources in each phase of study—including document analysis, direct observations, and interviews—I intended to reduce the "systematic biases or limitations of a specific method"[17] and adequately address the multifaceted subject of relationships. During data collection and analysis, I also considered the "dissonant voices"[18] that ran counter to general trends in the data (e.g., NETR residents who voiced critical interpretations of the program), and I collected additional data or conducted further analyses to adequately evaluate these. Because the study of relationships is by nature a subjective process, I also wrote copious process memos in an attempt to monitor my own biases and reflect on my positionality as a white woman doing research in this space.[19] Moreover, I completed member checks by meeting and discussing my inchoate findings with individuals from each residency and shared snippets of data and discussed my initial theories with colleagues who "have some distance from the study" to gain further perspective.[20] In these ways, I attempted to ensure the rigor of my data analysis and the validity of my findings.

Because this study is small in scale, and the research sites offer a unique take on education and relationships, the findings here cannot be generalized to the teacher education landscape at large. The field needs more research on how traditional teacher education programs attempt to prepare teachers to form relationships with students and how graduates of these programs integrate this learning into their beginning relational practice. Further research should also explore how teachers in a range of schools construct relationships with their students to identify whether the trend toward unequal teacher–student relationships is more pervasive.

Nonetheless, this study adds a substantive addition to the literature by conceptualizing teacher–student relationships—in the forms of knowledge, dispositions, and actions—to understand how different programs approach this work. It also contributes to the growing body of work on teacher residencies, providing insight into how teacher residency programs with a no excuses or progressive ideology may approach relational work. Finally, it establishes the "I–Thou" relation as a useful framework for evaluating teacher–student relationships in different contexts. According to Freire and Buber, dialogical relationships with educators can build community, advance critical consciousness, and promote social change; whereas objectifying relationships dehumanize, humiliate, and oppress students.[21] This study, as designed, provides insight into how teacher education programs can powerfully advance a particular vision of teacher–student relationships, with great implications.

NOTES

1. Grossman, Pam, & McDonald, Morva. (2008). Back to the future: Directions for re-search in teaching and teacher education. *American Educational Research Journal, 45*(1), 188.

2. Fine, Sarah. (2017). *Struggling toward humanization: Restorative justice, deeper learning, and the pursuit of transformed relationships at an urban charter school* (Doctoral dissertation). Cambridge, MA: Harvard University, p. 39.

3. Patton, Michael Quinn. (2002). *Qualitative evaluation and research methods.* Thousand Oaks, CA: Sage; Yin, Robert. (1994). *Case study research: Design and methods.* Thousand Oaks, CA: Sage.

4. Lawrence-Lightfoot, Sara, & Davis, Jessica Hoffmann. (1997). *The art and science of portraiture.* San Francisco, CA: Jossey-Bass, p. 13.

5. Lawrence-Lightfoot & Davis, *Art and science of portraiture*, p. 188.

6. Lawrence-Lightfoot & Davis, *Art and science of portraiture*, p. 159.

7. Stake, Robert E. (2013). *Multiple case study analysis.* New York, NY: Guilford Press.

8. Patton, *Qualitative evaluation and research methods*, p. 57.

9. Emerson, Robert M., Fretz, Rachel I., & Shaw, Linda L. (2011). *Writing ethnographic fieldnotes.* Chicago, IL: University of Chicago Press.

10. Maxwell, Joseph A. (1996). *Qualitative research design: An interactive approach* (Vol. 41). Beverly Hills, CA: Sage.

11. Calderhead, James. (1981). Stimulated recall: A method for research on teaching. *BritishJournal of Educational Psychology, 51*(2), 211–217.

12. Stake, *Multiple case study analysis.*

13. Boyatzis, Richard E. (1998). *Transforming qualitative information: Thematic analysis and code development.* Thousand Oaks, CA: Sage.

14. Lawrence-Lightfoot & Davis, *Art and science of portraiture.*

15. Miles, Matthew, & Huberman, Michael. (1994). *Qualitative data analysis: An expanded sourcebook.* Beverly Hills, CA: Sage.

16. Stake, *Multiple case study analysis.*

17. Maxwell, *Qualitative research design*, p. 75.

18. Lawrence-Lightfoot & Davis, *Art and science of portraiture.*

19. Boyatzis, *Transforming qualitative information.*

20. Maxwell, *Qualitative research design*, p. 93.

21. Freire, Paulo. (1970). *Pedagogy of the oppressed.* New York, NY: Continuum; Buber, Martin. (1965). *Between man and man.* London: Routledge.

Bibliography

Alexander, Michelle. (2010). *The new Jim Crow: Mass incarceration in the age of colorblindness.* New York, NY: New Press.

Anyon, Jean. (1981). Social class and school knowledge. *Curriculum Inquiry, 11*(1), 3–42.

Argyris, Chris. (1977, September). Double loop learning in organizations. *Harvard Business Review.*

Aspen Institute. (2019). *From a nation at risk to a nation at hope.* Retrieved from https://www.aspeninstitute.org/programs/national-commission-on-social-emotional-and-academic-development/.

Ball, Deborah Loewenberg. (2000). Bridging practices: Intertwining content and pedagogy in teaching and learning to teach. *Journal of Teacher Education, 51*(3), 241–247.

Berry, Barnett, Montgomery, Diana, Curtis, Rachel, Hernandez, Mindy, Wurtzel, Judy, & Snyder, Jon D. (2008). Urban teacher residencies: A new way to recruit, prepare, develop, and retain effective teachers in high-needs districts. *Voices in Urban Education, 20,* 13.

Berry, Barnett, Montgomery, Diana, & Snyder, Jon. (2008). *Urban teacher residency models and institutes of higher education: Implications for teacher preparation.* Chapel Hill, NC: Center for Teaching Quality.

Bonilla-Silva, Eduardo. (2014). *Racism without racists: Color-blind racism and the persistence of racial inequality in America.* Lanham, MD: Rowman & Littlefield.

Bowles, Samuel, & Gintis, Herbert. (1976). *Schooling in capitalist America: Education reform and the contradictions of economic life.* New York, NY: Basic Books.

Boyatzis, Richard E. (1998). *Transforming qualitative information: Thematic analysis and code development.* Thousand Oaks, CA: Sage.

Boyd, Donald, Goldhaber, Daniel D., Lankford, Hamilton, & Wyckoff, James Humphrey. (2007). The effect of certification and preparation on teacher quality. *The Future of Children, 17*(1), 45–68.

Brilhart, Dan. (2010). Teacher conceptualization of teaching: Integrating the personal and the professional. *Journal of Ethnographic & Qualitative Research, 4*(4), 168–179.

Brinkworth, Maureen, McIntyre, Joseph, Juraschek, Anna D., & Gehlbach, Hunter. (2017). Teacher–student relationships: The positives and negatives of assessing both perspectives. *Journal of Applied Developmental Psychology, 55,* 24–38.

Brooks, David. (2016, November 1). Read Buber, not the polls. *New York Times.* Retrieved from https://www.nytimes.com/2016/11/01/opinion/read-buber-not-the-polls.html.

Buber, Martin. (1958). *I and thou.* New York, NY: Scribner & Sons.

Buber, Martin. (1965). *Between man and man.* London, England: Routledge.

Calderhead, James. (1981). Stimulated recall: A method for research on teaching. *British Journal of Educational Psychology, 51*(2), 211–217.

Callahan, R. E. (1964). *Education and the cult of efficiency*. Chicago, IL: University of Chicago Press.

Carter, Prudence. (2005). *Keepin' it real: Why school success has no color*. Oxford, England: Oxford University Press.

Clark, Christopher, & Lampert, Magdalene. (1986). The study of teacher thinking: Implications for teacher education. *Journal of Teacher Education, 37*(5), 27–31.

Clift, R. T., & Brady, P. (2005). Research on methods courses and field experiences. In M. Cochran-Smith & K. M. Zeichner (Eds.), *Studying teacher education: The report of the AERA panel on research and teacher education* (pp. 309–424). Mahwah, NJ: Erlbaum.

Cochran-Smith, Marilyn, Villegas, Ana María, Abrams, Linda, Chavez-Moreno, Laura, Mills, Tammy, & Stern, Rebecca. (2015). Critiquing teacher preparation research: An overview of the field, part II. *Journal of Teacher Education, 66*(2), 109–121.

Cooper, Kristy. (2013). Eliciting engagement in the high school classroom: A mixed-methods examination of teaching practices. *American Educational Research Journal, 51*(2), 363–402.

Cooper, Kristy, & Miness, A. (2014). The co-creation of caring student/teacher relationships: Does teacher understanding matter? *The High School Journal, 97*(4), 264–290.

Darling-Hammond, Linda. (2012). *Powerful teacher education: Lessons from exemplary programs*. San Francisco, CA: Jossey-Bass.

Darling-Hammond, Linda, & Bransford, John. (2007). *Preparing teachers for a changing world: What teachers should learn and be able to do*. San Francisco, CA: Jossey-Bass.

Darling-Hammond, Linda, & Oakes, Jeannie. (2019). *Preparing teachers for deeper learning*. Cambridge, MA: Harvard Educational Press.

Delpit, Lisa. (1988). The silenced dialogue: Power and pedagogy in educating other people's children. *Harvard Educational Review, 53*(3).

Delpit, Lisa. (2012). *Multiplication is for white people*. New York, NY: New Press.

Dewey, John. (1900). *The school and society*. Chicago, IL: University of Chicago Press.

DiAngelo, Robin. (2011). White fragility. *International Journal of Critical Pedagogy, 3*(3), 54–70.

DiAngelo, Robin. (2018). How white people handle diversity training in the workplace. *Medium*. Retrieved from https://medium.com/s/story/how-white-people-handle-diversity-training-in-the-workplace-e8408d2519f.

Dobbie, Will S., & Fryer, Roland G. (2016). Charter schools and labor market outcomes. *NBER Working Paper Series*.

Duncan-Andrade, Jeff. (2007). Gangstas, wankstas, and ridas: Defining, developing, and supporting effective teachers in urban schools. *International Journal of Qualitative Studies in Education, 20*(6), 617–638.

Duncan-Andrade, J. M. R. (2009). Note to educators: Hope required when growing roses in concrete. *Harvard Educational Review, 79*(2), 181–194.

Duncan-Andrade, J. M. R., & Morrell, E. (2008). *The art of critical pedagogy: Possibilities for moving from theory to practice in urban schools*. New York, NY: Peter Lang.

El-Amin, A. (2015). *"Until justice rolls down like water": Revisiting emancipatory schooling for African Americans—A theoretical exploration of concepts for liberation* (Unpublished doctoral dissertation). Harvard University, Cambridge, MA.

Emerson, Robert M., Fretz, Rachel I., & Shaw, Linda L. (2011). *Writing ethnographic fieldnotes*. Chicago, IL: University of Chicago Press.

Fallace, Thomas. (2015). *Race and the origins of progressive education, 1880–1929*. New York, NY: Teachers College Press.

Feiman-Nemser, Sharon. (2012). *Teachers as learners*. Cambridge, MA: Harvard Education Press.

Feiman-Nemser, Sharon, Tamir, Eran, & Hammerness, Karen. (2015). *Inspiring teaching: Preparing teachers to succeed in mission-driven schools*. Cambridge, MA: Harvard Education Press.

Fine, Sarah. (2017). *Struggling toward humanization: Restorative justice, deeper learning, and the pursuit of transformed relationships at an urban charter school* (Doctoral dissertation). Harvard University, Cambridge, MA.

Fredricks, Jennifer A., Blumenfeld, Phyllis C., & Paris, Alison H. (2004). School engagement: Potential of the concept, state of the evidence. *Review of Educational Research, 74*(1), 59–109.

Freire, Paulo. (1970). *Pedagogy of the oppressed.* New York, NY: Continuum.

Freire, Paulo. (1973). *Education for critical consciousness.* New York, NY: Continuum.

Freire, Paulo. (1998). *Pedagogy of freedom: Ethics, democracy, and civic courage.* Lanham, MD: Rowman & Littlefield.

Furrer, C., & Skinner, E. (2003). Sense of relatedness as a factor in children's academic engagement and performance. *Journal of Educational Psychology, 95*(1), 148–162.

Gay, Geneva. (2000). *Culturally responsive teaching: Theory, research, & practice.* New York, NY: Teachers College Press.

Gay, Geneva. (2006). Connections between classroom management and culturally responsive teaching. In C. M. Everston & C. S. Weinstein (Eds.), *Handbook of classroom management: Research, practice, and contemporary issues* (pp. 343–372). Mahwah, NJ: Erlbaum.

Gehlbach, Hunter, Brinkworth, Maureen E., & Harris, Anna D. (2012). Changes in teacher–student relationships. *British Journal of Educational Psychology, 82*(4), 690–704.

Ginwright, Shawn A. (2015). Radically healing black lives: A love note to justice. *New Directions for Student Leadership, 148*, 33–44.

Golann, Joanne W. (2014). The paradox of success at a no-excuses school. *Sociology of Education, 88*(2), 102–119.

Golann, Joanne W., Debs, Mira, & Weiss, Anna Lisa. (2019). "To be strict on your own": Black and Latinx parents evaluate discipline in urban choice schools. *American Educational Research Journal, 56*(5), 1896–1929.

Gomez, Mary Louise, & Lachuk, Amy Johnson. (2015). Teachers learning about themselves through learning about "others." In D. J. Clandinin & J. Husu (Eds.), *The SAGE handbook of research on teacher education* (pp. 457–472). London, England: Sage.

Graham, Patricia A. (2005). *Schooling America.* New York, NY: Oxford University Press.

Green, Elizabeth. (2014). *Building a better teacher: How teaching works (and how to teach it to everyone).* New York, NY: Norton.

Griffin, Glenda. (1997). Teaching as a gendered experience. *Journal of Teacher Education, 48*(1).

Grossman, P. (2005). Research on pedagogical approaches in teacher education. In M. Cochran-Smith & K. M. Zeichner (Eds.), *Studying teacher education: The report of the AERA panel on research and teacher education* (pp. 425–476). Mahwah, NJ: Erlbaum.

Grossman, Pam. (1990). *The making of a teacher: Teacher knowledge and teacher education.* New York, NY: Teachers College Press.

Grossman, Pam, & McDonald, Morva. (2008). Back to the future: Directions for research in teaching and teacher education. *American Educational Research Journal, 45*(1), 184–205.

Guha, R., Hyler, M., & Darling-Hammond, L. (2016). *The teacher residency: An innovative model for preparing teachers.* Palo Alto, CA: Learning Policy Institute.

Guilherme, Alex, & Morgan, W. John. (2009). Martin Buber's philosophy of education and its implications for adult non-formal education. *International Journal of Lifelong Education, 28*(5), 565–581.

Hallinan, M. T. (2008). Teacher influences on students' attachment to school. *Sociology of Education, 81*, 271–283.

Harcourt, Bernard. (2005). *The illusion of order: The false promise of broken windows policing.* Cambridge, MA: Harvard University Press.

Haviland, V. (2008). "Things get glossed over": Rearticulating the silencing power of whiteness in education. *Journal of Teacher Education, 59*(1), 40–54.

Hawkins, David. (1974). *The informed vision: Essays on learning and human nature.* New York, NY: Algora.

Hirschman, Albert O. (1970). *Exit, voice, and loyalty: Responses to decline in firms, organizations, and states* (Vol. 25). Cambridge, MA: Harvard University Press.

Hollins, Etta, & Torres Guzman, Maria. (2005). Research on preparing teachers for diverse populations. In M. Cochran-Smith & K. M. Zeichner (Eds.), *Studying teacher education:*

The report of the AERA panel on research and teacher education (pp. 477–548). Mahwah, NJ: Erlbaum.

Horn, Jim. (2016). *Work hard, be hard: Journeys through "no excuses" teaching*. London, England: Rowman & Littlefield.

Hsin, Amy & Xie, Yu. (2014). Explaining Asian Americans' academic advantage over whites. *Proceedings of the National Academy of Sciences of the United States of America*, 111(23), 8416–8421. https://doi.org/10.1073/pnas.1406402111.

Hyland, N. (2005). Being a good teacher of black students? White teachers and unintentional racism. *Curriculum Inquiry, 35*(4), 429–459.

Ingersoll, Richard, & Merrill, Lisa. (2014). *Seven trends: The transformation of the teaching force*. Philadelphia, PA: Consortium for Policy Research in Education.

Johnson, Susan Moore, & Birkeland, Susan E. (2003). Pursuing a "sense of success": New teachers explain their career decisions. *American Educational Research Journal, 40*(3), 581–617.

Jolliffe, Darrick, & Farrington, David. (2006). Development and validation of the basic empathy scale. *Journal of Adolescence, 29*(4), 589–611.

Kershen, Juliana Lopez, Weiner, Jennie Miles, & Torres, Chris. (2019). Control as care: How teachers in "no excuses" charter schools position their students and themselves. *Equity & Excellence in Education, 51*(3–4).

Kraft, Matthew A., Papay, John P., Charner-Laird, Megin, Johnson, Susan Moore, Ng, Monica, & Reinhorn, Stefanie K. (2012, June). *Committed to their students but in need of support: How school context influences teacher turnover in high-poverty, urban schools.* Paper presented at the annual meeting of the American Educational Research Association, Vancouver, BC, Canada.

Kreber, Carolin, Klampfleitner, Monika, McCune, Velda, Bayne, Sian, & Knottenbelt, Miesbeth. (2007). What do you mean by "authentic"? A comparative review of the literature on conceptions of authenticity in teaching. *Adult Education Quarterly, 58*(1), 22–43.

Kumashiro, K. K. (2010). Seeing the bigger picture: Troubling movements to end teacher education. *Journal of Teacher Education, 61*(1–2), 56–65.

Ladson-Billings, Gloria. (1994). *Dreamkeepers: Successful teachers of African American children*. San Francisco, CA: Jossey-Bass.

Ladson-Billings, Gloria. (2006). From the achievement gap to the education debt: Understanding achievement in U.S. schools. *Educational Researcher, 35*(7), 3–12.

Lampert, Magdalene. (2001). *Teaching problems and the problems of teaching*. New Haven, CT: Yale University Press.

Lawrence-Lightfoot, Sara. (2004). *The essential conversation: What parents and teachers can learn from each other*. New York, NY: Random House.

Lawrence-Lightfoot, Sara, & Davis, Jessica Hoffmann. (1997). *The art and science of portraiture*. San Francisco, CA: Jossey-Bass.

Lee, Carol. (2017). *Opportunity and equity inside classrooms: Teacher–child relationships and educational success.* Invited speaker session presented at the American Educational Research Association, San Antonio, TX.

Lemov, Doug. (2010). *Teach like a champion: 49 techniques that put students on the path to college*. San Francisco, CA: Jossey-Bass.

Levine, Arthur. (2006). *Educating school teachers*. Washington, DC: Education Schools Project. Retrieved from http://www.edschools.org/pdf/Educating_Teachers_Report.pdf.

Lipsky, M. (1980). *Street-level bureaucracy: The critical role of street-level bureaucrats*. New York, NY: Russell Sage Foundation.

Livermore, Craig. (2008). Unrelenting expectations: A more nuanced understanding of the broken windows theory of cultural management in urban education. *Penn GSE Perspectives on Urban Education, 5*(2).

Lortie, Dan C. (1975). *Schoolteacher: A sociological study*. Chicago, IL: University of Chicago Press.

Martin, Andrew J., & Dowson, Martin. (2009). Interpersonal relationships, motivation, engagement, and achievement: Yields for theory, current issues, and educational practice. *Review of Educational Research, 79*(1), 327–365.

Mason, Kevin O. (2014). *Preparing for the classroom: What teachers really think about teacher education.* Lanham, MD: Rowman & Littlefield.

Matias, C., & Zembylas, M. (2014). "When saying you care is not really caring": Emotions of disgust, whiteness ideology, and teacher education. *Critical Studies in Education, 55*(3), 319–337.

Maxwell, Joseph A. (1996). *Qualitative research design: An interactive approach* (Vol. 41). Beverly Hills, CA: Sage.

McAllister, Gretchen, & Irvine, Jacqueline Jordan. (2002). The role of empathy in teaching culturally diverse students. *Journal of Teacher Education, 53*(5), 433–443.

McDonald, Morva A., Bowman, Michael, & Brayko, Kate. (2013, April). Learning to see students: Opportunities to develop relational practices of teaching through community based placements in teacher education. *Teachers College Record, 115,* 1–35.

Mehta, Jal, & Fine, Sarah. (2019). *In search of deeper learning: Inside the effort to remake the American high school.* Cambridge, MA: Harvard University Press.

Mercado, Carmen I. (2016). Teaching for critical consciousness: Topics, themes, frameworks, and instructional activities. In A. Valenzuela (Ed.), *Growing critically conscious teachers: A social justice curriculum for educators of Latino/a youth.* New York, NY: Teachers College Press.

Meyer, John W., & Rowan, Brian. (1978). The structure of educational organizations. In M. W. Meyer (Ed.), *Environments and organizations.* San Francisco, CA: Jossey-Bass.

Michael, Ali. (n.d.). Treating racial competence as a skill to be learned. University of Pennsylvania Graduate School of Education. Retrieved from https://www.gse.upenn.edu/news/educators-playbook/treating-racial-competence-skill-be-learned.

Michael, Ali. (2015). *Raising race questions: Whiteness and inquiry in education.* New York, NY: Teachers College Press.

Miles, Matthew, & Huberman, Michael. (1994). *Qualitative data analysis: An expanded sourcebook.* Beverly Hills, CA: Sage.

Milner, Richard. (2003). Reflection, racial competence, and critical pedagogy: How do we prepare pre-service teachers to pose tough questions? *Race Ethnicity and Education, 6*(2), 193–208.

Morin, Monte. (2014, May 5). Study examines achievement gap between Asian American, white students. *Los Angeles Times.*

Noddings, Nel. (1984). *Caring: A feminine approach to ethics & moral education.* Berkeley: University of California Press.

Noddings, Nel. (1992). *The challenge to care in schools.* New York, NY: Teachers College Press.

Noddings, Nel. (2013). Freire, Buber, and care ethics on dialogue in teaching. In R. Lake & T. Kress (Eds.), *Paulo Freire's intellectual roots: Toward historicity in praxis.* New York, NY: Bloomsbury.

Oakes, Jeannie. (1985). *Keeping track: How schools structure inequality.* New Haven, CT: Yale University Press.

Ofer, Udi. (2011). Criminalizing the classroom: The rise of aggressive policing and zero tolerance discipline in New York City public schools. *New York Law School Law Review, 56,* 1373–1411.

Palmer, Parker. (1998). *The courage to teach: Exploring the inner landscape of a teacher's life.* San Francisco, CA: Jossey-Bass.

Papay, John P., West, Martin R., Fullerton, Jon B., & Kane, Thomas J. (2012). Does an urban teacher residency increase student achievement? Early evidence from Boston. *Educational Evaluation and Policy Analysis, 34*(4), 413–434.

Patton, Michael Quinn. (2002). *Qualitative evaluation and research methods.* Thousand Oaks, CA: Sage.

Pecukonis, E. V. (1990). A cognitive/affective empathy training program as a function of ego development in aggressive adolescent females. *Adolescence, 25*(97), 59–76.

Picower, B. (2009). The unexamined whiteness of teaching: How white teachers maintain and enact dominant racial ideologies. *Race Ethnicity and Education, 12*(2), 197–215.

Reardon, Sean. (2013). The widening income achievement gap. *Educational Leadership, 70*(8).

Roorda, D., Koomen, H., Spilt, J., & Oort, F. (2011). The influence of affective teacher–student relationships on students' school engagement and achievement: A meta-analytic approach. *Review of Educational Research, 81*(4), 493–529.

Sanders, W. L., & Rivers, J. C. (1996). *Cumulative and residual effects of teachers on future student academic achievement.* Knoxville: University of Tennessee Value-Added Research and Assessment Center.

Saphier, Jon, & Gower, Robert R. (1997). *The skillful teacher: Building your teaching skills.* Acton, MA: Research for Better Teaching.

Schonert-Reichl, Kimberly. (2017). Social and emotional learning and teachers. *The Future of Children, 27*(1). Retrieved from https://files.eric.ed.gov/fulltext/EJ1145076.pdf.

Schultz, Katherine. (2003). *Listening: A framework for teaching across differences.* New York, NY: Teachers College Press.

Seider, Scott, Jennett, Pauline, Graves, Daren, Gramigna, Kathryn, El-Amin, Aaliyah, Yung, Jennifer, Clark, Shelby, Kenslea, Megan, Soutter, Madora, Sklarwitz, Sherri, & Tamerat, Jalene. (2016). Preparing adolescents attending progressive and no excuses urban charter schools to analyze, navigate, and challenge race and class inequality. *Teachers College Record, 118.*

Shalaby, Carla. (2017). *Troublemakers: Lessons in freedom from young children at school.* New York: The New Press.

Sizer, Theodore. (1984). *Horace's compromise: The dilemma of the American high school.* New York, NY: Houghton Mifflin.

Sleeter, Christine. (2008). Preparing white teachers for diverse students. *Handbook of Research on Teacher Education: Enduring Questions in Changing Contexts, 3,* 559–582.

Solomon, Jesse. (2009). The Boston teacher residency: District-based teacher education. *Journal of Teacher Education, 60*(5), 478–488.

Sosa, Teresa, & Gomez, Kimberley. (2012). Connecting teacher efficacy beliefs in promoting resilience to support of Latino students. *Urban Education, 47*(5), 876–909.

Souto-Manning, Mariana. (2018). Toward praxically-just transformations: Interrupting racism in teacher education. *Journal of Education for Teaching, 45*(1), 97–113.

Stake, Robert E. (2013). *Multiple case study analysis.* New York, NY: Guilford Press.

Tatar, Moshe. (1998). Teachers as significant others: Gender differences in secondary school pupils' perceptions. *British Journal of Educational Psychology, 68*(2), 217–227.

Taylor, Charles. (1994). The politics of recognition. In A. Heble, D. Palmateer Pennee, & J. R. (Tim) Struthers (Eds.), *New contexts of Canadian criticism.* Peterborough, ON, Canada: Broadview Press.

Theisen-Homer, Victoria. (2020). Preparing teachers for relationships with students: Two visions, two approaches. *Journal of Teacher Education.* https://doi.org/10.1177/0022487120922223.

Valenzuela, Angela. (1999). *Subtractive schooling: U.S.–Mexican youth and the politics of caring.* New York, NY: SUNY Press.

Villegas, Ana María, & Lucas, Tamara. (2002). Preparing culturally responsive teachers: Rethinking the curriculum. *Journal of Teacher Education, 53*(1), 20–32.

Whitman, David. (2008). *Sweating the small stuff: Inner-city schools and the new paternalism.* Washington, DC: Thomas B. Fordham Institute.

Wilson, James Q., & Kelling, George L. (1982). Broken windows. *The Atlantic Online.*

Wubbels, Theo, Brekelmans, Mieke, Den Brok, Perry, Wijsman, Lindy, Mainhard, Tim, & Van Tartwijk, Jan. (2015). Teacher–student relationships and classroom management. In E. T. Emmer & E. J. Sabornie (Eds.), *Handbook of Classroom Management.* New York, NY: Routledge.

Yin, Robert. (1994). *Case study research: Design and methods.* Thousand Oaks, CA: Sage.